EGYPT'S LEGACY

EGYPT'S LEGACY

The archetypes of Western civilization
3000–30 BC

Michael Rice

London and New York

First published 1997
by Routledge
11 New Fetter Lane, London EC4P 4EE

Simultaneously published in the USA and Canada
by Routledge
29 West 35th Street, New York, NY 10001

© 1997 Michael Rice

Typset in Garamond by
Florencetype Ltd, Stoodleigh, Devon

Printed and bound in Great Britain by
Biddles Ltd, Guildford and King's Lynn

British Library Cataloguing in Publication Data
A catalogue record for this book is available from the British Library

Library of Congress Cataloguing in Publication Data
Rice, Michael, 1928–
Egypt's legacy: the archetypes of western civilization 3000–30 BC/
Michael Rice
p.   cm.
Includes bibliographical references and index.
1. Egypt–Civilization–To 332 B.C. 2. Egypt–Civilization–332 B.C.–
638 A.D. 3. Archetype (Psychology) I. Title.
DT61.R48 1997   96-36661
932–dc20   CIP

ISBN 0-415-15779-X

The Beautiful God,
Lord of the Two Lands,
Lord of Diadems,
Neb-Kheperu-Ra,
Tutankhamun,
Given Life for Ever,
Who opened
my ears and my eyes.

CONTENTS

———— •◆• ————

ILLUSTRATIONS

———— •◆• ————

PREFACE

———— •◆• ————

It may very well be asked, 'Why another history of Ancient Egypt and why should this author think himself competent to write it?' Having asked the questions myself, I will attempt to answer them and, in doing so, try to give some justification for the book which is before you.

It was suggested to me that I should write a history of Egypt, following the kindly reception which was given to my earlier book *Egypt's Making*, which reviewed the origins of the Egyptian state and which was published in 1990.[1] That book attempted to bring together the currently available material on the earliest phases of Egyptian history, a period which has always particularly interested me.

Egypt's Making was, I think, unusual in that it attempted to interweave some of the insights which C. G. Jung, the founder of analytical psychology, brought to the study of Egypt in ancient times. As I wrote the book I became more and more convinced of the validity of applying many of the concepts which Jung developed, although they were primarily conceived in terms of the analysis of individuals, to the study of the development of the Egyptian state, in the time of its beginnings and its first brilliant flowering.

I am aware, of course, that Jung's reputation in some intellectual circles has undergone a degree of eclipse. This is perhaps inevitable for one who was so multi-talented and who, particularly in his later years, often relied as much on intuition and inspiration as on analysis. It is also true that many of his most telling insights about the origin of societies came from the briefest acquaintance with people whom he would regard as 'primitive' – the African tribes, the Pueblo Indians, for example – but nonetheless such insights are powerful and, I believe, entirely valid in the study of man as a social animal, endowed with the equivocal gift of consciousness.

Egypt's Making drew attention to the quality, often disparaged, of early Egyptian technology and, in particular, emphasised the importance of stellar observations in the principal cults which emerged in the Nile Valley around the beginning of Egyptian history. It also attempted to set Egypt into the broader context of the ancient Near East, a consideration which has not always carried weight amongst some Egyptologists and other writers on the antiquity of Egypt who have preferred, not altogether unreasonably, to concentrate their analyses of the unique achievement of Egypt within its own frontiers.

When I came to writing *Egypt's Legacy* I decided that there was little point simply in trying to write *another* history of Egypt. There is no shortage of excellent, up-to-date surveys of Egypt's history, many written by scholars far better qualified than I to record the minutiae as much as the great events of that rich inheritance. I decided therefore to write a history of the Two Kingdoms which would offer the outlines of the principal events and the main personalities involved but which would be written from a particular standpoint which has for long interested me.

I have been fortunate in that I have been able to indulge a lifetime's fascination for ancient Egypt in generous measure, for I have spent much of my professional life in Egypt and in lands peripheral to it. Viewing Egypt therefore from both the north and east, as it were, I have been able to meditate above all else on why Egypt has been so important a country for so very long.

This is the issue which *Egypt's Legacy* particularly explores. It is sub-titled 'The Archetypes of Western Civilisation 3000–30 BC' because in considering the course of Egypt's history it examines what I believe to be the psychological imperatives which underlay and indeed largely determined the principal events in that history which in turn seem to have first given expression to the most familiar components of what we have come generally to regard as 'civilisation'. Egypt's supreme legacy to the world which came after it was the identification and naming of the archetypes which I believe sprang from the Nile Valley peoples' collective unconscious.

One of C. G. Jung's most compelling insights was the realisation that the collective unconscious is common to all men, in all times, everywhere in the world. The study of mythology from around the world and the great mass of anthropological evidence drawn from complex societies as much as from those which Jung, with no sense of political correctness, would have classified as 'primitive', gives irrefutable support to this contention. The acknowledgment of the common psychic inheritance of mankind is deeply exciting for it allows us to begin to comprehend the motivations of the series of mythically-based belief systems which have so bemused our unfortunate species, blessed and cursed, in equal measure, as it sometimes seems, with that faculty of consciousness.

If this principle be accepted, namely that it is possible to begin to understand the psychological imperatives which have driven humankind as a whole throughout its history, then it follows that the same principle can with advantage be applied to the study of history, the record of human societies and the acts of men considered collectively. Obviously historical circumstances, environmental factors and the conditioning applied to individuals (when they can be identified) by all societies will affect particular cases but in broad outline the principle will remain secure. What originated as a system for analysing the psychoses of individuals can be applied, with appropriate reservations, to the study of the group and hence of societies, considered in relation to their historical experience. The role of the group in determining essential behavioural characteristics is clear: given the common psychological inheritance of mankind it could not be otherwise.

My principal contention in *Egypt's Legacy* is that Egypt was the one truly *pristine* society which developed into a large-scale, centrally directed, coherent political structure which existed over a significant span of history. It was hierarchic and thus firmly rooted in the human past, for human societies derive ultimately from the primate group; its pristine nature is revealed by its role in defining the archetypes and giving them expression.

Throughout the book I have tried to set the principal events of Egypt's history against the psychological matrices which Jung defined. I realise that not all who read the book will accept this approach: for them, I hope that the presentation of Egypt's history which I have outlined will be agreeable. I have tried to give the sequence of Egypt's history a human dimension by relating events, wherever it is possible to do so, to the lives and personalities of individuals, at least in the later phases of the story. It is, I freely admit, an idiosyncratic book. Its review of the course of Egyptian history is, I believe, generally in accordance with contemporary Egyptological thinking. Some aspects of the interpretation of that history is more subjective, perhaps speculative, however.

The book falls into three parts: the first deals mainly with some of the general principles which underlie the history of Egypt which I believe to be especially pertinent. Then it follows a chronological sequence of the flow of the Egyptian royal dynasties. It may be thought here that I give particular weight to the earlier periods when compared with the later. This is true, for given the basic thrust of the book it will be clear that I believe that the vital elements of the historic Egyptian experience which were to be of such crucial importance to the history of the world which descended from it (which includes most of the people who are likely to be reading this) were determined in the first two millennia of Egyptian history, from *c.* 3500 BC to *c.* 1700 BC. The third part then considers, briefly enough, the transmission of Egypt's history to the West and the continuing appeal of 'the mystery of Egypt', over the past two thousand years of Western civilisation.

Much of my working life has been engaged with the states of the Arabian peninsula and the Gulf. I explored some of the possible areas of contact between the headlands of the Gulf and late predynastic Egypt in *Egypt's Making* and I have returned to the question here. More and more I am convinced that this was bound up with the emergence of the Kingship in southern (Upper) Egypt. I believe that it may have been the mechanism which actually triggered the series of extraordinary events, the outflowing of the archetypes, which began the process of the individuation of society in the southern reaches of the Nile Valley, culminating in the creation of the Egyptian state.

The two thousand years during which Egypt flourished, to an extent unequalled by any other ancient society, imprinted a series of *ideas* of what a complex society should be. These ideas became the dominant model on which all other societies in the ancient world based their own experience, consciously or not. Eventually, the same archetypes which streamed out of the Egyptian unconscious rose similarly from the unconscious of other peoples in all parts of the world who, whether they knew it or not, were themselves on the threshold of complex, hierarchic societies.

I have written another book in this period of my life dealing with what may seem to be a more arcane theme than *Egypt's Legacy*. This is *The Power of the Bull* which considers the millennia-long preoccupation of men with bovids, especially the wild bull, *bos primigenius*. Egypt is a very rich source for all sorts of material relating to bull-cults; some of it appears in this present book. I am particularly taken with the identification of the king of Egypt as a bull. This was a dominant idea in the archaic period and the Old Kingdom but 'Bull' remained prominent in the royal titulary throughout Egyptian history.

It is not the intention of this review of the Egyptian contribution to some of the most familiar aspects of advanced and complex societies to attempt to resurrect the belief, popular in an earlier generation, that all civilisation was developed in the Nile Valley and from there was diffused to a waiting world. This is clearly not the case; many societies in many parts of the world evolved their own civilisations which, because of the similarity of conditions, needs and environment, often demonstrate forms reminiscent of those first produced by the Egyptians. The case of the pyramids in Central and South American cultures, which flourished long after Egypt had declined, is the most familiar example of this phenomenon; another is the creation of something like a divine kingship in China, some three thousand years after it was first proclaimed in Egypt.

Other societies found solutions to their own challenges and opportunities comparable with those which evolved in Egypt. These responses too are the consequence of the universal workings of the collective unconscious, as first comprehensively expressed by Jung. In some cases of course there may have been a degree of direct influence, in and around the Mediterranean for example, but its importance would have been incidental rather than fundamental and will have served to stimulate further the capacity of the collective unconscious to find its own level of expression. The very existence of comparabilities between Egypt and other societies demonstrates the tendency to replicate the same relatively limited repertory of symbols and forms in providing solutions to the dilemmas confronting the development of complex societies. What the Egyptians did was to give form, substance and names to the archetypes. Egypt was, to adapt Stravinsky's comment about the composition of *Le Sacre du Printemps*, 'the vessel through which the archetypes passed'.

Michael Rice
Odsey, Cambridgeshire

ACKNOWLEDGEMENTS

——— •◆• ———

This book is the outcome of many conversations and discussions held over the years. Thus, the ideas, disagreements, observations, objections and help which I have garnered from many sources have contributed to its final content – for better or worse.

I would like to thank Andrew Wheatcroft of Routledge and Stirling University whose stimulating encouragement and skilled editorial advice have always been readily and agreeably given. I am deeply appreciative of the comments which Dr Harriet Crawford of the Institute of Archaeology, University College London, gave on an earlier draft of the text; in particular her advice on aspects of the Sumerian experience have been especially valuable. My old friend Dr Barrington S. Cooper also read the earlier draft and made a number of beneficial comments on some of the uses which I have made of psychological and psychoanalytical material. None of those named are, of course, in any way responsible for what I may have made of their comments and any inadequacies which remain are entirely my own.

Many of the illustrations which appear in the book are the work of my friend John G. Ross. Anyone familiar with contemporary Egyptological photography will know of the exceptional quality of John Ross's work and the remarkable sympathy and skill which he brings to the recording both of works of art and of Egyptian archaeological sites.

THE CHRONOLOGY OF
ANCIENT EGYPT

———— •◆• ————

The chronology of Ancient Egypt is of importance not only for the determination of the places of the long line of kings, and occasionally queens,
whose reigns provided the only means for the counting of the years in the
sequence of Egyptian history but also because Egypt provides the basis for
the chronology of the entire ancient Near East. The chronology of all the
great historic cultures of the region prior to the seventh century BC by
which time independent, often written evidence provides relatively secure
dating, depend upon comparisons with Egypt and on the evidence of
Egyptian artifacts found in foreign contexts or the evidence of military
excursions which can be attributed to a particular Egyptian ruler.

The chronology of the kings of Egypt is customarily expressed in terms
of the successive (or occasionally contemporaneous) 'dynasties', into which
the Hellenistic historian Manetho chose to organise them when, drawing
on sources long lost, he wrote his evidently monumental work *Egyptiaka*.[1]
To a remarkable extent Manetho's classification has survived the test of
nearly two centuries of intense academic scrutiny.

Manetho's method was to list the kings of the historical period, that is
to say, beginning with the probably legendary 'Unifier' of the Nile Valley,
Menes, in family succession. Prior to the supposed time of the unification,
c.3000 BC, he refers to the belief that Egypt was first ruled by the gods,
then by a race of demi-gods, finally to become the domain of the reincarnated Horus.

The kings of Egypt themselves would not have recognised such a classification into groups linked by familial descent in the way that Manetho
proposed. Each king was the descendant of all his predecessors since each
of them was the Horus reincarnated. Often the kingship was conferred by
marriage to the daughter of the previous holder of the kingship; to this
extent the family connection is often valid. In the Old Kingdom at least it
does appear that there were familial links between the dynasties, though
the later ones may have been fairly remote. Manetho provides an estimate
of the length of each king's reign and a summary of the total of the years
that each dynasty was believed to have held the kingship.

Manetho's original work was lost but it was extensively quoted by other
authorities, in late antiquity and subsequently. From such quotations a reliable compilation of his text has been made.

In addition to Manetho's listings there are several other 'king-lists' which were produced in Egypt in much earlier times. The oldest of these, the 'Palermo Stone', records the principal events of the reigns of the kings, including a number of predynastic rulers, up to the Fifth Dynasty.[2] The 'Turin Canon' takes the list up to the New Kingdom;[3] at Abydos, Seti I, the father of Ramesses II, erected a great relief in the temple of which lists, somewhat selectively, the 'royal ancestors',[4] reaching back to the reign of Menes. From all of these sources, as well as the evidence produced by archaeology, it has been possible to compile a reasonably comprehensive roll-call of the kings.

There has been considerable variation over the past century and a half of Egyptological study in the estimates of the actual beginning of the kingship in Egypt, the date of the reign of the first king who is now generally thought to have been Hor-Aha, the happily named 'Fighting Hawk'. One of the more recent studies of the chronology of Egypt[5] puts the beginning of the First Dynasty in the last quarter of the thirtieth century, c.2920 BC. This is somewhat later than has generally been the consensus of post-Second World War scholarship, though the authors warn that there is a margin of error of up to 150 years in either direction in the case of dates before 3000 BC. In *Egypt's Legacy* Baines and Málek have generally been followed; their dates for all the kings at least have the merit of consistency though my inclination is to move the beginnings of the First Dynasty closer to the earlier limits of their time-scale.

The acceptance of Baines' and Málek's date for the late predynastic period, c.3000 BC, allows for the division of Egyptian history into millennia: the fifth and fourth millennia represent the predynastic (or prehistoric) period, the third millennium the Archaic period and the Old Kingdom, the second millennium embraces the Middle Kingdom and the New Kingdom, and the first sees Egypt in the Late Period ruled by a succession of foreign dynasties, culminating in the Ptolemaic Hellenistic dynasty of Greco-Egyptian rulers.

Nonetheless, a reliance on Baines and Málek does produce its own problems. Thus they attribute only eight years to the reign of Horemhab at the very end of the Eighteenth Dynasty, c.1320 BC. Horemhab was one of the most successful kings of this period, coming between the rather unsatisfactory reigns of Akhenaten, Smenkhara, Tutankhamun and Ay, and the early Nineteenth Dynasty when Seti I and Ramesses II raised Egypt to new heights of power and substance. This is because no record of Horemhab's reign had been found, until recently, later than his eighth year. Manetho and others credited him with a twenty-eight-year reign, clearly a more realistic figure, given the substantial achievements of his kingship. It is very likely that twenty years should be added to Horemhab's reign above the term allotted by Baines and Málek and hence to the dates of his successors, down to the confused succession in the Third Intermediate Period, embracing the Twenty-First to the Twenty-Third Dynasties.

CHAPTER I

THE NATURE OF ANCIENT EGYPT

—— ·◆· ——

Egypt is the most ancient of all nation states. When virtually all the rest of the world was locked in the immemorial and seemingly unchanging life of the stone-age hunters and scavengers, a civilisation at once majestic and totally assured rose on the Nile's banks. Its very existence changed the course of human history, to an extent unequalled by any ancient people, only to be approached by the creative and intellectual inheritance bequeathed to the world by the Egyptians' near contemporaries, the Sumerians of southern Iraq.

That Egypt is the first community known to history which can be called a 'nation-state', makes it unique. The Sumerians have the lead over Egypt in terms of historical chronology in, for example, the invention of writing and, possibly in the creation of pervasive bureaucracies in the form of the temple administrations which were the principal system of government in the little cities into which the polity of Sumer was, from early times, fragmented. However, the Sumerians never developed an integrated and coherent political structure over a widespread area, uniting disparate local traditions and ideologies, as the early rulers of Egypt certainly did. The Sumerian city-states remain individual, often warring and certainly divergent political entities; in Egypt the idea of unity, of nationhood, was first an ideal and then, when the Kingship became fully potent, a political reality.[1]

To set what was about to happen in the Nile Valley into the historical perspective of those of its contemporaries with whom it may properly be compared and to explain why it is qualitatively different from them, it is necessary to look at what has come to be known as 'the ancient Near East', in the latter part of the fourth millennium BC. By this term, which at once reveals the Eurocentric nature of historical studies over the past two hundred years, is generally meant the lands which comprise Anatolia, the Levant, Mesopotamia (Iraq and parts of northern Syria), the Syro-Arabian deserts, the Arabian peninsula and the Arabian Gulf, and the north-eastern quadrant of Africa, especially the Valley of the Nile and the mainly desert regions contiguous to it. Sometimes parts of Central Asia and Western Pakistan (the Indus Valley) are included in the term but historically and geographically they are peripheral, though from time to time they were influenced by, as much as they themselves influenced, the 'Near East' proper.

It was in the northern boundaries of this region, in the Levant, northern Mesopotamia and northern Iran, that the crucial experience of the domestication of plants and animals first occurred on a scale which resulted in the eventual establishment of permanent, settled communities. These agrarian communities in time developed permanent architecture, the practice of art (of which they were not of course the forerunners), the codification of systems of belief and the formalisation of rituals and liturgies directed towards placating the influence of unseen forces in human affairs.

These patterns of existence broadly persisted from the end of the last glaciation, *c.*10000 BC (known in archaeological terms as the Epi-Palaeolithic), and throughout the neolithic, which is identified by the use of stone tools, often of a considerable sophistication of manufacture, and the practice of domestication. In its later phases the neolithic also developed the conversion of metal ores, either by cold-hammering or, latterly, by smelting, leading eventually to the more advanced societies of the Bronze Age.

By the beginning of the fifth millennium a profoundly significant development occurred in what was to become one of the key areas of the ancient Near East. This was in the southern extremity of the valley of the two great rivers which flowed southwards through an otherwise empty and generally desolate landscape, to debouch into the upper reaches of the Arabian Gulf, the inland sea which separates Arabia from Iran and which opens eventually into the Indian Ocean. Here an immigrant people, whose origins are still entirely unknown, entered the land and set about the creation of one of the most significant and enduringly influential ancient societies of which we have knowledge.

These immigrants into southern Iraq were the Sumerians. 'Sumerian' is, strictly speaking, a linguistic term which can with assurance only be used to describe the southern Mesopotamian civilisation some two thousand years later when its people conferred their greatest boon on mankind, the invention of writing. There is, however, little doubt that the immigrants of 5000 BC were the ancestors of the Sumerians, when they can be named as such, after two millennia of historical anonymity.

The characteristic unit of Sumerian society was the city. Whilst the earliest southern Mesopotamian communities were undoubtedly agricultural, the nature of the land, an eerie combination of desert, marsh and immensely fertile silt deposited by the swift-flowing and unpredictable rivers on which the people depended for their existence, was such that small permanent communities were established which, by a neucleonic process, coalesced and formed larger settlements. These in time could be called 'cities', with developed administrations and systems of government.

It appears that at first the dominant influence in Sumerian corporate life was the temple. For the Sumerians the belief which defines the relationship between the visible world and that of the gods was that each city was

2

the domain of an individual divinity. The gods were visualised as super-human in form and character: the temple was the focus of the city and, in so far as it was the earthly 'home' of the presiding god, the reason for the city's existence.

But the city as a place of corporate religious events was only one of its functions; it was also a centre for exchange and trade, a meeting place and a refuge in times, all too frequent in the Sumerian experience, of strife. The cities of southern Mesopotamia developed into independent political enti-ties, anticipating the Greek city-states of several thousand years later. The 'religious' emphasis of the city changed as its political character became the occasion for the assertion of the ambitions of secular rulers. These were termed in Sumerian 'lu-gal', literally the 'great man' who probably first assumed the leadership of the community in times of stress; the analogy with the 'dux bellorum', represents a precisely comparable phenomenon.

In addition to its contribution to human progress by the invention of writing, Sumer was responsible for two other introductions which entirely changed the lives of those who came after its comparatively brief existence. These were, on the one hand, the concept of law, by which the relation-ship of the individual to his fellows and of the individual to the community could be regulated, and, on the other, monumental architecture.

The origin of Sumerian architecture, whose buildings were the largest structures known before the erection of the Pyramids in Egypt, can be traced back to the beginnings of settled life in the south of Mesopotamia. At Eridu, the earliest known settlement in Sumer, a little shrine lies at the lowest level of a sequence of increasingly complex buildings, which culmi-nates three thousand years later in the ziggurat, which dominated the city, sacred to the god Enki, and which was built c.2000 BC.

As a distinct political entity Sumer really only survived for a millennium and a half, falling finally under the effects of its own fractious nature, demonstrated by the patchwork of little states, and the submersion of the communities by the Semitic-speaking peoples who by the latter part of the third millennium made up the bulk of the population. From this time forward the history of most of the ancient Near East is dominated by the fortunes of the speakers of Semitic languages.

It was not only the Semitic-speakers who sounded the knell of Sumerian civilisation. To the east, on the Iranian plateau and especially in the south-west, had evolved Elam, a civilisation which was comparable in some respects with Sumer, though its evolution was on somewhat different lines. For one thing – and that one fairly crucial – Elam seems to have created a far more centralised administration than did Sumer, though the temples of Elam were powerful and were even, apparently, to influence the devel-opment of Egypt in its early centuries. Although Elam adopted writing very soon after it had appeared in Sumer and borrowed Sumerian cuneiform as its script, the language remains untranslated; in consequence less is known about early Iran than is the case of its neighbour to the west. It will be seen that Elam's influence and hence its material and intellectual resources must have been considerable to have had the effect on Egypt which they certainly seem to have had.

Both Sumer and Elam developed one particular product which was to prove of great importance in the centuries which followed its appearance in the early fourth millennium. This was the cylinder seal which was used to identify property in preliterate societies, large caches of which have survived to provide a treasury of information regarding the lives of the peoples who employed them. It is from the evidence of the seals derived from Sumer and Elam that the connections between them and the emerging Egyptian state, far away to the west, can in part be charted.

Thus we have the situation at the dawn of history (or, more prosaically, in the last quarter of the fourth millennium BC) that three centres in the Near East, Sumer, Elam and Egypt, each stand at the threshold of a complex society. Each of them gives some evidence of the factors which permit a society to be classified as complex: urbanisation, writing, a system of law or government, large-scale or monumental architecture, the management of resources, formalised religious cults and organisation, trade and the production of surplus, the arts. To these may be added the establishment of hierarchies, social classes, specialisation of professions and trades and the creation of a standing or periodically levied army.

Whilst there are many similarities between Sumer and Elam, Egypt presents an entirely different outline, the consequence perhaps of its African roots, which gave it a dimension of experience wholly at odds with its contempories. It is this which accounts for Egypt's unique character and which marks out its legacy to the world as quite other, both in degree and in kind, from its Western Asian peers.

Two factors especially make the Egyptian experience of the development of a complex society different from its contemporaries. From its earliest beginnings Egypt was conceived as a nation-state. Once the objective of unification was, as it were, expressed by the first Egyptian kings the basic political, religious and social components of the society were seen as valid from one end of the Valley to the other; although there were local traditions these were swiftly subsumed into the distinctively Egyptian corporate identity. This was not at all the situation in Sumer, where individual variations, in religious practices for example and even in the titles adopted by the leading officials of the cities, were emphasised and retained tenaciously.

One compelling reason why Egypt was so wholly exceptional in the impact which it had on later cultures was that it simply endured for so long. Sumer disappeared as a discrete entity around 2000 BC and its very existence seems to have been forgotten, though the language continued to be retained in temple liturgies. An occasional antiquarian-minded ruler of the empires which eventually succeeded Sumer might preserve the records of earlier kings, or the rich corpus of myth which seeped through into the consciousness of later ages. Elam, though it brought down Sumer in the end, did not survive as a separate political or cultural entity and so had little direct influence on the rapidly developing societies which flowered all over the region in the third and second millennia.

For century after century Egypt flourished, the legends of its wealth, power and mystery constantly accreting until the reputation of the Two Lands was preserved as massively as the stone monuments which Egyptian kings so diligently constructed. By virtue of its unique celebrity Egypt swiftly became the archetype of all complex Near Eastern societies, its reputation coalescing into the very image of the pristine kingdom, the exemplar of the ways in which human societies should be governed – in an ideal world.

That the world was not ideal resulted inevitably in the decline of Egypt and the extinction of its unique culture. But the pattern had been set and, even in its ruined state, Egypt stood for later ages as the witness to what was once the Golden Age.

By the early decades of the third millennium before the present era that Golden Age was beginning to acquire a clear definition of its principal characteristics. Egypt developed a high and complex culture with all the trappings of statehood: Kingship, the flourishing of the arts and architecture, a sophisticated, elegant way of life and a profound sense of 'the other', the spiritual counterpart of the material existence. Nowhere else in the world was there anything like it.

That this was a very remarkable state of affairs seems to have been recognised by those foreigners who, early on, came into contact with Egypt. Herodotus, a highly perceptive and creative historian, clearly believed that the Egyptians' experience was quite unlike that of the people of any other lands of which he had knowledge. Then as now the material remains of the early civilisation of Egypt invoked awe: it might be said, rightly so. Herodotus had the advantage of speaking with men who were still in touch with the traditions which had given life to Egypt, no matter that in his time those traditions were largely ghostly images of the reality that once they had been.

For two thousand years at least before Herodotus' time the people of the ancient Near East had intimate and sustained knowledge (if not, perhaps, understanding) of Egypt. Traders had carried pottery, stone vessels, seals, ivory, gold inlays and all the riches of the courts of the Nile to the rulers of lesser lands: sometimes goods, or 'tribute' as the Egyptians not unreasonably preferred to consider them, were brought from the Aegean, from Syria or Palestine to the Nile. Thus was Egypt known, but its mystery grew rather than diminished as a result of those who had such contact with her and who carried back to their own lands tales, not lessened in the telling, of all the wonders of which the King of Egypt was master.

The prevailing impression of Egypt, then as now, was of the splendour and scale of its buildings, the only works of men which seemingly defy time. Herodotus wrote 'Concerning Egypt itself I shall extend my remarks to a great length, because there is no country that possesses so many wonders, nor any that has such a number of works which defy description.'[2] This was the view of Egypt current long before Herodotus' lifetime and it was to persist long after it.

The Greeks marvelled at Egypt's civilisation and the remains of its greatness. They were the Egyptians' most ardent admirers, and attributed much of their own culture to the influence of the Nile people, even accepting that the knowledge of the Olympians, the Greeks' own fractious pantheon, originated in Egypt. The Greeks believed that the Egyptians were the first people to introduce the worship of the gods and to give them names.

The Egyptians themselves asserted, and the Greeks agreed with them, that their way of life, its institutions and the beliefs which informed it, were god-given. In times before memory Egypt had first been ruled by the gods, then by a race of semi-divine beings. The arts of civilisation were transmitted to men by the mysterious Followers of Horus, the Spirits of the Dead; Egypt had been favoured beyond all other lands by these divine and semi-divine presences.

Plato complicated the picture of Egypt's ancestry considerably by introducing the idea of Atlantis to the world. His story, with its portrayal of a sort of idealised Greek island kingdom with marked Egyptian overtones, has persuaded many, not all of them romantics or fantasists, that Egypt was the offspring of a lost continent, its rulers a class of priest-kings who escaped its destruction, so graphically described in the *Timaeus* and the *Critias*.

Those for whom the Atlantis myth was too rational an explanation turned to other, more exalted sources for the origins of Egypt. These saw the Nile civilisation being brought to earth by visitors from the stars, extraterrestrials who, for reasons best known to themselves, came down and implanted the seeds of high culture in the fertile soil of the Nile Valley. Such ideas, despite all reason, are still with us.

Although it is easy to dismiss the wilder explanations of Egypt's origins as the nonsense which they no doubt are, the fact remains that the appearance of so high a culture as Egypt's, suddenly and with virtually no antecedents, is deeply perplexing. In the space of a few centuries, on either side of 3000 BC , when the whole of the rest of the world had little to show by way of the refinements of living, Egypt stands fully realised, with a material culture whose influence still resonates across the world. Egypt's belief systems and principles of ordered government still determine much of what is accepted as civilised living in societies which are governed by considerations of order, a concept which, it will be demonstrated, is wholly Egyptian.

Most scholars, who are not encouraged to speculate about the mistier realms of Atlantean kings or beings from distant stars, have tended to eschew the question of the more remote origins of Egyptian civilisation, preferring to present such evidence as they have been able to unearth, either by way of excavation or in their libraries, and to allow the evidence to speak for itself. This is an entirely proper procedure, but it is one which leaves a void at that very point when Egypt suddenly soars away into a creative and social empyrean, leaving far behind the simple neolithic origins from which it must be presumed to have developed.

Before the middle of the fourth millennium, *c.*3500 BC, Egypt presents a cultural configuration little different from that of the rest of the ancient Near East. Some of its later preoccupations are already to be seen, certainly: the protection of the dead, the making of fine if simple artifacts, the origins of the cults honouring the supernatural forces which were to be such powerful presences in later centuries. But nothing here would have predicted the burst of energy which created 'pharaonic' Egypt, signalled by the appearance of the first kings, just before the end of the fourth millennium BC.

Even after 3500 BC, when the evidence of more advanced cultures appears in the sequence which scholars identify by the site at Naqada in southern Egypt where first they were recognised, the products of the Valley people are handsome, demonstrating a concern for form and a commitment to high standards of aesthetic and technical excellence. But in this their products were not *significantly* different from the pottery, stoneware and adapted raw materials made by contemporary peoples of Mesopotamia, Syria and parts of Iran (see, for example, Mellaart 1967). Then, at the beginning of the First Dynasty of kings, the situation changes totally and Egypt takes on a character different, not merely in degree but in kind, from all of its contemporaries.

Historic Egypt seems to have no beginnings but suddenly springs, apparently autochthonous and entire, from the rich black land of the Valley. The history of human societies has shown that the presence of a man or men of genius and determination in a particular society can bring about change and the advancement of technology or culture to an entirely unforeseen degree. Such men may be great kings like Alexander or the promoters of revolutionary ethical or religious ideas like Confucius or Mohammed. In their own generation or later they may exercise the sort of charismatic influence which changes the lives of those who come after them forever.

In Egypt it is possible, even likely, that the whole process was begun, as it was certainly continued, by such a man or men of exceptional attainment and genius. In the early dynasties the kings and their ministers were clearly exceptionally talented and exceptionally well focused: in the first two dynasties, for example, which lasted for some five hundred years in all, most of the essentials of ancient Egyptian society were defined and laid down. In the Third Dynasty Imhotep, the builder of the complex raised to ensure the immortality of King Djoser Netjerykhet, is to be numbered amongst the handful of supreme creative innovators whose names are known, from all of human history.

Some scholars, writing from the standpoint of the late twentieth century and bred in the traditions of scientific humanism, have been inclined to assess the achievements of the early Egyptians, remarkable though they acknowledge them to be, as little more than the outcome of a benign empiricism, with chance, a fortunate discovery, or the natural evolution of a fairly simple idea, being set into a canon of practice which led on, in the fullness of time, to the Pyramids.[3] This view sees no *essential* difference in the Egyptian experience from many others in the history of complex societies: it assumes that the great public works built in the early centuries of Egypt's existence are the products of an essentially simple technology.

The importance of technology in the development of even so high-flown a society as Egypt is well demonstrated by the remarkable ease with which the Egyptians, from very early on in their progress towards nationhood, manipulated stone. No other people, certainly not in the fourth millennium BC, handled stone with the delight in its variety of colours and textures and in its qualities as a medium for the expression of form, as did the Egyptians, treating it almost as if it were a plastic substance. Their ability to handle the most intractable stones with such assurance was clearly the result of an early specialisation of craftsmanship and the organisation of such craftsmanship over many generations.

The methods used for cutting the stone vessels which are amongst the most beautiful of Egypt's early artifacts remain largely unknown, for none of the techniques suggested allow for the perfection of the shapes which, apparently resulting from the use of only the simplest tools, evolved very early on in Egypt's history. A phenomenal degree of skill must be allowed to the craftsmen, relatively as great as the skills demonstrated by the early kings and their ministers who built the Egyptian state, itself the greatest artifact produced by the Egyptian genius.

That such skills were phenomenal is demonstrated by the precision with which the Pyramids are built, the virtually exact orientation of the sides of the Great Pyramid to the cardinal points for example. These skills are legendary yet some scholars persist in belittling the Egyptians' grasp of mathematics,[4] or their use of sophisticated engineering practices, largely because no examples from early times exist either of Egyptian mathematical theory or of the resolution of an engineering problem theoretically. The mathematical exercises which do exist are all from times later than the highest achievements of Egyptian architecture and are often simply textbook studies intended for the instruction of children or of scribal apprentices.

To such authorities the Egyptians cannot be credited with any real understanding of or achievements in what the modern world defines as science. The acquisition of knowledge as a result of experiment, repetition, peer review and the formal procedures adopted by the modern scientific community were indeed probably remote from the Egyptian experience. It is thus asserted that Egyptian astronomy was essentially simple and utilitarian, concerned with the regulation of calendars, perhaps with navigation and with the round of the seasons.

Yet herein possibly lies the key (or, more accurately perhaps, one of the keys) to understanding the achievements of the Egyptians of the early third millennium. The Egyptians were exceptionally skilled observers of natural phenomena: the acres of brilliantly recorded and executed reliefs and paintings in the many hundred tombs which have survived from the first centuries of Egypt's history are ample testimony to this exceptional ability and to the generous measure in which it was expressed. All life and all phenomena were analysed and recorded. The finished products of such records are to be seen everywhere that ancient Egypt survives: comparatively little, however, survives which shows how such observations themselves were made.

It is much the same with the most disputed area of Egypt's 'scientific' knowledge, the observation and recording of the night sky. It is evident, again from the contents of the tomb walls - and particularly from their ceilings in later times - that the stars, constellations and planets were skilfully charted by the Egyptians. That this was the case from early times is clear, for in the Pyramid Texts,[5] which were first recorded in inscriptions in the late third millennium but which possibly derive from a much earlier period, the emphasis is on stellar phenomena: the king is hailed as a star and there are many references to stars and to the cults which are identified with them. These references, indeed, are far more frequent than those which concern the sun, though from the Fourth Dynasty onwards solar cults generally prevailed over those which involved the stars, when the King became *Sa Ra*, the Son of the Sun.

There can be no doubt that the architects of the greatest monuments of Egypt aligned their buildings by the most precise observations of the stars.[6] Recently, the intriguing possibility has been proposed that the whole Giza complex and those of Abusir and Dahshur nearby may be aligned directly on the constellation of Orion and reproduce its celestial configuration in terrestrial terms, presumably on the principle, 'as above, so below'.[7] If this suggestion is proven in fact then an even more remarkable case for the Egyptian observation of the stars must be admitted.

Linked with the question of the extent of the Egyptians' scientific knowledge and, in particular of their understanding of celestial mechanics, is whether they had knowledge of the phenomenon known as the Precession of the Equinoxes.[8] This is the process by which the celestial equator appears to undergo a very slow, very stately movement which has the effect of changing the orientation of the earth in space. The Precession is fundamental to an understanding of what powered the development of Egypt.

If we put aside both the survivors of Atlantis and the visitors from outer space as sources for such knowledge, we are left with two alternative explanations: either the Egyptians (and the Sumerians) developed their astonishing degree of technological ability entirely by their own efforts in the course of a few generations, or they were the inheritors of a long tradition of observation and response.

There has from time to time been speculation about a great neolithic culture which embraced much of the ancient world, whose records were impermanent and which was dependent largely upon an inherited oral tradition. There is no evidence for the existence of such a culture, nor, by definition is there much prospect of the survival of such evidence, at least in so far as it might be expected to hand on, or inspire, such advanced technical capabilities as the Egyptians demonstrated very early in their history. However, there are some, very tentative, indications that there may have been centres in which hitherto unsuspected degrees of technology flourished in times which otherwise were still deep in the neolithic period.

One such possible centre is of special significance in this connection. On the Konya plain in central Anatolia lies the extraordinary settlement of Catal Huyuk, which was nothing less than a proto-city (perhaps, indeed, *the* proto-city), founded in the *mid-seventh millennium BC*, which flourished until the mid-sixth.[9] For a thousand years Catal Huyuk (its modern name; its ancient name is lost, presumably for ever) was a large agglomeration of houses, shrines and public buildings, in every respect a city which existed three thousand years before what are always accepted as the first true cities were established in southern Mesopotamia at centres such as Eridu, Uruk, Ur, Lagash and Shurrupak.

Only a small part of the 32-acre site of which Catal Huyuk consists has been excavated but what has already been revealed indicates that it is one of the most remarkable in the ancient world; indeed, in some respects it may yet be seen as the most remarkable currently accessible to archaeology. Though its way of life was clearly neolithic, dominated by hunting and gathering, there is evidence of incipient agriculture and the manufacture of sophisticated artifacts – pottery, wood, seal-cutting, textiles – and, most remarkably of all, of what is obviously a long-standing tradition of painting and modelling of remarkable diversity and richness. Many of the buildings which have been excavated appear to be cult shrines, which reveal evidence of a goddess-dominated religion, with some notably dark aspects to it. Of equal importance to the cults which feature the goddess are those which are consecrated to the bull, whose supreme ancient cult centre Catal Huyuk appears to be.

The bull-cult, which has the earliest evidences of its developed form at Catal Huyuk, was to persist for longer even than the cult of the goddess and to spread throughout the ancient world; Egypt was to be one of its most important centres.

It is a very singular fact that, from the very beginning of the arrival of the kings, the land seems to display many aspects of the bull-cult which are first identified at Catal Huyuk. This might not be so remarkable were it not that Catal Huyuk's precocious civilisation disappears *c.*5400 BC, though a smaller, less advanced settlement was for a relatively short time established nearby. This is some two and a half millennia before the arrival of the royal administration which was for so long to give life to Egypt. It is thus just possible (though perhaps barely so) that some form of inheritance in architecture, decoration and craftsmanship was taken from central Anatolia and by means of which we have no knowledge survived over this long and apparently unrecorded period. If the bull-cult drew its character and form to so great an extent from Catal then at least the possibility of other aspects of the culture of ancient Egypt may also have had their origins across the Mediterranean, to the north. The idea is not original; the best part of a century ago Flinders Petrie, who did much to establish Egyptology as a respectable academic discipline, speculated similarly.

At much the same time as Catal flourished a remarkable culture of painters, who practised a particularly vibrant form of their art, were at work in the Sahara, laying down their rich and mysterious depictions of the animals which they hunted and the creatures which haunted their imaginations, on the rock shelters and overhangs in the central Saharan deserts.[10] Some of their work seems to anticipate later Egyptian forms, though the connection is an uneasy one since the Saharan painters would be contemporary with the early predynastic period in Egyptian chronology, yet the paintings which suggest Egyptian styles are much more like the figure and animal representations which the Egyptians evolved in the New Kingdom, at least two and a half millennia later.

The people of Catal Huyuk and the painters of the Sahara share in a mysterious and still little understood period which intervenes between the Epi-Palaeolithic, after the end of the last Ice Age, and the emergence of complex societies at the end of the fourth millennium BC. It is a long time-scale, lasting over some four or five thousand years, and the material evidence for the life of whatever communities there were at that time is sparse indeed. But there is still another, more readily accessible source from which the dynamic to produce such immense changes in the life of our species may have drawn its power: this proposes that the brilliance of early Egyptian civilisation, its material forms and the complexity and enduring quality of its institutions all erupted directly from the collective unconscious (a term which is further examined in Chapter II) of the inhabitants of the Nile Valley, living at this crucial time, in the latter part of the fourth millennium BC.

Though it clearly gained some part of its inspiration from contact with both Sumer and Elam, Egypt drew the overwhelming majority of its essential characteristics from its own soil. The influences which percolated into the Valley in the second half of the fourth millennium BC contributed to, rather than detracted from, the civilisation which was developing in the Valley, which was rapidly and wholly 'Egyptianised'. Because Egypt is pristine, its institutions are truly innovative. They are the first of their kind to take on a tangible reality, and, in doing so, contribute to the creation of a sophisticated, ordered and centrally controlled society, with a well-defined, coherent political and social ideology which eventually united a body of previously unrelated communities.

From the collective unconscious of the Egyptians of the late fourth to early third millennia BC streamed the mighty archetypes, representatives of that phenomenon whose definition by C. G. Jung was one of his most enduring contributions to the understanding of the human condition.[11] Egypt was the first advanced community to give the archetypes expression and, hence, existence. It is precisely because such archetypal images have their origins in the unconscious of men, and not in the stars or in the remnants of some lost civilisation, that they exercise their power. From their origins in the unconscious they derive their enduring ability to engage the minds of all receptive members of our species and to provoke a response of something like immediate recognition.

The world which succeeded Egypt's long period of high achievement owes its concepts of social order and organisation to the first men called kings who existed anywhere in the world. The rulers of the unified Kingdom of Egypt were not only the makers of the first nation-state, they were the first to wear crowns and to carry regalia to denote their office. They were the first men to bear elaborate titles proclaiming their rank, which were recorded and given permanent status. They were also, so far as we know, the first rulers to be acknowledged as divine, an audacious and supremely imaginative conceptual leap which was to have profound consequences in the centuries to come. More than any other factor the equation of king and god marked out the Nile civilisation from all others.

The kings of Egypt were the first of whom we have knowledge to be attended by a pervasive, organised bureaucracy, a company of great and lesser officials who managed every aspect of the corporate life of the country. These officials, too, from at least the latter part of the fourth millennium BC, bore titles which denoted their offices and which already had considerable pedigrees (see Chapter V). In the temples which sprang up all over the Two Lands to serve the king and his fellow gods, temple bureaucracies were created which, in the manner of such institutions everywhere, were self-reproducing and contributed much to, if they did not actually cause, Egypt's eventual decline.

The first two thousand years of Egypt's recorded history reveal the extent to which man was capable of managing a community which harmonised with the world in which it existed. Under the direction of its incarnate, divine ruler, the community fulfilled the need for a belief that it was in contact with a reality beyond the visible world. This the society of ancient Egypt, especially in its early centuries, seems peculiarly to have accomplished, to a degree not achieved by any other human group of which we have knowledge.

To a creature which has come so recently onto the world scene as our particular brand of conscious-bearing ape, to whom we have awarded the proud classification *Homo sapiens* (without, it may be said, the least intention of irony), it is the sheer antiquity of Egypt which often seems so compelling. Egypt endured, not without occasional more or less calamitous interludes to be sure, but always somehow surviving with its essential character, its ethos or essential spirit, largely intact. Egypt's survival as a political and social entity over three millennia ensured the transmission of its psychological, societal, religious and architectural archetypes to the world of later antiquity and so on to the modern world.

When we conceive of 'the gods', we most frequently visualise them as the Egyptians imagined them. When we attend or observe some great public occasion, some national festival, religious pageant or solemn parade, we are sharing in an experience which began in the forecourts of the mighty temples which the Egyptians built, in their view to ensure the perpetuation of the life of Egypt and, hence, of the cosmos. On such occasions even today a Great Individual, of whom the King of Egypt is the first example, will serve to mediate between the people and whatever divinity, abstraction or ideology is being celebrated or propitiated.

The Egyptians achieved an extraordinary degree of integration between the trappings of statehood, the organisation of society and the natural world. To a large extent this was the consequence of the Egyptians' particular idea of the Kingship: since the king was also god (originally, *the* god) all nature was subsumed in him. Since he was the archetypal Great Individual, all of Egypt was expressed in him: thus it was of such importance that the life and prosperity of the king be preserved, in this life and in the next when he reigned in the regions beyond the stars.

It is also the countryside of Egypt, not only its man-made splendours, which evokes such responses. Despite the fact today that, as in the rest of the world, the Egyptian countryside is being obliterated, it is still possible to find places where it seems to be as it always has been, or at least has been since neolithic times: dusty tracks worn by the animals, the fields awaiting harvest, stands of trees along the roads or on the river banks, a sprinkling of people working, often cruelly hard it is true, with the animals who are their companions, their fortune and, in the end, their victims. Such scenes will always seem peculiarly *right*, to the perceptive observer. It was Egypt's singular achievement to have created a society which manifested all the characteristics which later ages have come to associate with complex societies yet at the same time was wholly at one with the natural world.

The economy of Egypt was rooted in the rich alluvial soil which the river deposited along its banks when it flooded each year. From south to north the people of the Valley were peasants tilling the soil, either as small farmers or as the retainers of a noble or official. Egypt's wealth was really to be reckoned in terms of its highly productive arable land and the herds of animals which, despite the harshness of the climate in summer, the land sustained.

The essentially agrarian nature of Egypt was reflected in much of the symbolism which was so powerful an expression of the Egyptian psyche and even in the way in which the Egyptians of ancient times spoke of their country. The counterpoint between the Red and the Black, the one the harsh, unyielding desert and the other the beneficent, life-bearing alluvium, was very telling; even Egypt's ancient name, 'Kem-t', meant 'The Black' and acknowledged the debt which the people owed to the land that served them.

The unifying factor which bound the people of the Valley together and made them all the recipients of an exceptionally bountiful nature was the river. When the Kingship first emerged at the end of the fourth millennium, the presence of the river and the similarity of its peoples' way of life, through the soil, made the political union of the Valley a feasible objective. When the campaigns for the unification of the Valley were launched, their eventual success, despite the inevitable checks brought about by local conservatism and an abiding concern for regional loyalties, was reasonably assured. Egypt the nation-state was the product of the land and its economy.

The king was the greatest unifying force in the politics of ancient Egypt. From the earliest times he is depicted as conducting ceremonies designed to ensure the land's fertility and the recurring sequence of flood, silt and abundance. In late predynastic times, the king who is known by the glyph which identifies him, a scorpion, is shown breaking the banks of a canal so that the life-giving waters may flow out and fertilise the land.

The Egyptian preoccupation with the idea of order and the balances which ensured the life of Egypt, and indeed the cosmos, was locked on to the return of the seasons and the cycle of the farmer's year as much as it was the product of the observation of the apparently perpetual revolution of the celestial bodies. The wonder was that, given so total an integration between the people, the land, its exploitation and the state, the Egyptians also very early on developed generations of engineers capable of raising great monuments and artists who produced works which stand amongst the noblest human achievements. Such achievements are as much reflections of the balance and order prevailing in the society as is the tilling of the earth, to make it capable of supporting the entire structure of the state.

As did no other ancient people the Egyptians responded to the land on which they lived with wonder and delight. The mountains, especially in Upper Egypt, are continual anticipations of the monumental in architecture and statuary. The constant interplay of sunlight, shadow, moonlight, haze or the dawn inspired numberless generations of artists to experiment and to capture the essence of Egypt in whatever medium they might employ. These range from the earliest predynastic painters representing a wonderland of little pyramidal hills and wavy-lined stretches of water, to the triumphant expressions of the power of the human spirit in the work of Old Kingdom sculptors and architects, the fusion of power, elegance and proportion in the Middle Kingdom, latterly to the still more sumptuous expressions of divine and royal power in the New Kingdom.

Indeed, the true mystery of Egypt lies in the work of its artists, craftsmen and engineers. Though they made the most majestic works of art yet to be produced over an extended time-scale by any society, Egyptian art, even at its mightiest, is still human in its proportions. Those proportions may be multiplied far beyond human scales but still they are within the comprehension of man. Take the greatest temple facade and reduce it to the size of a jewel and it will still be invested with proportion and hence with humanity: take a jewel and enlarge it to the scale of a pyramid and still it is comprehensible.

This degree of integration and the balance which the central role of the king ensured can best be observed in the work of Egyptian artists when they are concerned with the observation and recording of the natural world. There has never been so patent a delight in the life of animals and their companionship with man as the Egyptians displayed, especially, in the work of artists in the earliest periods of their history. This is a point to which we shall advert not infrequently.

For a thousand years Egypt was in truth 'the Peaceable Kingdom'. Secure from external threat, prosperous by the beneficence of the gods expressed in the gift of the Nile, confident in the sense of election as the chosen of the gods who lived amongst them, they were free to give rein to their prodigious creative energies. They were able to reach far beyond the normal limits of human achievement and to touch whatever divinity there may be (or may be imagined to be) in themselves or beyond the stars, a region which greatly intrigued the early Egyptians, as it has all thoughtful men.

It could not last: the Egyptians were human and human achievement is as limited as are human life-spans. But throughout the nearly five thousand years with which this book is concerned, from the middle of the fifth millennium BC to the coming of the Romans to Egypt, the precepts and aspirations which were first clearly articulated, notably in the third millennium before our era, continued to inform and suffuse life in the Valley. This was so even in the centuries most distant from the beginning, when much of the early inspiration had been transmuted into an inferior metal and the repetition of forms became a preoccupation of those who, with commendable if hopeless loyalty to the past, attempted to recall something of what Egypt once had been.

But though Egypt was unique in its creation of the first society which can be termed a nation, it was yet part of the larger world; its history, therefore, is not to be entirely isolated from the world around it. Ultimately, it was the impact of that larger world which was to bring the majestic sequence of the centuries of Egypt's greatness to a conclusion. Nor could it avoid the influence of the natural world which, though it must usually have seemed benign, yet could suddenly deliver a devastating shock even to the most secure of human societies. One such blow was experienced as the third millennium ended and the ancient Near East underwent one of its near-cataclysmic shifts of climate, introducing a regime of arid conditions very similar to those which have persisted to the present day. Such changes had been signalled in the latter part of the Old Kingdom, when hitherto virtually unknown misfortunes began to afflict the people of the Valley: a succession of low Niles may have contributed to the conditions which created the unrest which is taken to have been one of the reasons for the collapse of the royal authority which ended the Old Kingdom. The Causeway leading to the Pyramid of Unas, the last King of the Fifth Dynasty, *c*.2450 BC, where the earliest recension of the Pyramid Texts is to be found has, carved on its walls, graphic representations of the dreadful effects of famine on the people and their animals. Such scenes would perhaps have served as a reminder to the dead King on his last journey of the conditions which it would be his duty to alleviate when he was united with the sun-god in the eternity for which he was bound, as he had no doubt sought to do when he had reigned as an earthly sovereign.

The changes in climate were not peculiar to Egypt nor were their consequences confined to the Nile Valley. In the Arabian Gulf similar conditions prevailed, resulting in a quite dramatic fall in the level of the Gulf waters, by as much as two metres to something like their present level. In Arabia proper the brackish lakes which had run into the desert at the edge of what is now Ar-Rub al-Khali finally disappeared.[12] With them went the last vestiges of the old neolithic settlements which had clustered on the shores of the lakes, from the sixth millennium onwards. The process of desiccation had been at work in the peninsula for centuries before this time: it is possible to trace the decline of viable conditions there by the movement of one of the least expected communities of the ancient world, the cattle hunters and herders of Arabia.[13] They had flourished from the eighth or seventh millennia, as witnessed by the drawings on the rocks which they left wherever they followed the herds. It has been suggested that the style of engraving found in the earliest periods around Jubba in the north of Arabia, where a great lake once provided ample water for the herds of wild cattle, finally disappeared, several thousand years later, on the edge of the Rub al-Khali in the far south.

Deserts are created often as the result of a change in the direction of the prevailing wind and this is probably what affected the peninsula at this time. It is very likely that a similar phenomenon was the cause of Egypt's increased desiccation, added to the dire consequences of a fall in the Nile flood, brought about by adverse conditions far to the south, in the mountain ranges of East Africa.

Egypt's great contemporary Sumer also underwent radical changes at this time. The Sumerian city-states had fallen initially under the weight of the desert-born Akkadians in the twenty-fourth century BC. Then Sumer reasserted itself in a final burst of creative energy to disappear at last, at the end of the third millennium, submerged beneath the mass of Semitic-speakers, and the opportunistic invasions of the Elamites from south-western Iran, who were always ready to take advantage of any weakness of the Sumerian cities.

The arrival of the Semitic-speakers from the Syro-Arabian deserts was to have a profound effect on the history of the ancient Near East and ultimately of the world, most of it melancholy. The tribes who were forced to move from the deserts because of the adverse climatic conditions which they experienced were numerous, barbarous and undisciplined and at first destroyed whatever they encountered. They were also to have an enduring effect on the people of the Nile Valley and the civilisation which they had built.

To this time also is it possible to attribute the rise of nomadism which was to become one of the most potent and influential social systems to emerge in the ancient Near East, since the discovery of agriculture. Nomads, in the sense of unsettled hordes, had certainly been known for a long time – 'the people who know not grain', the Sumerians disparagingly called them – but nomadism is also a deliberately chosen and highly sophisticated way of life, intensely disciplined and dependent upon rigorously controlled cycles of pasturing. It first became a permanent factor in the life of the peoples of the Near East at this time, probably as the consequence of the deterioration of the climate at the end of the third millennium.

The contribution of Semitic-language speakers to the Egyptian gene-pool, though present in early times, was not especially important. The nomads of the desert lands which abutted the Valley were always considered the enemies of the settled agriculturists who made up the large part of the Egyptian population.

*

The Egyptians were not primarily city-dwelling people, unlike their Sumerian contemporaries. It is the more remarkable, therefore, that the Egyptians produced such powerful examples of monumental architecture, so early in their development. Without an understanding of the architecture of ancient Egypt, at all its most formative periods, particularly the earliest, it is impossible to understand the motivations which drove the society and which produced its vision of the world.

From the earliest moment of the Egyptian monarchy's existence great buildings began to fill the Valley. They were both functional, in that they supplied the setting for the king and his court and for the rounds of ceremonies which attended him, and symbolic, as they represented the power and authority of the state. Similarly, the king-as-god and his fellow divine powers were honoured in temples which became more and more splendid just as the tombs in which the living god and his closest associates were to spend eternity became ever larger, grander and more elaborate in construction. To understand the extraordinary quality of Egypt's achievement in the first phase of its existence and the influence which that achievement had on its subsequent history, it is necessary to consider the work of the builders of the great monuments which express so much of the essential Egyptian genius.

That genius expressed itself most dramatically in the ability to plan and build monumental buildings, of enduring presence and power. No people before their time and few since have been able to manipulate structures in space with such assurance and elegance, on so great a scale. Not only are many of the buildings themselves immense – the Great Pyramid, built *c*.2550 BC, is still one of the largest structures ever erected – but there are so many of them which have survived the ravages of time and the depredations of centuries of invasion or neglect. That they survive as they do is in large part the reason for the enduring fame of Egypt.

There was nothing in Egypt's prehistory, in the fourth millennium BC, to suggest that, in the space of a very few centuries, a built civilisation would arise in the Valley, which was so original and so magnificent. Those buildings which have survived from predynastic times are either simple houses,[14] with little to distinguish them from those of other contemporary cultures, or graves and funerary buildings;[15] our knowledge of the early shrines is mostly derived from sealings, ivory labels and, from later times, from hieroglyphs and carvings on the walls of tombs. In the case of some of these often very simple structures a line of descent can be detected which links them with the monumental buildings of Egyptian civilisation at its height. There is, however, a qualitative difference between a little wicker shrine of around 4000 BC and its simulacrum in stone in the heart of an immense temple of, say, the New Kingdom in the middle of the second millennium. But the great New Kingdom temple derives, ultimately, from the little wicker shrine.

It is instructive, as always, to compare the situation in respect of the development of an advanced architectural tradition in Egypt with that of Sumer. The city had much less significance in Egypt than was the case in southern Mesopotamia, where it became dominant from the middle of the fourth millennium. Cities require walls, gates, often defensive towers, all of which will accustom their architects (when such a calling actually exists) and their builders to work on a large scale using substantial, relatively long-lasting materials. The administrators of the city, both secular and religious, demand imposing structures in which to conduct their respective businesses and to encourage proper respect in those who are governed or who are required to worship (and, more important, to provender the worship) of the city's gods. These considerations led, early on, to the development of monumental architecture in Sumer, with the temple of the principal divinity taking its special place in the heart of the city and with the palace of the ruler and the offices of his bureaucracy providing another quarter, regularly to be found in Mesopotamian town plans.

The Sumerians have a significant chronological lead over the Egyptians in the creation of monumental buildings, with substantial religious buildings appearing in the middle of the fourth millennium, whilst large-scale buildings in Egypt date from the early First Dynasty, at the end of the millennium.[16] The association between architecture and the Kingship is crucial and, as in so many other departments of Egyptian life, it is the arrival of the kings and the need to provide quarters for a living and ruling god which give the impetus to building on a monumental scale in the Valley.

Another important factor in the contrasting development of the architectural traditions of the two peoples is the materials which their builders had at their disposal. In Sumer, with its lack of good-quality stone and, very largely, of timber the only material readily to hand was the inexhaustible supply of alluvial mud which was formed into sun-dried bricks, the shape of which became standardised by the fourth millennium. Egypt, on the other hand, was provided with every sort of stone in abundance.

However, in the very early centuries of the royal rule over the Valley, stone was only occasionally used and then on quite a small scale. The surviving monumental buildings of the Archaic period, the first two dynasties, representing the first four hundred years of Egyptian history, are built from brick, with stone appearing rarely and then only in quite modest usages, such as the flooring of an important tomb chamber. The buildings which do survive are almost without exception tombs, indicating that the houses of the living were built from less enduring materials. The use of brick at this time, given the evident enthusiasm with which the Egyptians were later to build in stone, is somewhat puzzling.

The apparent correspondences between Sumerian precedents and the architecture of Egypt in the Archaic period are intriguing. Though Sumer was generally bereft of good-quality stone, the foundations of one of the earliest monumental buildings in Mesopotamia, the Limestone Temple in the Eanna complex at Uruk, is a huge stone platform. This building dates from the middle of the fourth millennium; it thus anticipates the earliest large-scale stone building in Egypt, the Step Pyramid complex at Saqqara, by nearly a thousand years.[17] What survives today at Uruk are the stone foundations, a limestone platform on which the temple's superstructure was raised. It is not known whether this was also built in stone or in the Sumerians' customary material, mud-brick.

The stone for the Limestone Temple was quarried and transported to Uruk from beds some eighty miles to the west. The experiment, which must have demanded formidable logistics, appears never to have been repeated. Nonetheless it is clear that the Sumerians, by some process of which we have no inkling, had the technology available at so early a date to build a substantial structure in stone, its plan measuring 70 by 30 metres.

The extent of Western Asiatic influences on Egypt is highlighted when we consider the architecture of the earliest large structures in the Valley. The ground plans of the great tombs of the First Dynasty, with their recessed and panelled walls, c.3000 BC,[18] are so markedly similar to those of the earlier temples in Uruk (including the Limestone Temple) that it cannot simply be a matter of coincidence. Similarly, the Egyptian use of brick at this time recalls a development which is precisely paralleled in Sumer, of a slightly prior date. Yet, why should this be so? Why should the tombs of the great magnates in Saqqara, which may replicate the palaces of their living existence, be built to a Mesopotamian plan in mud-brick? Why should the walls of the royal funerary complexes in Abydos feature the recessed panelling and buttressing which are distinctive features of the walls of early Mesopotamian and south-west Iranian temple buildings? Why, indeed, did such panelling, later abstracted to an element in the design of sarcophagi, dominate the Step Pyramid complex at Saqqara, and survive even into the New Kingdom?

Stone was occasionally used in the First Dynasty and its use was continued in the latter part of the Second Dynasty, though still rather tentatively. Then, in the Third Dynasty, during the reign of Djoser Netjerykhet its second king, architecture in stone suddenly explodes into the miracle of the Stepped Pyramid and its ancillary buildings raised on the escarpment above Memphis. From this point onwards still larger, more elaborate and sophisticated buildings are erected all over the Valley.

Two categories of monumental architecture predominate in Egypt, the temple and the tomb. As Egypt in its origins was said to be ruled by the gods it was proper that their dwelling places should reflect the highest skills and most refined craftsmanship of every age which honoured them. The development of the Egyptian temple is nothing like as clear-cut as that which led to the temples of Sumer. There the sequence was, first, a little shrine which later becomes a long-sided rectangular building, later still with sharply articulated recessed panelling, which, by the end of the third millennium, has become the ziggurat, the stepped tower, the construction of which was determined by the dismantling and burying of each discarded or outmoded building, to be replaced by a usually grander and certainly higher platform on which the new temple itself was raised. On the summit of the temple mountain, with its succession of stepped platforms, stood the shrine of the god, in which the most sacred rituals were conducted. In Egypt the process is quite different.

Though the Pyramid in the centre of the Djoser complex at Saqqara is a very fair example of the *idea* of a ziggurat, clearly it is not one. The Step Pyramid began its life as a mastaba, the rectangular, box-like brick structure familiar from the First and Second Dynasties but, taking advantage of the new technology available to the Third Dynasty, it was built in stone, not mud brick.[19] Gradually the basic design was modified with successive steps being added on to the considerably extended base of the structure, in which the original mastaba was embedded. The development of the Step Pyramid is thus quite different from the ziggurat, which achieved general acceptance in the Sumerian cities, several hundred years later. The appearance is uncannily similar nonetheless and, again, as in the case of the First Dynasty tombs, it is difficult to believe that there is no connection between the two architectural forms, were it not for the problem of chronology. But it is likely that both represent the nearly simultaneous appearance of an identical archetype, the stairway to the stars.

Like the pyramid, with which it shares many mythological qualities, the Egyptian Temple is also a product of the most profound levels of the people's creative expression. According to the Egyptians' own explanation of the origin of the temple, this was connected with the journey made by the Falcon, the mystical first god-King of Egypt accompanied by a most ancient and mysterious divinity, Ta-Tanen, in search of the land which was to become Egypt. This sequence is also bound up with the very ancient Egyptian idea of the 'Divine Emerging Island', the original place of creation and the first home of the gods. The island is itself also an archetypal form, representing the unique in human experience, isolation and a location which customarily suggests a divine or numinous presence. In all mythologies islands are places of origins, as much as the need to reach them is the object of the quest. The archetypal island is contained within the most ancient form of the tomb in Egypt, a little mound which is both the island itself and a commemoration of the mounds of sand which were raised over the earliest burials on the outskirts of Badarian villages in the middle of the fifth millennium.

The earliest temples, to judge by the evidence of representations on First Dynasty ivory 'labels', were reed structures built in the shape of animals. This is a remarkable confirmation of the profound importance of the animal world to the Egyptians and is another example of the identification of the animal and the god which is one of the most frequently encountered Egyptian perceptions.

Although the Egyptian temple went through many developments, its basic plan remained remarkably consistent. A high, impressive facade, usually pillared, leads from a great forecourt through a portico into one or more immense halls, with pillars rising, often to great heights in New

Kingdom and later temples, like an immense stand of trees. The floor of the temple, laid in stone, rises imperceptibly towards the building's heart, the most sacred shrine concealed in its deepest recesses. The shrine reproduced in stone the archaic structures, built of reeds or wattle, which were considered to be themselves touched by the divine power.

There are few temples from Old Kingdom times and those which have survived are varied in their architectural design. Many are associated with the pyramids in which the kings of the Fourth, Fifth and Sixth Dynasties were buried. One of the most imposing is that associated with the Pyramid of Khafra (Chephren), he of the second of the Giza pyramids, who is identified with the Great Sphinx. The Valley Temple of Khafra is built of great red granite blocks and is really not at all typical of other Egyptian temples. It is however wonderfully conceived, for in its interior, which was never intended to be penetrated by human sight, a series of exceptionally fine sculptures of the king was placed so that light from clerestories, reflected on the polished stone on which the statues' bases stood and on the columns which surrounded them, gave the appearance of living flesh to the portraits of the king. The concept is extraordinary and its realisation approaches genius.[20]

Khafra's Valley temple has been the subject of a good deal of speculation, much of it hinging on the question of its date of construction. Some researchers believe that the temple, which is so unlike other Egyptian temples, is of a very much earlier date than is generally supposed and was built long before Khafra's reign. Cited in support of this opinion is the casing of some parts of the temple's exterior blocks which are dressed with granite. This was probably carried out in Khafra's time, say the proponents of this view, as the original stone had become considerably degraded. This is the result, it is suggested, of long exposure to the elements including a much more substantial regime of rainfall and flooding than has ever been the case during the centuries which have elapsed since Khafra's lifetime.

This proposition, and the similar questions about the age of the Sphinx, which is also said to be much older than is customarily accepted, flies in the face of all conventional Egyptological thought.[21] At present there seems to be no certain way of resolving the issue, other, perhaps, than by substantial excavations at the Valley Temple which the Egyptian authorities, understandably, do not seem inclined to authorise.

However the argument which questions the age of Khafra's temple on the grounds of its unusual appearance may not be entirely well-founded. The Archaic period and the early Old Kingdom were both times of great creative experiment in Egypt, with the royal designers and craftsmen producing a wide variety of forms in, for example, pottery and stone carving which, for one reason or another, were never taken into the canon of accepted designs. So it may have been with Khafra's temple, an experimental design (the clerestories and reflective floorings referred to earlier are quite unprecedented and were never repeated) which was simply not retained. But the evidence of the recasing of the temple's exterior stone-work is puzzling.

In the Middle Kingdom, in the beginning of the second millennium BC, the more austere conventions which become evident in the portrait sculpture of the Eleventh and Twelfth Dynasties are present also in the monumental architecture which the kings, passionate builders almost to a man, erected so prodigally. Middle Kingdom temples are often angular but are most elegantly proportioned. The funerary complex of King Nebhetepre Montuhotpe II at Deir el-Bahri for example is brilliantly conceived and is almost as much without precedent as the Step Pyramid of King Djoser. Not only is the building designed as a succession of rising terraces, ornamented with fine statuary and set within an artificial garden, beautiful in both concept and execution, it also enhances magically the powerful landscape in which it is so boldly set.

The Egyptian temple reached its apogee, at least in terms of size and grandeur, in the New Kingdom. The kings of the Eighteenth and Nineteenth Dynasties vied with each other across the generations in building yet more grandiose sacred palaces in which to house the divinities to whom they paid especial honour. Karnak and Luxor ('the Palaces', in Arabic) still amaze by the scale and prodigality of the buildings which went to make ancient Thebes the most imposing city in the world in the second millennium BC, to the extent that it became the archetype of the city consecrated to the gods, inspiring wonder in all who saw it. Even in the days of its decline it was marvellous in the eyes of Herodotus; today, two and a half millennia later, it is still an architectural marvel which draws visitors from across the world to its time-defying, ruined splendours.

Even in the centuries of apparent terminal decline the kings still built temples which proclaimed Egypt's paramountcy in the empire of the spirit. Successive Libyan, Ethiopian and Greek dynasts, the successors of the native-born Egyptian kings, continued to raise great monuments or to repair and extend the structures left by their predecessors; even the Romans contributed to the tradition which, by their time, stretched back more than three thousand years.

It is remarkable that, having so early on mastered the exploitation of stone so brilliantly, it seems always to have been used for buildings which had other than a secular purpose. Stone architecture was reserved, apparently, for temples, tombs, sometimes for funerary monuments and, of course, for portraiture. There are no surviving examples of stone-built palaces, even of the greatest kings, who seem to have been content to spend their lives in brick-built structures, relying on stone to accommodate their eternity.

The quality of Egyptian architecture, as much as its quantity and scale, has inevitably prompted much speculation about the nature of Egyptian technological and scientific knowledge. It *is* very remarkable that stone building on so monumental a scale was perfected in Egypt effectively in one generation and then exploited with absolute assurance thereafter, to achieve the splendour of the pyramids in the Fourth Dynasty, in what amounts to a few short decades. The manipulation of huge masses of stone and the precision with which the stone was worked rightly induce admiration where they do not provoke amazement. The subtlety of the mathematics employed in the surveying, site preparation and actual construction of some of the largest and most complex structures raised by men demands respect even from the least committed observers.

Again, there would seem to be only two alternative explanations for the high quality of Egyptian engineering management. As would seem to be the case with the Egyptians' understanding of the principles of celestial mechanics, their engineering and architectural skills can only be the product of an evolved body of knowledge, of exceptional refinement, the evidence for which is now lost, or it is the product of an ability to absorb precedents and to respond empirically to creative challenges which is unknown on this scale in any other culture at the time.

The second of these possibilities will be favoured here. The Egyptians, as early as the Pyramid Age, set the orientation of their buildings by the stars; the precise orientation of the sides of the Great Pyramid and its alignment with the cardinal points, with a minuscule degree of error, are examples of the application of what is surely empirically-gained knowledge raised to the level of genius. There has been much consideration of the extent to which the Egyptians had knowledge of transcendental numbers, as π (pi), which can be obtained by the distinctly arcane method of observing a drum revolving and ϕ (phi) which is also known as the Golden Section. This has been defined as 'the division of a straight line into two unequal parts, in such a way that the smaller part is in the same ratio to the larger part as the larger part is to the whole';[22] the proportion of the greater part to the total line length is approximately 0.618. The Golden Section is found in nature, in, for example, the spiral of a shell. It was widely employed in Renaissance and later classical architecture: it is said to have been demonstrated to be present in many Egyptian buildings, obviously of much greater antiquity.

The matter is, however, disputed. Several of the principal authorities on the history of Egyptian architecture have argued that the inhabitants of the Valley in antiquity were well acquainted with the Golden Section;[23] they propose, for example, that it is basic to the mathematics of the Pyramids. Others, particularly some recent historians of science, have denied that the Egyptians had any such knowledge, believing that when the Golden Section, or something like it, appears in an Egyptian building this is the result of chance. This conclusion seems less likely than that the builders did at least understand the effects of such a system of proportion.

For essentially the Golden Section is concerned with proportion. Constructions which contain it are peculiarly aesthetically satisfying, a fact known to architects and builders for millennia; it is therefore that unusual phenomenon, a mathematical formula which determines a subjective response in those who observe its effects. The ratio of the Golden Section is to be found also in the Fibonacci Series, in which each successive quantity is the product of the previous two numbers. Thus the Series runs: 0, 1, 1, 2, 3, 5, 8, 13, 21, 34, 55, 89 ... and so on. If any one of the numbers above is divided by the next higher, the ratio of the Golden Section, 0.618 (or a value close to it), is produced. It has been argued that the Egyptians recognised the Fibonacci Series and incorporated its expression in many of their buildings. The most powerful advocate of this belief in Egyptian architectural skills was the late R. A. Schwaller de Lubicz whose views, often derided by orthodox scholars, are now coming, guardedly, to be considered more objectively.[24]

There are no examples from the surviving Egyptian literature which can be accepted as demonstrating the conscious or planned use of the Golden Section in any theoretical or abstract sense. It may be quite simply, that the Egyptians' extraordinary instinct for form and balance produced the *effect* of the Golden Section without the need actually to define it.

If the Egyptians can be said to have had one principle that governed their entire existence, which determined the management of their society (was, indeed, the very reason for its existence) and which accounted for the overwhelming importance of the Kingship, it was the maintenance of order, stability and proportion. The basis of Egyptian civilisation was the reconciliation of all the elements which were required to be in balance, to ensure the continued ordered existence of the cosmos. Order, which embraces proportion and, in a practical as much as in a philosophical sense, truth, was identified with the ancient goddess Ma'at, the daughter, according to later theologies, of the King of the Gods, Ra. In her name the king was said to rule. Order also governed the practice of architecture and the creation of monumental structures as much as it did the making of a statue of a king or an image of the gods.

Clearly, much Egyptian architectural practice was essentially pragmatic, its disciplines empirically established, with frequent adaptations being made even to the largest structures (the Step Pyramid is an example) demonstrating changes both of mind and of direction. Until comparatively late times there is very little evidence of Egyptian architects working out their projects in any sort of mathematical or engineering detail before the commencement of the project itself. They seem to have been quite prepared to adjust either to a new situation, produced perhaps by the topography of a site or by the demands of a royal client. But above all else it is clear that they saw architecture as yet another expression of the harmony which was Egypt's unique contribution to the management of the world as it was.

It may therefore be that the exceptional quality of the architecture of ancient Egypt was the product of the clear light of Egypt and the phenomenal 'eye' of those who directed the creation of the monuments.

This does not explain how Imhotep, the builder of the Step Pyramid complex for Djoser, was able to create so vast, elaborate and superbly executed a complex of buildings with absolutely no precedent on which to work (for surely he did not know of the Limestone temple?) and to direct a workforce with no experience whatsoever of the effects which he was seeking to achieve, in materials whose properties he could have had virtually no prior knowledge. Yet so assured was their ability that there seems little doubt that Egyptian builders could vary the orientation of an entire temple when the star to which it had at its construction been aligned no longer threw its light into the far reaches of the temple on the appointed day, as it was originally planned to do. Indeed, this seems to have happened on several occasions.

Observers of these matters, if they are not prepared to accept a mystological explanation for what must otherwise seem strange and enigmatic, can only recognise that the genius of Egyptian architects was as it was precisely because they were working in new, untried fields of endeavour and in materials which they were the first to encounter. Even such firmly material products of the human genius as the great monuments of Egypt originated first in the mind's eye, before they found expression in three dimensions. Thus it must be with the Golden Section, whose frequency of exploitation in many cultures and as many different periods suggests that it is locked into the human unconscious, ensuring an appropriate aesthetic response to the choices which need to be made to provide an aesthetically satisfying result. If this presumption is accepted, then the implications for much, perhaps all, human creative endeavour are very great. It would be wholly consonant with the underlying theme of this book that the unique Egyptian contribution to civilisation was to be the first in which all these elements were articulated and, being so articulated, were liberated, to take their place amongst the acknowledged archetypes which determine human behaviour.

CHAPTER II

THE ANCIENT EGYPTIAN PSYCHE

——— •◆• ———

To understand why Egypt exercised so profound an appeal to the imagination of men living in antiquity and why it has continued to do so over the past four thousand years of the history of what was to become the Western world, it may be helpful to turn aside from the more ordered recital of Egypt's history. I shall try to probe into such issues as the nature of the individual, of individual consciousness and what may seem to some to be the still mistier regions of the collective unconscious as they were relevant to, and affected the lives and attainments of, the early inhabitants of the Nile Valley. Though such concepts are now part of the familiar jargon of many studies related to man as a social animal, they have not been applied so generally to the study of societies themselves. Yet there is little doubt that the psychological principles related to the individual can, with some qualifications as to scale and the influences of the social environment, be applied also to the study of those groups which make up societies themselves. The attempt will therefore be made here to examine the emergence of complex societies, specifically the proto-typical complex society which arose in the Nile Valley from the middle of the fourth millennium onwards, in the light of these principles.

The psychological paradigms which most usefully contribute to an understanding of the mechanisms which drive human groups and which hence lend themselves to the examination of the origins of complex societies, are those developed by C. G. Jung and his followers. Jungian analytical psychology is less dogmatic than that formulated by Freud and his associates; it is more concerned with the effects on the individual psyche of those common psychological drives which are universal in their application. Jung sought to identify the common psychic inheritance of humankind and to explain human behaviour in terms of and as a consequence of, that inheritance.

At various times during his long life (1875–1961) C. G. Jung seems to have felt himself strongly drawn to Egypt and to the study of its place in antiquity. As a boy he had developed an interest in Assyriology and Egyptology;[1] however, there was no faculty at that time for the study of archaeology in his local university at Basle and his original ideas of a career as an archaeologist had to be abandoned. He turned, therefore, to medicine, one of the professions which had engaged his family for generations.

Egypt features frequently in Jung's writings, in various contexts. Much more directly than Sigmund Freud he seems to have understood that there was a deep and very special stratum of experience underlying the familiar stereotype of 'Ancient Egypt'. Even in the early years of the twentieth century this stereotype was already well formed. Egypt, seemingly, was mysterious, remote and was often represented as being, in some unspecified way, alien to the humanistic tradition of European culture which, as every educated man knew, ultimately drew its inspiration from Greece, heavily overladen with the revealed truth of the Judeo-Christian sacred texts. This view inevitably prejudiced an understanding of the unique nature of the Egyptian experience, certainly of the experience of the earliest periods during which its distinctive character was being laid down.

Jung's recognition of the deeper levels of human consciousness and, in particular, of the collective unconscious, drew him on to speculate about pre-conscious levels and what he tends to describe as the nature of the 'primitive'. It can be confidently asserted that Jung came closer to apprehending the nature of pristine societies, of which Egypt was the only enduring example, than any observer before him.

Jung travelled to Egypt in 1925. This, his sole journey there, was towards the end of a visit to Africa, an experience which was of profound importance to him. He does not seem to have written of his Egyptian visit, other than in letters to some of his correspondents, until *Memories, Dreams and Recollections* was published in 1961.[2] Jung was a child of his time and of his own cultural inheritance which inevitably influenced, though it did not imprison, him. The attitude which characterised African society as 'primitive' was to make him think of the Africans whom he met as being on a level of cultural development less advanced than that of his own European background. In setting out, he later recalled, he felt that in Africa 'one meets men of other epochs'.[3] 'The desire then grew in me to carry the historical comparison still further by descending to a still lower cultural level.'[4]

He came to Egypt from the south, travelling up from east Africa, observing that he wished 'to approach this cultural realm ... from the South, from the sources of the Nile. I was less interested in the complex Asiatic elements in Egyptian culture than in the Hamitic contribution'.[5] Jung recognises here the importance of the essentially African character of Egypt but he does not appear to have written further about this aspect of Egypt's cultural inheritance. He would certainly have been unusual in his time in rejecting what might be called the Semitic substratum in the Egyptian psyche, recognisable as a component in the ancient Egyptian language, which many commentators of his day would have seen as being far more important than the Hamitic or African element.

Jung continued to meditate on Egypt and on the particular nature of the Egyptian psyche. His most extended consideration is recorded in the

Collected Letters, in which many of his references to Egypt are contained; in particular he attempts to identify the nature of the psychology of the Egyptians in high antiquity. Thus in one letter written in 1939 he describes the king as 'the self and individual of the people'.[6] He speaks of the dual nature of the ruler and the importance of the king's placenta,[7] which fulfilled the function of a twin, existing in the celestial sphere awaiting reunion with the king after death. He suggests that the idea of the *ka*, the etheric double and the vital essence which gave life, descended from the placenta.

The idea that the king represented the individuality of the Egyptian people, becoming in effect their 'self', is very telling, as is Jung's awareness of the significance of opposites which was always one of the identifying marks of the Egyptian psyche in social organisation, religious belief, and art. The suggestion that the placenta represents the King's twin provides a reasonable explanation for its place in the line of royal standards which were borne before the Archaic kings, as early as *c*.3000 BC ; indeed, it is the only wholly convincing explanation for the appearance of the placenta in Egyptian rituals of the Archaic period and later.

During his African journey Jung was deeply moved by the realisation that the very ancient cult of Horus of the Horizon was that of the 'newly risen divine light', the first light at dawn, the glimmer on the eastern horizon. In the New Kingdom, for example, it was believed that the Sphinx at Giza represented Harmachis, a manifestation of Horus in the Horizon, and was worshipped as such.

Jung observed the phenomenon of the Nile baboons who seem to wait for the first rays of the sun, to greet its glory.[8].This moment is brilliantly captured in the great temple of Abu Simbel where a line of cynocephalus baboons is sculpted on a frieze at the top of the temple's facade. The baboons sit on their haunches, their paws raised, seemingly applauding the sun's rays as they strike them in the first light of dawn. The allegorical significance of the baboons' action is not in the least diminished by the knowledge that their response is primarily physiological, for they are in fact wakening themselves and boosting their circulation, torpid after the night's sleep.

The sensitivity of the Egyptians to the world around them and their capacity for synthesizing disparate phenomena into a single poetic image is nowhere better demonstrated than in this celebration of the sun returning to the world. The Egyptians were fascinated by the band of light which appears at the eastern horizon heralding the appearance of the sun each day. They expressed this moment as the god returning after surviving the perils of the night, when he travelled in his divine barque through the underworld.

The moment immediately before the dawn was of special importance in many of the rituals associated with the 'heliacal' rising of the great constellations. As the light on the horizon intensifies a constellation can be seen moments before it disappears in the light of the sun. To the ancients this was an especially charged event. The constellations which appear heliacally included Sirius, the most important of all to the Egyptians, associated by them with the renewal of the year, and those which were identified as dominant in the cycle of the Precession of the Equinoxes.

Horus was represented in later Egyptian mythology as Osiris' son; as such he personified the living king. But Horus was much older than Osiris in the Egyptian pantheon for as the Falcon Prince he was identified as the first unifier of the two lands, Upper and Lower Egypt. Jung, however, believed Osiris to be the 'patriarch' of Near Eastern Saviour figures.[9] This he was not, but Jung perhaps was not to know this, reliant as he was on the strongly biblically-influenced scholarship of the time.

Jung, like many others who came after him, was inclined to regard the divinities of ancient Egypt as representations of celestial or astronomical phenomena. He was perhaps more liberal than most in his acceptance of what have come to be regarded as the more speculative, even arcane areas of scholarship. He was much interested in that greatest demonstration of celestial mechanics, the Precession of the Equinoxes, which is also revealed by the appearance of one of twelve constellations on the eastern horizon immediately before the sun's appearance at dawn.

Jung was convinced of the importance of the Precession on the course of human affairs, a view which is coming increasingly, if still guardedly, to be accepted by some historians of science.[10] The entire cycle of the Precession is said to represent a Great, or Platonic, Year. This is an idea which seems always to have had a special meaning and significance to Jung, as he returns to it on several occasions.[11] In speaking of the uncertainties of his own day he often attributes them to the fact that the world was passing from the sign of Pisces to that of Aquarius, a transition bringing in its train changes which he considered as calamitous as those which heralded the transition from Taurus to Aries, sometime around the year 2000 BC, after the Old Kingdom ended.[12]

He saw these periods, when the universe is conceived as moving from one sign in the Great Zodiac to another (just as the solar zodiac moves from one to the next through the twelve signs), at intervals of 2160-year periods, as times of particular distress and melancholy when cataclysmic events are likely to beset mankind. Jung described these periods as 'transitions between the aeons'.

It is generally agreed that knowledge of the Precession does not extend back into the third millennium but was first defined in late antiquity, in Hellenistic times, by Hipparchus of Bithynia. He drew on somewhat earlier records, compiled a century and a half before his lifetime. But this may not be the full extent of the matter for it is clear that empirical observation of celestial phenomena can predict the Precession over a more limited time-scale than its 25,920-year sequence would seem to demand. The observable constellations apparently retrogress by one degree of arc in seventy-two years; thus in only two or three lifetimes, or with longer recorded observations retained for example by a temple community a discernable shift of a constellation or star marked against a natural feature, such as a hilltop or a stand of trees, would become evident. The quality of ancient Egyptian observation is unquestionable and the deduction of the effects of the Precession would have been well within their capabilities.

To Jung the recurrence of symbols associated with certain of the constellations in the several epochs of human history during which the great civilisations of antiquity emerged and flourished was compelling. Their recurrence indicated that the choice of a certain image as the archetype of the aeon and identified as the dominating constellation in the dawn sky, which was reflected in the art, architecture and cults of the period, is not merely accidental or the outpouring of excited imaginations. The Twins, the Bull, the Ram, and the Fish all feature in the catalogue of ancient symbolism during the epochs attributed to them, extending, roughly, from the seventh millennium to the end of antiquity; all were important to Jung and indicative of their choice as significant forms amongst the societies which were directly ancestral to our own. Each of the constellations with which they were identified rose 'heliacally' in the dawn light, at the vernal equinox, at approximately two thousand year intervals from *c.*6500 BC to the end of the ancient world.

The evidence that the most refined astronomical observation was practised in Egypt in the third millennium BC (and probably even before that date) is clear from the precision with which the Pyramids at Giza are aligned to the cardinal points, a precision which could only have been achieved by their alignment with the stars.[13] This fact alone makes Jung's belief in the Egyptians' knowledge of the Precession a good deal less speculative than once it seemed.

Jung's understanding of the nature of the Egyptian Kingship led him to view the development of early Egypt as being determined by those profound levels of consciousness to which the individual psyche may have access but is probably itself unable to recognise or define. The exceptional quality of the Egyptian psychic experience, the rapid development of its institutions, rituals, hierarchies and canons of belief which is the consequence of the outflowing of the archetypes, make it possible to identify something very like an emerging 'self' in archaic Egyptian society.

To compare the processes at work in the earliest phases of the Egyptian state and which were manifested in the arts and social forms which flourished there, with the condition which Jung defined as 'individuation' will demonstrate this point.[14] Egypt's development as a complex society permits the drawing of analogy between the experience of the individual growing to self-awareness and the emergence of what was to become the first fully articulated nation-state in human history, for the state may be considered to be the 'self' of the extended group. It is precisely this moving towards a fully realised awareness of statehood that allows the comparison to be made with the progression of the self to the realisation of its own discrete identity.

In many respects the progress of the early rulers towards the unification of Egypt is directly analogous to the process undergone by the psyche when moving towards its own individuation. The definition which expresses the acquisition by the individual of the awareness of its own discrete existence, and its interaction with the world around it, is precisely mirrored in the unfolding of the campaigns of the early kings to achieve the unification of the Valley.

The concept of unification was the 'Great Idea' which the early kings of Egypt pursued with such remarkable determination, and its ultimate formulation into a unitary political state. This was a very singular concept in that, as in the case of so many other Egyptian innovations, it was entirely without precedent. No other people had ever attempted to produce a nation out of an extended region with a diversity of traditions and social organisation.

Undoubtedly one of the most important mechanisms available to Egypt in its early progress towards the realisation of its own statehood was the invention of writing. This allowed for the very rapid creation of a system both of record and of creative expression. As with the extraordinarily swift flowering of the other arts at this time, it contributed to a sustained release of creative energy on a scale never before experienced by any other human society.

The experience of living in societies which flourished immediately after the invention of writing and the creation of sophisticated political structures in the form of states and cities was wholly unlike that of earlier groups, which ultimately derived their character from the primate experience. At a psychic level (this term is used here in the sense that Jung used it in the original German, meaning of or appertaining to the psyche) at least they were still strongly linked with the primeval primate communities; their experience was unlike that of later societies which were subject to the inflow of many diverse external influences of a value approximately equal to their indigenous experience.

Jung demonstrated that the concept of the collective unconscious explains many of the less rational or otherwise inexplicable apprehensions and motivations of the human psyche at its most profound level. In the pristine society which was Egypt it is possible to see the influences of the collective unconscious at work in ways quite different from the experience of later cultures. The collective unconscious is the fountain from which the archetypes flow. The collective unconscious in Egypt is as powerful and as pristine a phenomenon as the society itself.

Jung observed that 'the unconscious is infinitely more common to all men than are the contents of their individual consciousness. The unconscious is, in fact, the condensation of the average run of historical experience'.[15] The remarkable consistency of the Egyptian response to the promptings of the collective unconscious during the early centuries demonstrates the truth of this observation admirably. It is in this sense too that all Western societies, and many in Western Asia, can claim themselves to be the heirs of ancient Egypt.

Jung's contribution to the uncovering of the deeper levels of the human psyche focused in particular upon definitions of the collective unconscious, the concept of the archetypes, and of individuation. Each of these needs to be examined, though to do so briefly (or even succinctly) runs the risk of dealing inadequately with what are extremely complex and many-levelled propositions. However, for the purpose of this review, the definitions provided by Jung himself offer a starting point.

> The hypothesis of a collective unconscious belongs to the class of ideas that people at first find strange but soon come to possess and use as familiar conceptions.

This has been the case with the concept of the unconscious in general. After the philosophical idea of the unconscious, in the form presented chiefly by Carus and von Hartmann, had gone down under the overwhelming wave of materialism and empiricism, leaving hardly a ripple behind it, it gradually reappeared in the scientific domain of medical psychology.

At first the concept of the unconscious was limited to denoting the state of repressed or forgotten concepts.

> A more or less superficial layer of the unconscious is undoubtedly personal. I call it the *personal unconscious*. But this personal unconscious rests upon a deeper layer, which does not derive from personal experience and is not a personal acquisition but is unborn. This deeper layer I call the *collective unconscious*. I have chosen the term 'collective' because this part of the unconscious is not individual but universal: in contrast to the personal psyche, it has contents and modes of behaviour that are more or less the same everywhere and in all individuals. It is, in other words, identical in all men and thus constitutes a common psychic substrate of a suprapersonal nature which is present in every one of us.[16]

Regarding 'the archetypes' Jung observes: 'Primitive tribal lore is concerned with archetypes that have been modified in a special way.'[17]

> The term 'archetype' . . . designates only those psychic contents which have not yet been submitted to conscious elaboration and are therefore an immediate datum of psychic experience. . . . The archetype is essentially an unconscious content that is altered by becoming conscious and by being perceived, and it takes its colour from the individual consciousness in which it happens to appear.[18]

'Individuation', the third concept described by Jung as the maturation process of personality induced by the analysis of the unconscious, is the process whereby the psyche becomes aware of its own discrete existence and its relationship to other individuals and entities with which it is required to deal.[19]

The concept of individuation describes the progress towards maturity experienced by the self. Individuation makes possible the transition from the collective experience and from the pervasive influence of the collective unconscious to the identification by the individual of distinct and specific responses to his or her environment, at all levels. It will be suggested here that this procedure is comparable with the transition to self-awareness which the Nile Valley culture underwent, particularly in the period from the end of the fourth millennium to the last centuries of the third.

These three concepts depend upon the understanding that *all* humans, of all periods and backgrounds, share a common psychic inheritance. This inheritance will, of course, be conditioned by particular circumstances, of environment, education, societal pressures and the inculcation of particular systems of belief. In essence the inheritance of our human past, and that of the period which preceded the attainment of our present state of 'modern' humanity, is common to us all no matter in what age we may live or where we pass our lives.

With this in mind it is possible to examine the history of past societies in the knowledge that the same imperatives, motivations, apprehensions and rationalisations link today and yesterday in one seamless fabric of existence. That this must be so has been further demonstrated by the work of other scholars who, working from a more mechanistic basis than Jung, have shown that the common neurophysiological system which all humans share produces identical neuropsychological responses.[20] This has been demonstrated most convincingly in the context of work carried out amongst shamans of the !Kung San bushmen. When in trance the shaman will produce drawings of what the researchers concerned have described as 'entoptic phenomena', that is to say shapes and formations glimpsed at the edge of vision which are identical to those found in cave or similarly located paintings and rock engravings of virtually every other 'primitive' culture anywhere in the world.

Identical phenomena have also been reproduced under laboratory conditions from subjects drawn from impeccably advanced Western societies; they also manifest themselves in conditions of stress, in hallucination and migraine. The researchers involved have identified a similar process at work in the art of Upper Palaeolithic cultures; there is no doubt that it is a principle of universal application in time and place. It may be said that the laws which govern neuropsychological responses are, within the limitations of the human psyche, as unchanging as the laws of physics.

Against the background of some of the basic principles on which his system of analytical psychology was constructed, it is obviously relevant to consider what is known of Jung's own preoccupations with ancient Egypt. It will be evident that, as in so many other of the areas of human experience with which he concerned himself, many of his ideas on Egypt and particularly of the development of Egyptian civilisation were remarkably prescient, often far in advance of Egyptological thought in his lifetime.

To apply the ideas of individuation or of the collective unconscious to Egypt in the earliest centuries of its corporate existence is not, of course, to deny the role of the individual, nor the variety and diversity of the experiences undergone by individuals living in the Valley. But in the collective phase of the Egyptian experience may be found an explanation for the swift and apparently ready acceptance of forms, customs, beliefs and social organisation over extended distances and time-scales which are evident at this time and which are otherwise difficult to explain. It is even possible that the Egyptians themselves had some sense of the psychological implications of the transition from the collective unconsciousness to that of the individual; such an awareness would account for their personification of the strange, indeterminate, bisexual divinity called Atum, who is sometimes spoken of as the 'Undifferentiated One', whom they saw as the *primum mobile* of the whole process of creation.

The comparison between the experience of individuation at the level of the individual self and what was happening collectively in Egypt at this time is demonstrated by the appearance at an early date in Egyptian art and ritual, of an almost obsessional pairing, the constant linking of apparent opposites in everything concerned with the emergent Egyptian state. As Jung wrote, 'the One is never separated from the Other, its antithesis'.[21] Jung also called individuation 'a mysterious conjunction, the self being experienced as a nuptial union of opposite halves'.[22]

It is to this phase of the experience that the widespread idea of the Twins belongs: the pair of something more than mortal beings who encapsulate different, often opposing, characteristics but yet are ineluctably bound together, two halves, almost, of some more total being. In this remarkable Egyptian preoccupation with dualism, the essential idea was that everything has its counterpart or opposite; even the king himself was conceived as a twin. In the ancient world twins were always regarded as uncanny, the possessors of unusual powers. The Egyptians believed that at the time of the fashioning of the king prior to his birth, a task discharged by the ram-headed god Khnum who had charge of such matters, his twin was created and translated at once to the Beyond, where he existed in a sort of parallel state to the king's; it is from this concept that the deference paid to the royal placenta derives. The royal twin is not the same as the *ka*, an etheric double possessed by everyone. The idea of the twin as the eternal counterpart of the living king is another African, probably originally Nilotic, concept, for twins have always exercised a powerful and mysterious attraction in African societies.

A striking demonstration of this idea of the dual identity of the king which gives support to Jung's analysis is provided by his invocation as the 'two-dwellers-in-the-palace, that is Horus and Set'. Here the king seems to be accepted as the personification of the two eternal opposites, the two perpetually warring divinities who are only reconciled in his person. The queen was 'she who looks on Horus and Set'; only the great King Khasekhemui, whose name means 'the Two Powers are Reconciled', proclaimed the resolution of this duality of personality at the end of the Second Dynasty, *c.*2700 BC. By displaying it in the *serekh*, the enigmatic badge which contained his name as the Living Horus, surmounted by both the falcon of Horus and the hound of Set, Khasekhemui came closest to the declaration of the twinship of the two gods.

In Egypt the need to reconcile apparent opposites is one of the most powerful psychological imperatives of the early royal state. The Two Lands, the union of Upper and Lower Egypt, the Horus of the north and the Horus of the south, the two contenders Horus and Set, the gods and goddesses produced in pairs at the time of their creation, the Lions of Yesterday and Tomorrow, the two shrines of Upper and Lower Egypt, the Two Ladies (one of the royal titles referring to the tutelary goddesses of the Kingdoms), the Two Crowns, even the remarkable repetition of red and white symbolism (a fact which intrigued Jung[23]) in the crowns, palaces, and the lands themselves, all emphasise the dual nature of the evolving state and the deliberate expression of that duality.

With the experience of individuation on a national scale came a streaming out of the archetypes, a phenomenon of the condition, for, as Jung states, 'in this still very obscure field of psychological experience, where we are in direct contact, so to speak, with the archetype, its psychic power is felt in full force'.[24]

In early Egypt many of the archetypes are already apparent in the art of the time, when associated with the king and the state; the devices employed are already dominant and immensely powerful, having their origins in a past far distant.

The greatest and most enduring of all the archetypes which ancient Egypt released was undoubtedly the king himself. He was the centre of the universe; sometimes indeed he was simply titled 'Lord of All', an honorific otherwise held by the exalted god Ptah. In early times one of the royal titles was *ity* which seems to be associated with the idea of fatherhood; the king was father of his people, just as he was their shepherd and, occasionally, their herdsman. This last idea is obviously connected with the cattle-cults of the peoples of the remoter reaches of the Nile Valley from whom the dynastic Egyptians were in part descended. The people were sometimes called 'the cattle of god' and the influence of cattle was to be of lasting importance, signalled by the power of the bull in Egyptian art and symbolism and the identification of some of the great goddesses as cows.[25]

The relationship between the gods (it will be suggested later that 'Divine Power' is a better term to apply to these entities) and the Egyptians of the early periods was essentially a collective one. There is no sense of a direct or personal connection between the individual and the gods, other than through the mediation of the king and of his worship as one of the company of divinities. As with the king so with the gods, of whom he was both the peer and, originally, the ruler. As expressions of the inexpressible the divine powers of Egypt have never been surpassed; their extraordinary power comes from the fact that they are products of Egypt in its pristine state, at the point where the society's progress towards the manifestation of its own individuality demanded the definition of its specific dynamic characteristics and those less material but still profound influences which the people recognised around them. It is entirely to be expected that, in the collective state of mind represented by the inhabitants of the Nile Valley in the fourth millennium, even before the first appearance of the Kingship, the archetypes should come into existence themselves in the form in which they could be recognised when the collective unconscious demanded that they manifest themselves. They were then personified as beings or powers beyond nature as, indeed, in the way in which they were conceived, they assuredly were: the Egyptian word for them is *ntr* which is inadequately represented by the word 'god'. The nature of the gods and the changes which the idea of the divine powers underwent in the course of Egyptian history is further described in Chapter III.

The Egyptians appear to have invented the idea of the Divine Kingship and elevated it to a supreme and audacious degree; no man before the kings of unified Egypt remotely approached their splendid paramountcy. In creating the idea of the all-powerful king, isolated in majesty, the Egyptians were laying down for later ages the idea of the all-powerful god, enthroned, remote and eternal.

Before the creation of the Egyptian state no human had been elevated to the rank of Kingship. The Egyptians were a logical people, though their processes of thought may seem obscure to minds of the present day. Having conceived of the Kingship as the linchpin of the unitary state which was emerging along the Nile's banks it was by an entirely consistent intellectual synthesis that they combined the idea of the mortal Kingship with that of the undying divinity. Thus the king and his office were perfectly reconciled: though the holder of the office might die and be recalled to his other realm beyond the stars, the Divine Kingship continued unchanging. The king was the Good God (an Egyptian ascription): he was also the Wise King and the Prince, in the sense of being the First, or Great, Individual.

The king is seated on a throne with seven steps. He wears a crown, a ritual costume and carries objects associated with the Kingship, such as the flail and the crook. He is attended by deferential followers, courtiers who are designated to discharge responsibilities related to his person or dress, and sometimes by a retinue of gods. He has power of life and death and destroys the enemies of Egypt. In all of these acts, as in every other function, the king of Egypt discharges an archetypal role.

The king of Egypt was the first example in recorded history of the archetype identified in psychological parlance as the 'Great Individual'.[26] This enduring figure is often encountered in epic and mythological contexts. He is heroic in scale and action; Gilgamesh and Herakles are good examples of the type.

The Great Individual is an agent of profound change, by his actions or example releasing great charges of psychic energy into the society or community with which he is engaged. He is, in the generally employed sense of the word, 'charismatic'. In addition to his heroic qualities he may also be a sacrificial figure, who suffers or dies for his followers. Osiris is such a figure, as is Christ.

According to the Pyramid Texts, the most venerable series of sacred writings in the history of the world, which emphasise the unique nature of the king and are designed to ensure the king's survival after death, the king existed before the creation of the world. However, in the way of the Great Individual, he will eventually decline from his position of primacy, to assume something more like a mediatory role, a process which the Kingship in Egypt precisely experienced. Eventually the figure of the Great Individual will disintegrate, a process which is often also undergone by the society of which he was, once, the prime mover. This disintegration may actually be mirrored in the Great Individual's physical dismemberment, as was mythically expressed in the death of Osiris.

Egypt was unique – and uniquely fortunate – in having at its disposal not merely one but a number of Great Individuals amongst the kings of the earliest dynasties. Their powerful influence, which effected such dramatic developments in the early centuries, continued to resonate throughout the Valley for many hundreds of years after their lifetimes. Whilst they lived their unique status was preserved and identified by their being represented on a superhuman scale, or raised high above their followers, whenever it was necessary actually to represent them. Thus they were preserved forever in their archetypal roles.

When considering the ceremonies which attended the king in his archetypal function Jung was much taken by what he saw as the special importance to the Egyptians, corporately, of the Heb-Sed festival. This was the elaborate series of rituals which the king underwent at certain points in his reign. Its purpose was to renew his psychic forces, effectively to bring him to rebirth. The Heb-Sed was especially important in the case of a long-reigning king; its usual first occasion was on the thirtieth anniversary of his coronation though this could be varied.

The king seems to have undergone a symbolic burial and resurrection, on which he once again took possession of the lands of Egypt. He mounted his throne in the company of the gods and great priests of Egypt and signified his possession of the four quarters of the world. Jung suggested that the king's acts on this occasion and his assumption of the crown, robes, insignia and regalia of the Kingship proclaimed him the *Anthropos*, the archetypal universal man.[27]

The king and the great gods such as the supreme creator, Ptah, are attended by a flock of animal archetypes, each displaying not only his own potent nature but also symbolic of a larger dimension. The tremendous bull which in the earliest dynasties personifies the king in his conquering, most potent aspect and which was the archetype of the epoch of Taurus in which all the early, crucial developments of Egypt occurred, was one of the first of these, as was the majestic lion, like the bull another early symbol of the king. They were followed by the swift hound, the soaring falcon (the exemplar of Kingship itself), the alert and watchful dog, the 'Opener of the Ways', the wise baboon; eventually an entire menagerie of theriomorphs surged out of the unconscious of the emerging Egyptian corporate psyche. Jung expressed it thus : 'The archetypes are the imperishable elements of the unconscious but they change their shape continuously'.[28] The Egyptians were not, of course, the first people to employ animal forms to express ideas so profound that they were beyond words, even beyond abstract symbols, but they fixed them so completely that no mythology could ever equal either their endurance or their penetration.

The perception which Jung so frequently displayed when considering the nature of ancient myth and the outpouring of the archetypes is nowhere more acutely set out than in his observation (quoted by James Hillman in 'Senex and Puer'),

> Zarathustra is an archetype and therefore has the divine quality, and that is *always based upon the animal*. Therefore the gods are symbolized as animals; even the holy ghost is a bird, all the antique gods, and the exotic gods are animals at the same time. *The old wise man is a big ape really*, which explains his peculiar fascination.[29]

This is a quite remarkable insight into the process of god-making, particularly when the gods are realised in animal form. It was the special genius of the Egyptians first to recognise the nature of the archetypes and, in so doing, to recognise their correspondence to animal forms when they are manifest. The majority of the high gods of Egypt have their animal persona; only Ptah, who is one of the greatest of the gods, is shown invariably in human form though even he can be recognised in the bull which in several instances – Apis, Mnevis, Buchoris – is sacred to him. The Egyptians went further still in interpreting the animal forms in which the gods appear as archetypes by merging their physical shape with humans; the gods are animal-headed when they appear in the rituals and when they are attendant on the king.

The researches to which earlier reference was made, relating to the art of the !Kung San people of southern Africa, demonstrate another part of the process of unravelling the fabric of the Nile Valley's ancient culture. In conducting experiments on the art of the !Kung San shamans produced when in a trance state, a condition of special psychological value both by reason of the shamans' function and because of the stress which the trance induces, it became clear that in the third, profound level of trance the shamans began to produce not only the 'entoptic phenomena' which were earlier noted, but also conflations of human and animal forms. The theriomorphs which the !Kung San shamans experience are conflations of humans and the eland, the animal on which their hunting economy largely depends.[30]

The studies conducted clearly suggest the universality of such experiences. Cultures to which a particular animal or animals was of special importance would in trance or conditions of stress, produce theriomorphs of that animal or animals combined with human characteristics.

No society in ancient times was so prodigal in its production of therianthropes as was Egypt. Most societies which have conceived of the mixture of human and animal forms have confined themselves, like the !Kung San, to one animal especially significant to them or to a few which had their origins in myth, like the cases of both Sumer and Elam – though it may reasonably be asked how they got there. The Sumerians tended to depict animals with human characteristics which were connected with the pastoral life of the people: a number of Sumerian theriomorphs represent animals which threatened the herds, like the lion or the eagle. In Elam monsters appear drawn entirely from the imagination and were, by a process which is not yet understood, passed on to Egypt. Elam also gave birth to a range of Disneyesque figures, of rather engaging animals represented in human activities.

In Egypt on the other hand, therianthropes fulfilled a special mission as manifestations of the *ntrs*, the divine powers who are usually called 'gods'. Virtually every important creature amongst the fauna of the Nile Valley was portrayed in this way: dogs, lion, lionesses, rams, monkeys, cows (but, significantly, not bulls), ibis, owls, crocodiles, ichneumon, geese, even beetles form a train of animal-headed divinities in attendance on the king.

It is not by chance that the conflation of humans and animals becomes widespread iconographically in the somewhat later periods of Egyptian history, especially from the time of the New Kingdom onwards. In Egypt it is surely significant that theriomorphs play little part in the symbolism of the Old Kingdom, when all was assured and the Valley was entirely secure, or at least so it must have seemed to the people living there. Even when the therioanthropes do appear there is nothing menacing about them. They minister to the king or perform a variety of functions attributed to them by the priesthoods of the temples of which they were frequently the patron divinities. In later times there is evidence that the priests assumed animal masks when impersonating the divinities in the ceremonies which formed much of the public face of Egyptian religious cults.

As Jung observed, the archetypes always manifest themselves in animal form. Very frequently in myths which arise from archetypal sources, the animals are helpful to man, aiding them in trials or rescuing them from danger. In Egypt an ancient myth, that of the Shipwrecked Sailor, is full of archetypal images, and has as its principal character a most obliging serpent, who is the prince of the distant island on which the Sailor is ship-wrecked. The serpent helps the sailor to recover from the effects of his misfortune, comforts him and then loads him with gifts. As the Sailor sails away from the serpent's island it sinks beneath the waves.

Animals were of great importance to the Egyptians of all periods. They never tired of observing them and of recording their ways. Animals were of course an important food resource; the Egyptians were skilled stockmen and bred their animals selectively. They domesticated a large number of different strains and experimented with the domestication of unlikely candidates such as the hyena and the gazelle.

They were enthusiastic keepers of animals as pets. Dogs were important members of the greatest households; cats were regarded with something approaching veneration, to the extent that to kill one was a capital offence. Monkeys were often kept as pets too, and are shown taking part in the affairs of the family.

The Egyptian attitude to animals probably explains the generally friendly nature of the theriomorphic divinities. Animals were part of the natural world which they shared. As such they were worthy of respect, even of veneration in later times, which earlier on would probably have seemed strange, if not perverse. Certainly there is no doubt that the study of the Egyptian attitude to animals reveals much about their collective psyche.

Jung was responding to his own unconscious when he remarked, in the extract quoted above, 'the old wise man is a big ape really'. The Egyptians were in advance of him in this perception, for Thoth was the god of wisdom, the embodiment of the wise man, and is very frequently represented as a baboon. The cynocephalus baboon, the same species that so impressed Jung at Abu Simbel, was sacred to him.

Jung's recognition of the role of the ape is particularly penetrating. The acknowledgement of mankind's primate nature is fundamental to an understanding of what happened in Egypt in the early centuries of its corporate existence. There were two special qualities which determined the nature of archaic Egyptian society: it was hierarchic and it was pristine. Egypt is the first, most perfectly realised complex society because it is organised on firmly hierarchic principles. Man belongs to the order 'Primate'; he is a particularly developed form of primate, with special skills and qualities but none of these obscures his essentially primatial nature. Most primates, and all the higher primates, live in structured bands, most, though not all, under the leadership of a dominant or alpha male. He will be attended by (and eventually compete with) a group of lesser-ranking males.

Dominance over the group by an individual is an inheritance which is drawn from the most distant history of our species. The Egyptians clearly apprehended the role of the dominant leader of the group, 'the big ape'. The leap from this simple concept to the idea of the Kingship, with all its attendant rituals and the overlay of divinity, is immense but entirely logical. In conceiving of the Kingship the Egyptians recognised the primatial nature of human society and by its creation seem to have attempted to maintain a connection between the impending complex societies and the small bands which for all of mankind's previous history, as a primate and as an evolved human, had provided the hierarchic structure which made the group viable. This the Egyptians attempted to do; that they could not, ultimately, reconcile the condition of humans living in groups numerically so vastly beyond anything that primates could endure does not diminish the nobility of the attempt.

The pristine quality of Egypt is still more simply expressed.It was the first in the sense that the archetypes and all the elements which would eventually become the characteristic marks of all complex societies had their first expression and were first named in Egypt as the foundations of the state.

Underlying much of the ancient Egyptian perception of the visible world is another world of symbols and symbolism. The subtle psychology of the early Egyptians seems often to have led them deliberately to represent one object or concept by another.[31] This capacity permeated their works and is fundamental to an understanding of their world.

An important event in the development of the corporate Egyptian psyche, which exercised a considerable influence on later events, was the shift in the middle of the third millennium from predominantly stellar cults to those which took their inspiration from the sun and which, from the Fourth Dynasty onwards, dominated the royal cults. Stellar cults have stronger Mesopotamian affinities than solar cults: it may be that the worship of the stars was a vestige of the ancient Western Asiatic influences which percolated into the Valley to such notable effect in the late predynastic period. As such they were perhaps considered inappropriate for a belief system which was based on the idea of the supreme divinity of the king. The sun is apparently unique whereas the brightest star is one of a myriad of celestial bodies. The significance of the stellar cults, however, was not forgotten, as witnessed by the constant identification of the king as a star in the Pyramid Texts.

If something of the sort happened, just as the Fourth Dynasty came to power, it would account for its expression in an architectural form by changing the shape, though not the essential nature, of the pyramid tomb.

The Step Pyramid is demonstrably a staircase to the heavens, a concept which also is retained in the form of the stepped platform on which the king's throne stood. The true pyramid represents the rays of the sun petrified and made eternal, to protect the body of the king for ever. After some experiments with other shapes, the true pyramid took its canonical form early in the Fourth Dynasty. It then assumed its place as one of the great archetypes, standing splendid and initially alone on the plateau at Giza.

The pyramid is the archetypal Egyptian symbol. Four thousand five hundred years later it evokes instant recognition; it has probably been reproduced more frequently in more media than any other human artifact. An administrator-architect of genius such as Hemionu, who is credited with the building of the pyramid of Khnum-Khufu (Cheops to the Greeks) may well have been inspired to confine the sun's rays in stone, and so create the monument which was to be associated with the king for all eternity one winter afternoon in the desert to the north of Memphis, where the phenomenon of the sun's rays breaking through the clouds and forming a perfect pyramid of light can on occasion be seen.

There is another symbolic form which lay even deeper, it would seem, in the Egyptian unconscious, which was to achieve three-dimensional expression in the pyramid. This is the frequently depicted line of triangular hills which appears on the pottery of Naqada II, in the late predynastic period. It is found in other societies, long after it appeared in Egypt. The Nile Valley is not generously supplied with sharply-peaked hills; the limestone and sandstone hills which it does possess are usually not particularly isolated in such a way as to suggest the triangular shape. It may be that the shape of the Naqada hills was actually locked in the collective unconscious of the Egyptians, whose basal population were immigrants into the Valley and who may have retained some recollection of a mountainous or at least a hilly landscape with which they were once identified.

More likely still is it that the Naqada hills and the pyramid are expressions of the same archetype. The three-dimensional triangle is a peculiarly satisfying shape and one which is replicated in many forms, in many different contexts throughout human history. It is the Egyptian version of this basic image which has become the paramount expression of the archetype, a product of the human unconscious and hence common to all mankind. Geometric shapes, of which the triangle is one of the most frequently encountered, appear as 'entoptic' phenomena in trance-induced art.[32]

In recent years there has been a revival of the debate as to the nature and purpose of the Pyramids. The belief, hitherto generally held, that they are royal tombs, has been questioned, at least as far as the Giza group is concerned. There is no doubt that the majority of pyramids, from the earliest built for Djoser Netjerykhet to those which entombed the Middle Kingdom kings, were tombs. It has been fair to assume therefore that the three Giza Pyramids also served the same purpose though, since there is actually no certain evidence that anyone was ever buried in any of them, this can not be asserted unequivocally. The weight of probability suggests that such was their purpose, though this does not of itself exclude their having served other purposes as well. The exquisite mathematics of the Giza group certainly could be taken to indicate that they served a function more complex than merely the interment of even the most formidable god-king.

But whatever may be the case the development of the Egyptian tomb and its culmination in the pyramidal shape is revealing of the workings of the Egyptian psyche. The earliest burial recorded in the Nile Valley is from an astonishingly remote time and far to the south, at Tushka in Nubia.[33] There a number of graves of cattle were found and with them a human burial surmounted by two wild bull skulls; it is dated to the fourteenth *millennium* before the present and was the work of the hunters who followed the herds of wild cattle. The use of the bull heads to mark the site of the burial and, presumably, to give protection to it, is remarkable evidence for the survival of ritual and cultic practices in Egypt, for nine thousand years later wild bull heads were mounted around high-status burials at Saqqara and a wild bull's skull is buried in the southern court of the Step Pyramid complex, also at Saqqara.

The earliest identifiable group in predynastic Upper Egypt, the Badarians, buried their dead in shallow graves, with a little mound of earth raised over them to mark the place. By late predynastic times, notably at Hierakonpolis, tombs are marked by a lightweight superstructure, a sort of canopy raised over the grave which may contain the burials of cattle and dogs as well as human occupants.[34]

By the period immediately before the appearance of the kings of the First Dynasty, the burials have become more elaborate. The famous Tomb 100 at Hierakonpolis, now lost, is the most notable of this type – a rectangular grave, divided in two, with the walls plastered and painted with vivid scenes many of which seem to be of Western Asiatic, particularly early Elamite, inspiration.[35]

After the coming of the kings and the unleashing of the archetypes, an entirely new style of architecture prevailed. For the kings themselves immense 'funerary palaces' were built with high mud-brick walls, the king's tomb being built inside the enclosure.[36] The great magnates and close associates of the king were buried in the so-called mastaba tombs, of which those excavated at Saqqara are the largest group to survive.[37] The earliest are huge rectangular mud-brick buildings with extensive structures below ground, allowing the stacking of large quantities of offerings for the tomb's occupant, who reposes in a central grave. The tombs became larger and more complex as the First Dynasty advanced but they all seem to have retained a common feature: in the centre of the tomb, over the actual burial, was placed a little mound, sometimes of sand alone, sometimes contained within brick. In some cases the brickwork enclosing the mound is stepped.[38]

It is the latter feature which gives the clue to the connection between the simple predynastic graves and the later, immense tombs which were built for the kings. The first monumental stone complex of buildings, not only in Egypt but in the entire world (with the single, perplexing exception of the Limestone temple at Uruk) is the stepped structure raised to a monumental scale in the pyramid complex built for King Djoser Netjerykhet at Saqqara. From this, the prototype of the pyramid, all the other 'true' pyramids sprang. The eruption of the pyramid, apparently fully realised, from the earth in which it had been germinating is a very exact metaphor for the emergence of the nation-state, also apparently fully realised, from the land of Egypt.

Similar considerations apply to the development of the other archetypal Egyptian structure, the temple. The earliest representations of ritual buildings show them probably to have been animal in shape and made from reeds.[39]. The simple reed shrine was retained in the most elaborate of the largest temples built of stone, hidden in the darkness of the temple's centre, made of stone itself but reproducing the little reed shrine of the remote past. The manifestation of the god in animal form is again demonstrated in the shape of the shrine itself.

The temple is a microcosm of the world, its roof the sky. The forest of columns which supports the roof are both the pillars which in Egyptian myth were the supports of the sky and the primeval grove of trees or the banks of reeds in the primordial island from which began the gods' original journey to found the Egyptian Kingdoms. In the Jungian canon the forest is also a synonym for the unconscious,[40] a quality undoubtedly shared by the temple. Within the temple, as in the recesses of the unconscious, lie the most obscure but at the same time the most potent symbols. The mystical nature of the temple may be recognised by the forest of columns which at once conceals its interior and at the same time leads the hierophant deep into its further recesses, where the most sacred part of the building stands, a place for the living presence of the god. This was a simple shrine originally built of reeds; its shape, if not its substance, was retained in every Egyptian temple, no matter how immense. The worshipper, if he is permitted to enter at all (as he probably was in later times), goes further and further into the darkening interior as if he were pursuing some ideal form, as it might be of an animal, barely glimpsed, into the heart of the forest.

The notion of the temple as a forest, witnessed by its columns reaching high into the darkness of the roof, also reveals both temple and forest as symbols of the unconscious. This archetypal function the Egyptian temple admirably fulfils and the fact of it doing so accounts for much of its mysterious and numinous quality.

It is this archetype of the temple with its high and majestic portico that defines the public building, consecrated to the powers and aspirations of the community, in most societies which have come after Egypt and which have absorbed the archetypes which were released there. Whether it is the god who is worshipped within the forest of columns, or even the wealth of the community and the status of its citizens proclaimed and enhanced by it, such buildings are the means by which authority, power and mystery are expressed in terms which both intimidate and reassure the members of the community.

Egypt's gradual descent from the heights of the third-millennium experience, when it had approached nearer to the idea of the gods than any other people before or since, to the empty shells of the temples of later times, parallels the individual's progress towards maturity and beyond. Once Egypt's maturity was attained and its historic achievements fulfilled, the period comparable with that of individuation in the individual was left behind. Egypt's coherence and the integrity of its pristine personality began to fragment, never wholly to be rejoined.

Egypt was the first nation to leave behind a coherent, multi-faceted and multi-disciplined corpus of art practised over an extended and sustained period. To appreciate Egyptian art fully it is necessary to recognise that the artists were intensely responsive to the influences of the world around them but it was almost entirely a secure and tranquil world, ordered and safe. In this they were very different from their Sumerian contemporaries over to the east, in a world determined by the vagaries of two unpredictable rivers and the whims of a collection of largely hostile divinities.

Thus, in contrast to the Sumerian or Elamite experience, monsters rarely appear in Egyptian art; when they do, they are often of Western Asiatic inspiration, like the Elamite serpo-pards of the Archaic palettes from the end of the fourth millennium BC. They are confined largely to the period of the presumed Unification, itself a time of turbulence and the influx of alien influences into the Valley. Scenes of violence occur but they are somehow ritualised, like the representation of Horus presenting the king with his decapitated enemies on the Narmer Palette, or the defeated foes on the throne base on which Khasekhemui sits, who seem to be tossed away in the winds of some violent storm. This indicates the source from which Egypt derived some of the Western Asiatic influences which can be detected at the end of the fourth millennium BC, for a similar scene is portrayed on a seal of the period from Susa in south-western Iran.

It has been said that 'the Ego of antiquity and its consciousness of itself was different from our own, less exclusive, less sharply defined'.[41] This truth is important in the understanding of the processes which were at work in the creative imagination, the often sublime works of art produced by men of the earliest high cultures. The lack of exclusiveness of the Ego is markedly true of the Archaic Egyptian personality. The Egyptian of the earliest historic periods was clearly less individualised than has come to be expected from someone living in a highly cultured, well-structured and organizationally very advanced society, such as was that which was emerging in the Nile Valley. The people of the Valley were still closer to the collective experience, the experience of the group. But parallel with this collective experience, manifested also by an intense sense of 'belonging' and of identity as part of the group, was a nascent awareness of the individual and the potentiality of the individual to express a separate identity. Initially this idea of individuality was, as Jung apprehended, yet another prerogative of the king and his closest companions, though doubtless it was not acknowledged in such specific terms.

Throughout the later phases of the Old Kingdom, as demonstrated by the increasingly naturalistic art of the tomb reliefs, for example, the emergence of the individual was evidently one of the factors which marked a most notable change in the society and which ultimately weakened the fabric of the state. At the end of the Sixth Dynasty (*c.*2200 BC), this led to its sundering and to the distress and general insecurity of the years preceding the reassertion of royal authority by the founders of the Middle Kingdom. When that authority was restored, it was notably different from what had gone before.

The original and formative Egyptian experience had been that of the extended group, highlighted with the occasional brilliant flash of individual genius. The images which are the common currency of Egyptian art and architectural design are archetypes, products, too, of the collective experience. The falcon perched on the *serekh* for example, the everlasting symbolism of the crowns, a poetic image such as the two lions joined back to back signifying Yesterday and Tomorrow, even the falcon as the eponym of the royal clan, are all examples of this process. Such archetypes are all the products of the early Egyptian collective unconscious; it is this which gives them their often mystical, faintly uncanny but hauntingly familiar character.

The momentous events of the last quarter of the fourth millennium, when the process towards the unification of the little principalities which it is presumed then comprised the Valley really began, led the Egyptians to undertake the creation of a complex political system and to extend it over a large if relatively contained area, embracing several local cultures with differing religious and social traditions. The Egyptian collective unconscious must have been dramatically activated by this process, releasing a variety of archetypes and creative initiatives which, in a relatively small and closely knit community such as theirs still was, could be apprehended rapidly from one end of the Valley to the other. It is a further tribute to the genius of the early kings that they realised this to be the case and pursued the unification of Egypt relentlessly, ultimately to achieve it despite many setbacks and frequent disappointments.

The concept of the Divine King is the supreme Egyptian political achievement and is the product of the unique Egyptian-African psyche. The idea of the Divine King emerged precisely at the point when the society over which he was raised was beginning its process towards the attainment of its own distinct and individual identity. The supreme status of the king, once he is recognised as such, is demonstrated by the fact that he is fully individuated in name, in function and in the numinous quality with which he and his office are invested.

It is tempting to see the characteristics of the individuation process which the Egyptian state exhibits as actually being designed to give expression to the king's own individuality; in this respect the king is, as Jung observed, Egypt's self and, in consequence, its paramount incarnate divinity. In the earliest periods the king's singular individuality is demonstrated most cogently by his unique experience of survival after death; his survival ensures the continued existence and prosperity of Egypt but not of every Egyptian, the mass of whom are, as it were, to be subsumed into his individuality.

The collective character of the society can be seen in the customs attending the burial of the king. As a consequence of some exceptional persuasion by the royal propagandists or by the evidently overwhelmingly charismatic figure of the king himself, the society was apparently prepared to accept the idea that only the king might, of right, avoid the dismal experience of death, and as the supreme divinity go on to an eternal existence beyond the stars, or in the easterly land where the gods were born.

All other creatures were fated only to continue to exist through him and through his survival; only by ensuring his continued existence could the future of the whole land of Egypt be preserved. The individual was nothing; Egypt, in the person of the king, subsuming all others to himself, was all. It is in this sense that the king is Egypt's self.

This belief had in it the seeds of its own change. The idea that the people survived through the survival of the king led in time to the belief that the retainers sacrificed at the king's death, and at the deaths of the very greatest nobles, would continue to serve them. This practice of the sacrifice of retainers appears in the First Dynasty and on a very much reduced scale in the Second; thereafter it disappears.[42] Subsequently the idea became accepted that proximity to the royal burial could ensure immortality for the king's family and his ministers.

Gradually the Great Ones (the nobles and high officials of the Two Kingdoms) began, particularly in the later centuries of the Old Kingdom, to adopt the forms of what had been the royal prerogatives of burial. Finally, in the Late Period, the god Osiris became the symbol of regeneration and the focus of the hopes of eternal life of even the most humble Egyptian.

The change which overcame the Egyptian view of the ceremonies appropriate after the death of the individual also reveals an awareness of the transition from the collective to that of the individual consciousness. In the earliest times the death of the individual may not have been considered as especially significant to the community, which, particularly in the person of its leader and personification, continued undying. As the process of individuation wore away the old communal and collective spirit of the society and the individual psyche began to flourish and to demand its own recognition, so the needs of the individual even after death began to be apprehended and all the complex industry associated with the care of the individual's immortality was introduced.

The Egyptians have been described as a people inordinately preoccupied with death. Such a view misjudges them: the Egyptians were wholly preoccupied with life and with its perpetuation. Death was an incident in man's experience of life; it marked simply a transition from one state of being to another. But, even more important, the process of individuation leads to an awareness of death as an aspect of life, as crucial and meaningful an experience as birth. In their preoccupation with the business of death, the preservation of the body, the building of the tomb as 'the mansion of millions of years' and the provisions for the afterlife, the Egyptians were working towards the individuation of their society and the full maturity of their individual consciousness.

The considerable activity which was directed towards ensuring survival after death, first of the king, later of his closest assistants and ultimately of all, had the effect no doubt of concentrating the Egyptians' minds on an acceptance of the inevitability of death. More than most people, therefore, their lives represented a preparation for the experience of dying. In thus preparing themselves they proceeded further along the path to a still more fully realised individuation. The acceptance of the fact of death as part of the process of life is one of the most significant gifts which the Egyptians have left to the world which succeeded them, the recognition of the value of the second part of life as a preparation for the fact of death. The need for the individual to understand death as part of life was an insight also expressed by Jung.[43]

The genius of the people of Egypt is most powerfully expressed in creative action, in the making of artifacts, from the relatively humble pottery vessel to the pyramid or the majestic image of the Divine King; the most sublime artifact they made was Egypt itself, splendid and richly complex. The eternal principles of Egyptian art and design are the products of the peculiarly Egyptian collective unconscious; there is another powerful manifestation of this same collective stream, that body of spells and incantations, the first recorded literary expression, anywhere in the world, of the striving after the Divine, known as the Pyramid Texts.[44]

The Pyramid Texts enshrine much of the collective memory of the Egyptian people of the process which defined the emerging state. These memories are the products of the earliest aspirations of the Egyptians as a group, when they were first experiencing that sense of election which led to nationhood. Some of the texts are in the form of dialogues, demonstrating how ancient is the form of antiphonal exchange, sometimes between spirits, sometimes focusing on the king as the principal actor in the drama, sometimes in the form of exchanges between priests officiating in a complex ritual.

The Pyramid Texts are known from a series of recensions carved on the walls of royal tombs of the late Fifth Dynasty and the Sixth Dynasty. This was the high point of the Old Kingdom's coherence and assurance; the society from which they emerged was in balance with nature and it must have seemed to be without threat, unchanging and eternal. The Texts do not display notable tensions such as, for example, those which the near-contemporary late Sumerian or Akkadian texts reveal; the Egyptians' characteristic state of psychic assurance seems unimpaired until it is finally blown away with all the rest of the mooring posts of the Old Kingdom world at the end of the Sixth Dynasty.

Though, most remarkably, the Pyramid Texts have come down to us over four thousand years uncorrupted by the hands of editors and thus quite unlike all later religious writings, the texts are still little understood. The obscurity of their language in translation and the strange images which they evoke are difficult to comprehend. Jung seems to have drawn on several recensions, published in the early years of the twentieth century, including that by E. A. Wallis Budge in an English translation. During Jung's lifetime, a version of the Texts was translated by the great German Egyptologist Kurt Sethe who, though some of his interpretations have been questioned by more recent authorities, was the first to make them generally accessible to a modern audience after the rather hasty publications of their original translators in the latter part of the nineteenth century. Jung was familiar, too, with Sethe's edition. Nonetheless, despite the authority of their translators, the language of the texts often seems wilfully obscure.

The Pyramid Texts were first carved in exquisite hieroglyphs on the subterranean walls of King Unas' pyramid at the end of the Fifth Dynasty (*c*.2350 BC) and originally infilled with a brilliant blue paste.[45] The Unas texts, like the others which succeeded them, are a compendium of the most profound and perplexing expressions of the ancient Egyptian spirit. They are peculiarly relevant to the study of the psychic drives which motivated Egypt in its most formative period. They are concerned, almost exclusively, with the perpetuation of the life of the king when he returns to, or travels beyond, the stars, of which region he will be the ruler after death. Many of the 'Utterances', the divisions in which the Texts are customarily published, deal with Osiris, with whom the king is identified after death. This is particularly interesting as Osiris is a relative late-comer amongst the gods.

Jung's recognition of the Pyramid Texts' importance was a natural corollary of his equation of the king with Egypt's self; he recognised that both the security of the person of the king in life and death and the office of the Kingship were fundamental to the understanding of the origins of the Egyptian state and the governing principles which underlay it. All the outpourings of the state, certainly during the Old Kingdom as demonstrated in the Pyramid Texts, and notionally even in later times, were directed towards ensuring the life, prosperity and health of the king – and hence of Egypt.

It is in this context too that the monumental public works which are so much a feature of the early centuries of the Egyptian state's existence must be seen. As the process of individuation advanced, and as the king assumed an ever more exalted position as a consequence, the essential Egyptian spirit began to find expression in massive works which engaged the whole society and absorbed much of its resources. Such resources were not wasted, nor deployed extravagantly; their employment was the inescapable consequence of the burgeoning of the individuality of the Egyptian state. The monuments were, initially, the product of the need to protect and nourish the king's individuality. Later, as the individual Egyptian begins to take on a more precise outline, the role of the king diminishes, first to that of a god among gods, later still to something like the mediator between gods and men, with what amounts to little more than a sort of honorary divinity. The decline of Egypt from its pristine greatness can be seen at this point as part of the process of the state's own individuation. In the New Kingdom in particular, monumental architecture is no longer solely identified with the king but becomes the preserve of the expanding temple bureaucracies just as the tombs of the great provincial magnates in the early Middle Kingdom will be seen to be a reflection of their accession of power at the king's expense in the late Old Kingdom.

But this is to anticipate, somewhat. The final seal of Egypt's progress to statehood and the full achievement of its historic personality was the building of the Pyramids during the Third, Fourth, Fifth and Sixth Dynasties. The Pyramid is the supreme artifact linking earth and heaven, land and sky, the mortal and the divine, and the most powerful simulation of light then possible to technology. The Pyramids came out of the deep levels of the unconscious of the Egyptian people and of the state in its first supreme manifestation. With their eruption into three-dimensional form Egypt was, in effect, fully mature, its historic destiny achieved.

CHAPTER III

EGYPT AND 'THE GODS'

—— ·◆· ——

The temples of Egypt were the repositories of various explanations for the origins of the Egyptian state. Different generations of gods and of divine and semi-divine kings were represented as the primeval rulers of the land, to be succeeded ultimately by the divine Horus reincarnated, generation after generation, in the living king.

To the Egyptians of the early periods this was the central fact of their existence. In mythological time Horus had been declared the ruler of all Egypt after an epic battle which took place in the celestial dimension. The king was Horus' incarnate successor and Egypt was the successor of the celestial region over which his sovereignty had been confirmed.

This essential fact made the necessity for any formalised religion, in any sense that the word would be understood today, superfluous. If an earthly people is ruled directly by an immanent divinity there is no requirement for revelation, for the god's will is manifest, no moral precepts enshrined in any form other than the daily evidence of the divine will, no gods or other supernatural beings who need to be persuaded and cajoled, other than to be acknowledged as the supporters of the living god.

In Egypt, the rituals and ceremonies involving the powers which existed outside the realm of nature were manifest as state, hence corporate, occasions. The great ceremonies in the temples were acts of psychic expression on a national scale. They bonded the land of Egypt, in the person of the king, with those psychic forces which the creation of the state had released. They were immense theatrical events whose audience was Egypt's self, designed both to release and to augment the nation's psychic energies. In later times, as the power of the priests grew, the ceremonies became more congregational, so that the political and material power of the temple could be made manifest.

The ceremonies in the temples focused the psychic energies contained in the people's unconscious, liberated by the releasing of the archetypes. The Egyptians were thus the first people to recognise and exploit the energy contained in large concourses of people in a state of heightened and directed excitement. Such events have become the common currency of most religions and many political gatherings. An occasion nearer our own time which brilliantly encapsulates both the religious and the political dimension of this phenomenon and which reveals the almost palpable presence of psychic energy in such a situation is recorded in Leni Riefenstahl's film *The Triumph of the Will*. Events such as the Nuremberg Rallies are the products of the most skilful manipulation of human consciousness in the mass.

No one has thus far explained satisfactorily the origins of human consciousness nor even, quite, what it is. It is elusive and difficult of definition; like many other human qualities it is a state which can be recognised by its presence even if it resists precise definition. It was Egypt's particular destiny to have been the first human community to harness the power of human consciousness by releasing the power of the archetypes. In doing so the people made a significant contribution to the management of complex societies and, in the process, contributed to the transformation of mankind.

The great rituals in Egypt, which centred on the king and on the divine powers who attended him, were intended to focus the psychic energy of the state and to release it into the society. There it would stimulate the profound creative resources which were the particular treasury of Egypt and the Egyptians. The direction of such ritual events was, as we have seen, one of the crucial acts of each of the early kings when appearing as the Great Individual.

The divine powers who attended the king, the *ntrs* who are to be thought of more as forces of nature than gods in the sense of discrete, anthropomorphised entities, are exceptionally complex. In the centuries before the arrival of the Kingship the presence of beings with a supra-natural status may be inferred, lodged in the collective unconscious of the people of the Valley. Large humanoid figures, sometimes with feminine characteristics, dominate smaller ones on the painted pottery of the predynastic period, strange bearded males are portrayed in ivory carvings, in stone and on the slate palettes, which are amongst the most important documents of the period immediately prior to the arrival of the Kingship. There are still more enigmatic figures amongst the products of the late predynastic period, who, if they are not divine, are certainly superhuman.

The schist and mudstone palettes, which are amongst the finest products of this period, provide the first evidence of the king as the Great Individual, standing apart from those around him and portrayed on a far larger scale than they. In several cases the king (if it is not too early to call him by that title) is actually represented by one of the royal animals, a bull goring his enemies or as a lion devouring them. Later, when the earliest kings, crowned and with the costume and regalia which will be retained throughout the next three thousand years with very little alteration, assume human form they are depicted in a variety of media, on the palettes as well as on small ivory plaques, or on large-size votive mace-heads.

The kings are shown in such contexts either towering above their companions or raised high above them on a throne which stands on a stepped platform. In some of the events represented they are attended by the bearers of standards of the various territories – nomes in Egyptological

parlance – into which Egypt was once divided and which are taken to represent the ancient chiefdoms which made up the Valley before the campaigns
to bring about the Unification were launched.

Many of the standards carried before the king display animal symbols.
Even in the First Dynasty some of the divine powers are manifested in
animal form, notably Anubis the dog (sometimes represented as a jackal)
and Apis the bull, who was a personification of Ptah. The very ancient
divinity Set, one of the most complex in the entire catalogue of Egyptian
powers and originally the patron of the South, appears with a human body
but the head of the animal with which he is identified, the noble, swift,
prick-eared hound. Set is the first of the powers to display himself in this
theriomorphic form.

By the Third Dynasty a number of the powers were depicted, generally
in human shape and, with the exception of the very greatest, such as Ptah,
as subservient to the king. This situation indeed persists throughout the
Old Kingdom. Some other of the oldest 'gods' are permitted entirely animal
forms. Such are Horus the Falcon and his mother Hathor, who manifests
herself as a cow, harking back, no doubt, to the cattle hunters and herders
who made up an important component of the ancient population.

As with the king and the state, so with the divine powers and their
realm. When the unconscious began to release its images and to give
expression to the otherwise largely inexpressible, it was necessary for the
Egyptians to give form and substance to what they represented. The multi-
plicity of the forms of the divine powers is part of this process; since
divinity can never be wholly encompassed or its infinite nature exactly
defined, it is inevitable that an infinity of forms and representations is
permissable, even necessary. The ethereal portion of life, life itself, the
storm, wind, wisdom, the Kingship, unity, all would be given expression
and, by the process of naming, actuality. Therein, incidentally, lies the origin
of the belief in the power of the name; in this the Egyptians came close to
the concept which the Sumerians expressed as *me*.

It is indicative of the forces which were abroad in the Near East in the
fourth and fifth millennia before the present era that the Sumerians, too, were
touched by the recognition of the archetypes, though in ways quite different
from Egypt. The Sumerians were moved much more by the promptings of
the intellect, to an altogether remarkable degree; the Egyptians, on the other
hand, were both more pragmatic and, perhaps paradoxically, more inclined
towards what the modern world might describe as the mystical, at least to
the extent of seeking to harness the influences of the unseen world and,
through the supreme archetype of the king, to bind it and Egypt together.

The Sumerians recorded their recognition of the archetypes through their
most particular medium, the written word. They produced a list – they
were, rather engagingly, much given to list-making – of what were defined
as the *mes*. This is an elusive concept. The *mes* have been defined as

a set of rules and regulations assigned to each cosmic entity and cultural phenomenon for the purpose of keeping it operating forever in accordance with the plans laid down by the deity creating it. In short, another superficial, but evidently not altogether ineffective answer to an insoluble cosmological problem which merely hid the fundamental difficulties from view with the help of a layer of largely meaningless words.[1]

This definition clearly shows the essential difference between the Sumerian and the Egyptian experience of the archeypes. To the Sumerians, they required definition; to the Egyptians, recognition.

The list which records the *mes* is in part obscure; it appears in a long, late third-millennium myth, 'Inanna and Enki: The transfer of the arts of civilisation from Eridu to Erech';[2] there are some sixty of these 'cultural traits and complexes'. They include *en*-ship (*en* was a Sumerian term for ruler or governor), godship, the exalted and enduring crowns, the throne of Kingship, the exalted sceptres, the royal insignia, the exalted shrine, the priestly office, and truth. Thus far they are not dissimilar from many of the qualities most highly regarded by Egypt; but the Sumerian list also includes much less exalted concerns: the eunuch, prostitution, sexual intercourse. Then there are the flood, the battle standard, law, art, music, heroship, power, the destruction of cities, straightforwardness, the craft of the builder, terror, wisdom, the troubled heart – and many more.[3] To the Sumerian mind the *mes* existed as entities and in the myth from which they are extracted are subjected to a form of piracy, being taken from Eridu, where they were in the charge of one of the greatest of the gods, Enki, to Erech, the city of Inanna, a goddess who steals them by the rather deplorable subterfuge of making the god hopelessly drunk.

The more intellectual character of the *mes*, when compared with the archetypes which defined the Egyptian apprehension of the divine, demonstrate an important difference in the psychology of the two peoples and, in consequence, of the nature of the legacies which they respectively passed on to the world which succeeded them. The Egyptian archetypes, in contrast to Sumer's, are essentially three-dimensional and material in nature – architecture, the person of the king, the regalia, the throne, the pyramid, the temple. These have profoundly influenced the forms of social and religious observance; the Sumerians and still more their Semitic-speaking contemporaries and eventual successors, were much more influential in determining the sort of religious beliefs which were to be adopted by so much of the world in later ages. The idea of sin, of a wrathful divinity, punishment, duty to the divinity, the direct intervention of divine, invisible powers in the life of men, all concepts which were wholly alien to the Egyptian mind, are to be found in Mesopotamia and thus became a large part of the foundations on which religious systems which draw their inspiration from Semitic sources are derived. In later times, as the status of the king was reduced, the consequence of the disintegration of his role as the Great Individual when the society as a whole was moving towards full maturity, the theriomorphic gods became much more significant and their cults more influential. It is in this form that the divine powers of Egypt are generally remembered.

Whilst there was no revelation of the gods' intentions, other than through the ordinances of the living god-king, there were several recensions of what might reasonably be called 'myth', which had no particular religious or moral sanctions about them. These sought to explain the origins of the institutions by which Egypt was governed. Some of these were of great antiquity, with those derived from the great temple-observatory (if that is not too provocative a description) at Heliopolis (Egyptian Iwnw) accorded a degree of primacy. There was also a school of theology, as it might be called, of Memphis, whilst another system drew its inspiration from Abydos, one of the most ancient centres of the Kingship and still other versions of teleological myths derive from Edfu and Denderah, which are known from very late versions of the texts on which they are based, though these are generally thought to draw on much earlier originals.

Most of the cosmogonies which sought to explain the origins of the universe, and Egypt's place in it, begin in a watery chaos, with all matter in a state of potentiality. The act of creation, since it apparently takes place in reality, is inherently contradictory: creation may be initiated by the High God (a generally obscure concept in Egypt, other than in the person of the king) raising Ma'at, the embodiment of Truth, to his lips, or by the cry of a waterfowl. Then the generations of the divine powers are born and the process of the making of the universe begins.

Many of the stories of the gods, particularly those which can be traced back to third millennium or earlier sources, seem to have an astronomical origin, from the time when Egypt was dominated by stellar cults; this seems certainly to have been the case, before the Fourth Dynasty. Many of the systems of cosmology which describe the origins of the Kingship and the gods can most satisfactorily be explained as allegories devised to retain the memory of significant astronomical events which were thought to have influenced the course of Egypt's development. The recognition of such events, as we have suggested earlier, presuppose an awareness of and a concern for the effects of the Precession of the Equinoxes. In a sense Egypt as a nation-state and the king of Egypt as a living god are the products of the realisation by the Egyptians of the astronomical changes effected by the immense apparent movement of the heavenly bodies which the Precession implies.

The connection between the observation of the night sky and the origins of the Egyptian state can be taken further. Like all desert peoples the Egyptians relied upon the stars for their navigation, on land or sea, over what were frequently long and dangerous journeys. Without a highly tuned awareness of the stars in their courses, the knowledge of those which remained in their stations and the mutability of others which from time to time vanished only mysteriously to reappear, it would have been impossible for the early kings to have set out on campaigns far to the south, to have ventured deep into the eastern or western deserts to put down marauding tribes or to march out, far to the north, to secure Egypt's frontiers.

The perplexing evidences of contact between the southern reaches of the Nile Valley and the headlands of the Arabian Gulf, especially with south-western Iran, in the late predynastic period could only have made by confident voyagers who travelled westwards to the Valley. To achieve such a journey they would have had either to conduct a long and treacherous sea voyage or to have crossed the deserts of the Arabian peninsula itself. In either case they would have needed the assistance of the stars to have completed the journey and, at least as important, to have returned home again. It is probably to such travellers, and their need for a workable mnemonic system to allow them to identify the major constellations, that the idea of the zodiac is due. The recognition of the assistance which the night sky could render to those who could read its secrets was one of the crucial intellectual achievements of mankind. Very early on in their history the Egyptians adapted the knowledge of the stars to give them an understanding of the imperishable principles which, as it must have seemed to them, underlay so vast a process as the watching of the night sky revealed.

The observation of the celestial bodies, the counting of the seasons and the certainty of the Nile's return each year, even in the heart of the deadliest season of summer, gave rise to that sense of order which governed the existence of the entire universe. From this acknowledgement of the principle of order came the naming of the divine power, the archetype who stood for the principle of order itself.

This was the goddess Ma'at, of very great antiquity, in whose name the king was always said to rule. Order is also truth and truth demands justice: the discharge of all these related concepts was central to the kingly office. The king, in the name of Ma'at, brought justice to the people and in doing so ensured the continuing prosperity of the Two Lands. Other than the idea of the king's divinity, the honour paid to Ma'at and to her archetypal qualities were the nearest that early Egypt approached to a religion, in any sense which might be recognised by the cultures which succeeded it in the ancient world.

It is Egypt's misfortune that so many of its institutions are judged by the evidence of them when they were in terminal decline. This was the time when travellers from the world outside Egypt entered the Valley and described what they saw. It is from many of such descriptions, borrowed and enhanced by writers of later antiquity, that the very unsatisfactory record of what is regarded as the religion of ancient Egypt has been handed on to the world of the present day. Even now, certainly at the level of popular response and interest, Egyptian beliefs are represented as little more than a mélange of mutually conflicting cosmologies, overblown rituals and a naïve dependence on animal-headed divinities.

Herodotus, to whom the study of ancient Egypt owes so much, was the first recorded observer to be mislead by the apparently all-pervasive nature of Egyptian religion. To Herodotus, the Egyptians were the most religious of all peoples. In his time, in the fifth century BC, this may well have had some truth in it but by that time the pristine nature of Egyptian society had very largely been eroded. In the early centuries the cults surrounding the king and his relationship with the 'gods' were far removed from the experience of the vast majority of the people living in the Valley.

The common misapprehension expressed by Herodotus is partly the consequence of the limitations of language and partly of the entirely alien character of the Egyptians' relationship with what we have come to call 'the gods'. Partly it is the consequence too of many more recent commentators having failed to notice the marked differences in the attitude of the Egyptians to the invisible world, the world beyond reality, which they demonstrated at different periods of their long history.

'Religion' is taken to mean an agglomeration of precepts, often declared to be the revealed will of a high god or group of gods, which is set to determine the behaviour of the society to which the revelation has been made and of the individuals within that society. Codes of behaviour will extend to the management of the society and of the individual's relationship to the society and to his fellows. Rituals will be established for the worship of the god or gods whose aid or goodwill will be invoked by ritual prayers and ceremonies and sometimes induced by offerings or sacrifices.

In Egypt the origins of the cults which eventually flowed together to form the great national rites were quite different. The fact that Egyptian religion did not consist of rules, did not concern itself with behaviour nor, except in one specific sense, with the management of human affairs makes the Egyptian approach to the divine wholly different from that of any other ancient people. The exception was the service of the king-as-god, to whose benefit all the energies of the state were directed and in whose name all the rituals and ceremonies, in the temples or elsewhere, were conducted. These rituals in the temples were initially another expression of the state's emerging awareness of its self. It was not the purpose of the temple priest-hoods to 'worship' the gods, whose equivocal nature in any case largely precluded their identification as discrete entities, with the exception of a very few. Unlike the gods of Sumer and particularly unlike the gods of the Semitic-speaking peoples of the ancient Near East, the Egyptian powers did not require the constant reassurance that these divinities seemed always to need. To praise the gods of Egypt would have seemed superfluous to a degree approaching the absurd. Even the king was beyond such low-level adulation since, by reason of the very fact of his existence, he ensured the continued prosperity of the land and people of Egypt.

It is in this sense therefore that it is misleading to speak of Egyptian religion. Differing explanations were offered by the priesthoods for the origins of the divine powers, for the creation of the world and for the government and sacred character of Egypt, but these were allegories which concealed, as much as they revealed, the psychic reality of which they were expressions. The archetypes do not require explanation, merely recognition.

The practices of the temples were not designed for the comfort or direction of the people of Egypt; ruled by an immanent divinity, they had no need of the sort of precepts, instructions or reassurance which it is both the function and the delight of religious bureaucracies to provide. The great ceremonies originally were not, in any sense, congregational. They were occasions for the king and the powers to recognise each other and for 'the gods' to uphold the king in the exercise of his functions as the pivot of the universe.

All the ceremonies, in every Egyptian temple, were conducted in the name of the king; even the greatest priest was, notionally, his surrogate. Only the king was deemed appropriate to communicate with the divine powers, since he was, after all, one of them.

Such was the situation throughout most of Egyptian history. What applied in predynastic times must largely be inferred but certainly by the middle of the fourth millennium BC, as revealed by the most important predynastic centres of the cult of the Kingship, structures were set up which are ancestral to the temples of the historic period and some of the powers already have the form and probably the names which they will ultimately bear.

The form of the principal Egyptian cults changed subtly throughout the course of the country's history. In the early periods a wide diversity prevailed, the inheritance, doubtless, of the different local traditions which the unification sought to bring together into one polity. The cult of the king as the Divine Horus appears at the outset of the monarchy; other of the great gods – Hathor, Ptah, Set and Anubis – are also present as were many local divinities, some of whom would achieve great prominence in later times.

Though the stellar imagery was retained in the rituals of the latter part of the Old Kingdom, particularly in relation to the king, its predominance seems to have diminished. At this point a new supreme divinity, other than the king who had hitherto occupied this role unchallenged, begins to rise, in the person of Ra, the personification of the sun.

The sun-cults are especially associated with the kings of the Fourth and Fifth Dynasties. For the latter part of the third millennium the sun is the primary expression of divinity; Ra is portrayed as an old man, the leader of a pantheon of other divinities. In a fashion not generally admitted of gods he grows old to the point of incompetence, to be mocked even by his own daughter, at least in the folk-tales which became popular in later times.

At the end of the Old Kingdom the divine power who was to be one of the most enduring, and certainly the most popular in the life of Egypt, first appears. This is Osiris, whose origins are obscure but who may have originated in Western Asia.[4] He is the king-in-death, the ruler of eternal Egypt, the underworld of justified spirits, the Duat. He became identified in the centuries following his first appearance with the prospects of individual salvation; his cult is thus the antithesis of the earlier rites which were concerned only with the life after death of the king.

Osiris was rapidly assimilated with existing, entirely Egyptian divinities like Anjedty and Khentiamentiu, both of whom were identified with the territory around Abydos with which Osiris was to be linked throughout Egyptian history. Gradually he became the leader of the pantheon, effectively displacing Ra.

The accessibility of 'justification', the term which the Egyptians employed to signify the right to eternal life, to an increasing proportion of the population, eventually indeed to all, made Osiris and his cult ubiquitous and exceedingly powerful. As access to salvation became possible for all Egyptians, the observances of Osiris' cult, and later the cults of the other divinities who were associated with him, became elaborate and public events wholly unlike the practices which prevailed during the Old Kingdom.

The idea of rebirth had always been close to the Egyptian psyche, as even the earliest Badarian burials, with the corpse lying on its side in a foetal position supported by grave goods, make clear. The cult of Osiris focused this search for immortality until it became a national preoccupation, to the increasing benefit of the colleges of priests which rapidly emerged to cater for its adherents. As the cults of regeneration, with all the attendant panoply of death, mummification, revivification and the supposedly eternal protection of the corpse, assumed the proportions of a national industry the nature of the cults themselves was transformed. They were no longer élitist, corporate events in which the king was both the celebrant and the object of the celebration, later to be modified to extend the benefits to his closest associates, but universal occasions for identification with the divinity through acts of public worship. This process further augmented the power of the temples in the life of the state, until Herodotus' statement about the religiosity of the Egyptians must have been no more than a simple expression of the state of affairs prevailing in Egypt in the Late Period.

The Pyramid Texts were the literary expression of the rituals relating to the king's immortality in the Old Kingdom. In the Middle Kingdom the Coffin Texts were the medium through which the incantations and liturgies were made available to the official class and down through the society, which was experiencing an increasing degree of prosperity and sophistication. By the time of the New Kingdom the Book of the Dead (literally, the Book of Gates, or of Going Forth by Day) brought the power of the ancient liturgies within the reach of all men, women and children, eventually even to domestic and sacred animals.

Osiris was ultimately challenged, though not entirely displaced, by Amun of Thebes, whose rise to paramountcy was the result of the importance which was given to his cult by the first line of Theban princes to assume the Double Crown at the beginning of the Eleventh Dynasty. From this time, at the very end of the third millennium, Thebes never lost its influence in Egyptian affairs; even if it were not always the capital of the country it was something of the country's principal religious centre, not necessarily its holiest shrine but certainly its most vigorous religious administration, its Rome or Canterbury.

Amun became assimilated with a number of other divinities, producing composite gods such as Amun-Ra, thus giving the old sun-god a new lease of life, and Amun-Min, in which he vigorously displayed the phallic attribute of that very ancient divinity of the Theban region. Amun survived throughout the remainder of Egyptian history, enjoying a final moment of particular triumph as the putative father of Alexander the Great. By this time the old Egyptian cults had largely been submerged beneath the accretions of foreign religious influences which poured into Egypt in the last phase of its history.

Throughout the Old and Middle Kingdoms the rituals in the Egyptian temples were concerned exclusively with the nature and functions of the king. Even in later times the king still occupies the centre of all the ceremonies but, just as there was a qualitative change in the nature of the Kingship, from the supreme divinity, to one in a train of gods, to something approaching an honorary godhead, so the nature of the rituals changed, becoming more directly the celebration of the power and glory of a particular divinity and hence of his priesthood. They then become directly comparable with the rituals conducted in every temple or sacred place in the ancient world.

By the New Kingdom the situation had changed again. The gods, now in form and attributes more closely resembling those of the other lands with which Egypt was increasingly in contact, became the focus of acts of worship which would have been unthinkable in earlier times. Part of the occasion for such changes undoubtedly was the influx of foreign, mainly Semitic, divinities into Egypt at the time of the Hyksos invasion in the centuries between the end of the Middle Kingdom and the reassertion of Theban autocracy by the Eighteenth Dynasty. From this time onwards, though the power of Egypt expanded on an international scale dramatically, the king-as-emperor replaced the even more exalted king-as-god of earlier times, though formal acknowledgement was paid to his official divinity, not far removed from the manner of the cults of the emperors in Rome.

This development was unfortunate for the understanding of the divine powers in their archetypal forms, which Egypt had so uniquely revealed. Their reputation suffered correspondingly when more and more foreigners, from societies which were taking over the supreme role which once Egypt had discharged, came into Egypt, saw the evidence of its mighty past and generally misunderstood it. The gods of Egypt were now dismissed as an assembly of animal-headed monsters, their priests little more respected than village magicians.

Yet something of the dignity of the Egyptians' recognition of the powers of the invisible world remained. The Greeks, always ready to be impressed, believed that it was the Egyptians who first named the gods; they paid tribute to Egypt as the source of their own culture, a fact which has too often been disregarded by observers of the ancient world.

By the second millennium BC, after the expulsion of the Hyksos kings and as the New Kingdom began, the temple bureaucracies, which had been geared to the king's service in the Old Kingdom and had been restrained in the Middle Kingdom, began to proliferate and greatly to increase in wealth and influence.

The later centuries of the history of Egypt saw the development of the administration, both in government and in the temples, lead to a much more complex liturgy and public ritual. Festivals celebrating particular gods, which once would have been small-scale, distinctly local affairs, now assumed larger and larger proportions, consuming much of the state's wealth and energy. In the temples themselves we find more frequent representations of great ceremonies, with huge teams of shaven-headed priests in procession, carrying images of the god where once they had borne the living god on his portable throne, a practice copied, however unconsciously, by the Roman pontiffs. In the temple ceremonies the king himself is virtually demoted to a priest exercising his office in the worship of the gods, censing them, offering them gifts, little more than a superior practitioner of the mysteries.

The role of the priests in Egyptian society is complex. They were certainly important functionaries, even in the early days. They were not, however, *religious*, either in the sense of being motivated by a sense of vocation or as professional clergy ministering to the people. They were temple bureaucrats in much the same relationship to the state as an official in the Chancellor's office might be considered a servant of the state. At some periods it was customary for an Egyptian of position, even quite a modest one, to serve for part of the year as a priest in one of the temples, rather in the same way that a public-spirited official might chose to serve for a time in the Territorial Army.

Priests were required to administer the pious foundations which were set up, generation by generation, to keep alive the memory – and hence the spirit – of a dead king or magnate. There is evidence of such shrines being maintained over many generations; the priesthoods were frequently hereditary and, as they were supported by substantial endowments, were prized. Most of the foundations specified the ways in which the priests were to be reimbursed for their services.

There were various categories of priest functioning in the temples at different periods of Egypt's development. The *sem* priest was responsible for the conduct of the funeral ceremonies; others were skilled embalmers. Lector priests were responsible, especially during the centuries of Egypt's decline, for the management of the temple ceremonies, the declamation of the liturgies and for the 'special effects' which became part of the process of astonishing the simple. There was also a class of physician priests, who presumably discharged a somewhat more valuable function.

The High Priests of the great temples were formidable figures who came to control considerable power and wealth. Perhaps they came nearest to the character of a great medieval prelate, the Abbot of an important monastery for example, who would be the equal of any territorial magnate and of whose power the king would need to take account.

It is deeply ironic that one of the oldest of the cults of Egypt, that of Apis, incarnate in a distinctively marked bull, which survived for three thousand years to the end of antiquity, should have been one of those which seemed most grotesque to those from other lands who encountered it. By the time that the Serapaeum was established, the site of the massive tombs built for successive generations of the Apis and his mother at Saqqara, the ancient cults had become sadly overblown. The same fate awaited the legions of ibises, monkeys, dogs and falcons which were mummified and buried in their own cemeteries where, three thousand years before, the great magnates of the earliest dynasties had been buried in their handsome brick-built tombs on the escarpment looking down on Memphis.

Nonetheless, something of the essential nobility of Egyptian philosophy (a word which here can be used in its literal sense of denoting the love of wisdom) survived. Behind all the plethora of divine powers which the Egyptians acknowledged was 'He whose name is hidden'. This is the unknown god, the reality behind all the gods, of whom it was said that Horus, the ever-reincarnating falcon prince, perched upon his battlements. The image is a powerful one and, like so many Egyptian literary expressions of the ineffable, reveals deep levels of awareness, the product of the unique surge of psychic energy which the creation of the Egyptian state released into the world.

CHAPTER IV

BEFORE THE KINGS: PREDYNASTIC EGYPT

——— •◆• ———

More deeply than most peoples the ancient inhabitants of Egypt were conscious of their land, keenly attuned to its physical properties and character. They were linked to it by ties of the most profound emotional power; constantly, in their later writings and in the graphic arts, they emphasise the bond between the Egyptian and his land. This deep psychical bond between Egypt and Egyptians contributed much to the historical Egyptian experience. The bond was also physical for, in the end the Egyptian would always return to the land of Egypt, there to await rebirth, either beyond the stars if he were king or, in later times, in a Valley transfigured and raised to a celestial dimension, if he were an ordinary mortal Egyptian.

The land of Egypt is physically very clearly demarcated. It consists, in large part, of the great valley which, over millions of years, the river which we call the Nile (and which the Egyptians themselves called, simply and rather grandly, 'The River') has cut through the sandstone and limestone rocks which underlie this north-eastern quadrant of Africa, the eastern reaches of the Sahara desert.

In the north, Egypt is bounded by the Mediterranean Sea, in the east and west by desert wastes. In the south the river runs on its course from its distant origins in the mountains of Ethiopia to its outpourings in the Delta, 4,000 miles away, through rocky cataracts which made navigation challenging but which made policing the access to deeper Africa relatively easy.

This quadrilateral containment of the land of Egypt had a considerable and lasting influence on the historic Egyptian personality. It gave the people a deep-seated sense of security which, for much of their history, was confirmed by the failure of foreigners (not a class of person greatly admired by the ancient inhabitants of Egypt) to penetrate the Valley by force. For most of the long centuries of Egypt's existence it was possible to contain the risk of attack by a sensible exploitation of Egypt's physical characteristics and topography.

Egyptian civilisation did not arise only on the Nile's banks. The deserts are as important as the rich and fertile river-borne land on which the farmers, the most typical of Egypt's inhabitants, raised their crops. The desert, known as the Red Land in contradistinction to the Black Land, was the source of Egypt's mineral wealth, which was immense. It was also the home of the animals, of the herds and of the chase, on which the people depended for much of their supply of food.

The physical character of the Valley and the desert changed dramatically over the millions of years during which the land was being formed. In the remote past a palaeo-Mediterranean stretched across much of what is now North Africa and ran far into the south of the Valley, forming a deep embayment. Beneath this region lie the oldest rocks in the Valley, diorite, granite and quartz, all of which were to become the favoured materials of the sculptors of Egypt. Sandstone and limestone are the most visible evidence of Egypt's sedimentary history in the south whilst shale and rocky clays form the upper surface of the northern reaches of the Valley and the oases in the western desert.

Eventually the land of Egypt experienced a significant 'tilt' which allowed the waters in the south to drain into the Mediterranean basin. This process was achieved slowly, with the result that the limestone underlay was longer in its formation in the more northern reaches of the Valley.

In the Miocene period another rise in the land levels in the Valley produced the gorge, much the same formation as that through which the Nile flows today. The ancient proto-Nile had flowed more or less where it listed; now, for the first time, the flow of the waters was contained and the process of cutting still deeper into the ancient rock formation was accelerated. This resulted in the exposure of the various geological strata which today are so much a feature of the river-scape.

Much more recently, over the past two million years, deposits of loose shales and rocky debris were laid down, near the centre of the Valley. These deposits would supply the terraces which form much of the Valley's profile today.

The Nile, as all the world knows, begins its life as two rivers, the White and the Blue. The great mass of water in the Nile's annual inundation (at least until the arguably catastrophic introduction of Lake Nasser and the elimination of the annual flood) came from the White Nile, rising in Lake Victoria. The Blue Nile rises in Ethiopia and its flooding brought with it the rich alluvial deposits of silt and topsoil which formed the cultivable land on which Egypt's agricultural prosperity was based.

The White and Blue Niles converge near Khartoum, in the Sudan. The two rivers' flood was essential to the life of vegetation, animals and, later, man in Egypt, for the rainfall, which had once been quite plentiful in north-east Africa, began to decline. It was around 10,000 years ago that the Nile became virtually the only source of water for irrigation in Egypt, for rainfall was, for all practical purposes, non-existent.

In the north of Egypt, not far from the modern capital city of Cairo, the Nile divides into two for its final journey to the sea; in antiquity there were three branches of the river running through the Delta which the flooding of the river at this point created. This is the fertile plain which runs to the Mediterranean and which, in the times of the early kings, was probably the centre of the domestication of cattle. Here the water level has always been relatively high, impeding archaeological exploration of many of the early levels of habitation, though modern techniques are beginning to change this situation and to make hitherto inaccessible levels possible of access.

Most of Egypt's population lives, as they have always lived, close to the river and its fertile banks. Fields could be cultivated during the time of the inundation by the skilful creation of a network of canals which drew off the water from the flood and allowed it to spread across the land, depositing its precious silt and topsoil. It was this process which also produced the *shaduf*, the device used to lift water from one level to another, whose rhythmic creaking was one of the most enduring and familiar sounds of the Egyptian countryside.

Until relatively late, perhaps around 10,000 years ago, the Valley was largely empty of human inhabitants. The period which followed the end of the last glaciation, around twelve thousand years ago, is still little understood. The melting of the ice in Europe had a considerable and prolonged effect on sea levels throughout the hemisphere causing them to rise over many centuries. Similarly, there was a marked change in local climatic conditions as the release of large amounts of water altered not only shore lines but also wind patterns and atmospheric moisture levels. One result seems to have been the beginning of the process of the drying up of the lakes and bodies of standing water which were to be found in the western and central Sahara. This drove the hunters and herders who lived on the herds of ruminants which had previously inhabited North Africa, increasingly towards the east. Thus they reached the Valley and the course of Egyptian history began.

They were met by other groups, moving up from the south, people who came from the southern Sudan and east Africa. They had been percolating into the Valley over many millennia but they were transient peoples, following the great herds of wild cattle, for example. Even in times which otherwise were unimaginably early for this part of the ancient Near East they seem to have been bearers of at least the rudiments of a culture. The burial found at Tushka,[1] which was protected by the skulls of two wild aurochs, is evidence for the existence of ritual in the Valley even in such early times, fourteen thousand years ago. Of all the influences which can be detected in the development of the character of Egypt in its earliest historical phases, that of the cattle people seems to have been especially powerful. This point will be further developed later in this study, particularly in the context of the early Kingship.

The desiccation of the Valley continued into historic times. Although the Valley must have seemed paradisal to its earliest inhabitants, the riverbanks and the steppe-lands teeming with game, this happy situation did not last much beyond the beginning of the third millennium BC; it had probably begun to be threatened even earlier, in late predynastic times. The stocks of game animals declined markedly and this decline is dramatically demonstrated by the rock carvings in Upper (southern) Egypt which show giraffe, elephant, hippopotamus and ostrich, all of which had disappeared by early historic times. To the effects of a reduction in available water resources must be added the effects on animal stocks of the increasing sophistication, and hence the deadliness, of the hunting techniques which drove the animals further and further to the south and out of the parts of the Valley which had come to be more densely populated.

The main influx of new people into the Valley seems to have begun around 6000 BC. From that point onwards it is appropriate to describe the development of life in the Valley in terms of the different cultures which can be associated with the people who lived on its generous, river-borne bounty and who laid the foundations of Egyptian civilisation.

The environmental division which is apparent between the southern and northern regions of the Nile Valley was to be perpetuated in the historic periods, expressed in the idea that there were originally two kingdoms, the South and the North, which it would be the historic role of the first Kings to unite. The idea of the division persisted throughout Egyptian history and was reflected at every level of the national life and organisation. However, it must be said that although the king bore two titles, one for each Kingdom, symbolised by the sedge and the bee, there is actually no archaeological evidence for the existence of a northern Kingdom before the unification.

But the notional division between south and north is evident before the unified Kingship which was to be so powerful and long-prevailing a principle in the Egyptians' management of their world. In the two thousand years or so before the date conventionally given to the unification of what were always called 'The Two Lands', c.3100 BC , the cultures which define the different groups which emerged in the Valley also reflect this division between south and north.

The division of the two Egypts was of great importance in establishing the Egyptians' own view of the world. To them Egypt *was* the world, not in microcosm but in reality. Other lands and other peoples were deprived of the full status of humanity by virtue of their misfortune in living outside the Valley. Egypt represented the matrix of the world as it was meant to be. The perpetual rhythm of the cosmos could be demonstrated by the balance of opposites: everything in creation had its pair. Thus Egypt was two lands and, correspondingly, one.

In the later predynastic period and throughout the history of Egypt as a unitary state it is the south which tends always to be the dominant half of the union. In the early predynastic period, however, it is generally accepted that northern cultures have a slight priority of time over those which appeared in the south. However, despite the fact that the high water-table has limited severely the opportunities of excavation of early sites in the Delta, in broad terms the four principal northern Egyptian predynastic cultures chime well with the three main cultures (with their subdivisions) from the south.

There are, however, few similarities between them. The northern cultures, associated with the sites of Fayum (from the mid-fifth millennium BC,[2] Merimde (early fourth millennium),[3] El Omari (late fourth millennium),[4] and Ma'adi (end of the fourth millennium),[5] are scanty and often very slight, with the exception of Ma'adi, the latest of them, which was quite substantial covering an area of 18 hectares. Generally they lack the evidence of the increasing sophistication, in art and social organisation, which becomes apparent in the south from early in the fourth millennium.

The earliest predynastic settlers in northern Egypt were probably immigrants, who camped around the shores of the Fayum Depression. Like many of the inhabitants of the north in historic times the predynastic northeners seem to have had contact with Palestine. The Merimde people, too, may have had links with the north-east and the architecture of their settlements has suggested connections with the much earlier inhabitants of Palestine, the Natufians, who lived there in the immediate aftermath of the migrations which took place at the end of the last glaciation.[6] These people probably followed a way of life still rooted in the old ways of the hunting and gathering bands but with some rudimentary attempts at cultivation; they may have domesticated some animals.

In the case of the last predynastic people of the north, those associated with the important site at Ma'adi, their settlements suggest a more developed life-style, with well-made pottery, stone vases and storage pits for grain. One of the more unusual of their practices was the burying of dogs and gazelles in their own graves in the cemeteries which were near their main settlement sites.[7]

Towards the end of the predynastic period there seems to have been some contact between north and south, witnessed by the presence of southern pottery in Ma'adi. But in general the northern settlements do not appear to have exercised the same degree of influence on the eventual development of the Egyptian state as did the south, though this may be the consequence of evidence having been destroyed by later settlements or submerged under the Delta's water-table, which has risen since predynastic times.

The predynastic cultures of the south seem to be much more developed than their northern contemporaries. The earliest of them, named for the site at El-Badari where the first pottery-making culture was identified, appears in Upper Egypt in the middle of the fifth millennium BC in the area immediately to the north of the point when the Nile turns to run due east before returning to its north–south orientation. The Badarians may also have been immigrants into the Valley, though this is by no means certain; however, they did maintain contacts, presumably by way of trade, with Palestine, perhaps mediated through the 'Fayum A' people in the north, and with the Red Sea. There is also some evidence of contact as far away as Syria.

Badarian pottery is very well made, with a wide diversity of shapes. The earliest ware is particularly fine, the walls of the pots being of an almost eggshell thinness but exceptionally hard.

The Badarians may have practised animal domestication. There is evidence for some sort of cult of the dead, with burials being carefully prepared and offerings to the dead being placed with them. The stone palettes which are to become so important a feature of the later predynastic period make their appearance and were used for the grinding of cosmetic materials, particularly kohl for the eyes, used to reduce the sun's glare. Unlike peoples in the north, the Badarians do not seem to have depended much on hunting.

The Badarian culture was succeeded by that first recognised at El Amra and hence called the Amratian. Nowadays the later southern predynastic cultures are generally grouped under the description 'Naqada'; Amratian is thus Naqada I. It represents quite a considerable advance on the Badarians, with exploitation of the river and the appearance of the first towns in Egypt, including Hierakonpolis, which was to play a most significant role in Egypt's history. The development of Naqada I (*c*.3500 BC) is highly distinctive, especially in the type of pottery which the people produced. Most authorities, however, consider that there was a close relationship between this phase of the Egyptian predynastic period and the Badarian which preceded it.

In the decoration of their pottery the Naqada I people demonstrate two of the most compelling characteristics of the culture of ancient Egypt: a genius for draughtsmanship and a delight in the observation of nature. The Egyptian propensity for drawing is truly remarkable and will be demonstrated in many different forms throughout Egyptian history. It has its beginnings in the Naqada I culture.

Naqada II (*c*.3300 BC), which is also known as the Gerzean, is especially important for it indicates strongly that at this time, towards the end of the fourth millennium BC, Egypt was subject to a not insignificant degree of foreign influence, certainly the only period in its early history when such influences are qualitatively significant. The Naqada II period was one of intense development and rapid change in all aspects of Upper Egyptian society. Many of these developments seem to have been stimulated by contacts with foreigners and, although the distances involved are very great, it seems most likely that such contacts were made with people from south-west Asia. In particular it is possible to detect foreign elements of design, in architecture, on pottery and in the manufacture of objects of daily use such as the slate palettes used for grinding cosmetics, some of which now assume superb and monumental form, and seals. These last show clear evidence of contact with southern Mesopotamia and, more particularly still, with Elam in south-western Iran. That they were rapidly Egyptianised and absorbed into the distinctive canons of Egyptian design and custom does not lessen their significance.

The standards of craftsmanship and the arts developed apace during Naqada II. Pottery, quite different in its fabric from the preceding cultures, is brilliantly and naturalistically decorated. Copper begins to be more generally used and the manipulation of fine stones becomes part of the craftsman's repertory, to remain one of the glories of Egyptian art throughout its history. Flint-knapping becomes exceptionally skilled, with some of the most exquisitely fabricated blades ever produced by any ancient society appearing at this time. Exceptionally finely made flint knives are now made, often married to superbly carved ivory hilts; it is generally considered that the knives were votive objects, because they are too fine and fragile to have had any ordinary use. Similarly, in late predynastic times in the important site of Hierakonpolis, exceptionally large knives, far too big for any practical purpose, were laid up in the temple there.[8]

Further evidence of long-range contacts is provided by the use of lapis lazuli, the brilliant blue stone which is extracted only from two known sites, one in Badakhstan and the other at Quetta in northern Pakistan. That trade routes were maintained over such distances as these sites imply at so early a time is truly remarkable. Gold and silver also begin to be used, particularly in beads and amulets: the presence of gold in Egypt may indeed be the reason why traders from the distant east penetrated the Valley in the first place.[9]

At the beginning of the historic period, that is after the development of writing, the Naqada culture reveals other forms which will be sustained throughout Egyptian history. Stone-carving, including statuary, develops most powerfully: in the statuary, eerie, rather menacing figures of bearded – and in one case, cloaked and hooded[10] – men appear. A good deal less menacing are a series of cheerfully abandoned figures of dancers fabricated in clay.

As the end of the fourth millennium BC nears it seems that the Valley, or at least its southern reaches, was divided into a series of small entities which it is usual to describe as 'chieftaincies'. There is ample evidence from the historic period that however much the polity of Egypt reflected not only the enduring idea of the Two Kingdoms (north and south), the country was already divided into an agglomeration of districts, each with its dominant divinity and, in times of national stress, the tendency to split off from the central royal authority, asserting something approaching independence. This period, the point of transition between the predynastic cultures and the arrival of the kings, is now classified as Naqada III.[11]

The division of Egypt into localities with their own traditions and cults was to influence the development of the country and its institutions even when it was at its most apparently coherent. However, movement towards the unification of the Two Lands does seem to have begun quite early in the historic period, ultimately to be achieved despite sustained and often successful resistance by interests opposed to the princes who promoted the unification.

The impetus for the unification of the country appears to have come from a family of princes who ruled from, or around, the great city of Hierakonpolis far to the south, where the heart of Egypt seemed always to beat most vigorously. Hierakonpolis (the name is, of course, Greek and means 'Falcon City'; to the Egyptians it was Nekhen) is the first great city in Egypt, a land not generally well-supplied with large urban centres. In the late predynastic period it was surrounded by a great double wall, a massive defensive structure built against who knows what enemy.[12]

According to tradition the unification was brought about by a young prince whose name was rendered as Menes, and who was revered throughout Egypt's history as the founder of the Egyptian Kingship. He has been identified with another early royal name, Narmer and also, more certainly, Aha. He is a mysterious but profoundly significant figure; his memory was to be invoked throughout the long sweep of Egyptian history. He was evidently very young when he set out from the city which was sacred to his symbolic protector, the falcon, which ever afterwards remained the particular badge of the King of Egypt, for he was said to have reigned for sixty-four years. There is no reason to doubt that, whoever he was, he did possess the Kingship for a long time.

The importance of the late predynastic period, of which the culmination is the more or less simultaneous appearance of the Kingship, writing and the state, is that it contained all the seeds of the later full flowering of Egyptian civilisation. All the aspects of Egyptian life which were to be formalised into the ceremonies, beliefs, art, architecture and traditions of the succeeding centuries are present by around 3000 BC. The predynastic period is the bedrock on which the entire structure of historic Egypt was to be built and which survived for the next thirty centuries.

However, in its physical manifestations, of art and, in so far as the term can be used, of architecture, the predynastic period is quite distinct and particularly its works of art are hardly, if ever, exactly recalled in the art of later periods. Given the notable coherence of the Egyptian world view (a coherence which is sometimes mistaken for conservatism) this is remarkable. But the scenes so brilliantly realised on the slate palettes, for example, seldom recur, except some of those which are associated with the king, notably his identification with a great wild bull. The decoration of predynastic pottery is quite unlike what follows; stone vessels do carry over, though the repertory of designs and techniques is greatly expanded in the coming Archaic period.

The most likely explanation for this sudden change of forms, associated both with the arrival of the Kingship and a very marked flowering of art and technique, is that the creation of the Kingship brought about the releasing of the archetypes, which in turn was the product of the liberation of the collective unconscious of the people of the Valley in which all the 'new' forms which were to appear, were previously locked. Since there is no evidence for the incursion of foreign peoples on any substantial numerical scale, such a psychological explanation seems the only one tenable, to account for the dramatic changes which occurred. Such changes, whilst they were clearly significant, were wholly consonant with what had gone before and with what was to follow. The explanation for this synthesis is probably to be found in the archetype of the king who was to appear precisely at this point and whose presence focused the forces which were present but unrealised in the collective Egyptian psyche.

It is clear that the *idea* of the Kingship is present in times which preceded the beginning of the First Dynasty. Royal names, enclosed in the *serekh* badge, are known including those names of at least six predynastic rulers, who may have had pretensions to the rule of all the Valley; what may be the oldest recorded royal name appears in the *serekh*.[13] The centre of these kings seems already to have shifted from Hierakonpolis to the region of Abydos, which was especially to be associated with the kings of the first two dynasties.

Already, too, there are signs that the king (if he may be so described) was buried in some state. Large late predynastic burials have been found at Abydos and, at the end of the nineteenth century, Tomb 100 at Hierakonpolis, the celebrated decorated tomb with its plastered walls painted with scenes and elements of design which were to persist throughout much of Egyptian history, was recognised as the burial place of a high-status individual. As such it was probably ancestral to the long line of royal tombs which was to be so important a part of the Egyptian state in succeeding centuries.

The late predynastic period is marked by the clear evidence of influences seeping into the Valley which have their origins in south-western Asia. Given the great distances involved, this seems remarkable for these influences have their origins in the region which opens out of the headlands of the Arabian Gulf, in southern Mesopotamia, which was to be known to history as Sumer and, in Elam, in south-western Iran. It is Elam which seems to have been the more important of the two sources for the introduction of ideas and symbols which were foreign to the emergent culture in the southern part of the Valley in the late fourth millennium, but which were to exercise a lasting and, symbolically at least, a most powerful influence on it.[14]

The development of complex societies in the fourth millennium BC is one of the most engrossing if obscure episodes in human history. In three main centres in the Near East at virtually the same time, societies emerged which were to be quite different in character from those which preceded them. These centres were the southern Nile Valley (Upper Egypt), southern Mesopotamia (Sumer) and south-western Iran (Elam). Each of these was culturally quite distinct and, in historical terms, apparently had little if any previous relationship with any of the others, though Sumer and Elam shared a common border region. In the mid- to late fourth millennium each shows signs of rapid, exponential development; at the same time Elam and to a lesser extent, Sumer, seem to have exercised a clear influence on Egypt, precisely at the point when the Nile Valley was to undergo the spectacular changes associated with the Kingship and the resulting movement towards the Valley's political unification.

It must not be forgotten that the culture which was growing in Egypt at this time was essentially African; whatever influences there may have been from the east were secondary, though of considerable significance. At the time that Western Asiatic elements were appearing in Upper Egypt, especially in the art and protocol associated with the Kingship, there is evidence that at Qustal in Nubia, to the south of Egypt, there were rulers established in the latter part of the fourth millennium who display, in their regalia and the representations of their state on religious occasions, much that seems to anticipate the trappings of the chieftaincies in Upper Egypt which led to the development of the Egyptian Kingship itself.[15]

On the face of it, the evidence from Qustal would seem to predate the earliest appearance of the Kingship in Egypt by several generations. It may be that this Nubian evidence is simply the consequence of the happenstance of archaeology and that evidence of a comparable time has not yet been found from Egyptian sites, further to the north. The work of the German Archaeological Institute at Abydos,[16] which has uncovered what seem to be royal burials from a date in the late fourth millennium, which is earlier than any hitherto recorded, may result in this view being qualified but at present the material from Qustal does appear to be very early.

Unlike this tentative evidence from Nubia, which is a very recent development, the existence of Western Asiatic elements in aspects of early Egyptian society and iconography has long been recognised. At the end of the nineteenth century Flinders Petrie identified a number of distinctive factors which could only have originated in the region which today would be described as lying to the north and east of the headlands of the Arabian Gulf.

The particular factors which Petrie,[17] and later scholars (especially Frankfort,[18] Baumgartel[19] and Kantor[20]), described may be summarised thus:

- a heroic figure dominating animals, especially lions, who appears on the Jebel El-Arak knife and in the paintings in the early high-prestige Tomb 100 at Hierakonpolis; this theme is to be found in both Sumer and Elam; the dominating figure on the Jebel El-Arak knife, in particular, is dressed in the manner of a late fourth-millennium Mesopotamian and is not in the least Egyptian;

- composite animals, with long intertwined necks, commonly described as serpo-pards, and 'griffins' with wings protruding from their backs, depicted on slate or mudstone palettes used in Egypt for both cosmetic and votive purposes, the designs of which originate on cylinder seals from Elam;
- high-prowed ships, unlike native Egyptian vessels, which appear on painted pottery, carved on palettes, and on the Jebel El-Arak knife are paralleled by Mesopotamian boats which appear on seal designs;
- recessed panelling with buttresses, on the facades and sides of public buildings, which appears first in Sumerian temples at Uruk c.3500 BC, and later in Elam, especially on the seals of the early period, c.3000–2900 BC. It is used extensively in Egyptian funerary architecture of the early periods and long survived in the decoration of sarcophagi;
- the temple or palace facade, incorporating the recessed panelling and buttressing, usually under a battlemented tower as the heraldic device which depicts the king's most sacred name.

The use of cylinder seals in Egypt appeared only in late predynastic times and was clearly inspired by Mesopotamian originals, where they had been used throughout most of the fourth millennium. A number of seals of actual Mesopotamian provenance have been found in Egypt, suggesting the presence of people who relied on their use in their daily lives. The most likely individuals who would require the use of a cylinder seal would be merchants or itinerant traders who, like their prospective customers or suppliers, would be illiterate. Other examples of cylinder seals from late predynastic times show Egyptian motifs, rather than ones which obviously originated in Mesopotamia, indicating that such seals were being made in Egypt.[21]

Other more random evidence includes a small limestone head (now in the British Museum) from Abydos which is evidently either of Sumerian manufacture or inspiration. It is similar in form to heads of figurines of the Early Dynastic period (c.2800 BC.) from the Diyala region, in the north of Sumer.

A still more problematical case of what may be the evidence of Western Asiatic influence in Egypt is the mound on which the archaic temple was built in the city of Nekhen (Hierakonpolis).[22] This is distinctly un-Egyptian, consisting of a layer of pure sand laid over the ground, retained by a revetment, for all the world like the 'Temple Ovals' known from several sites in Sumer, at el-Hiba, Khafajeh,[23] and Tel El-Ubaid. These are all approximately of the same date as the mound at Hierakonpolis. A similar construction is to be found far away in the Arabian Gulf, at Barbar in Bahrain.[24] This oval, however, is several hundred years later than either the

Egyptian or the Sumerian examples, dating from the very end of the third millennium, but it, too, is built on a mound of pure sand, held in place by a revetment.

It has been suggested that the Hierkonpolis revetment was the source of the hieroglyph ⌒ or ⓝ with which the name of the city, Nekhen, was written. If this is so it may reflect the singularity with which this particular architectural feature was regarded by the Egyptians themselves.[25]

Petrie seems to have believed that the spark which exploded into the dynastic civilisation of Egypt was borne into the Valley by seafarers from 'the Persian Gulf islands'.[26] Intriguing though this idea is, there is no evidence in the Bahrain islands, the principal group in the Gulf which Petrie identified as the most likely point of origin from which the voyagers came who carried Elamite influences into the Valley, for any settled (or indeed significant transient) population as early as the end of the fourth millennium, when these influences first appeared in the Valley.

There are other locations, however, in the southern part of the Gulf, where there were quite sophisticated settlements somewhat earlier than in Bahrain. In addition to the settlements which were established on the Arabian mainland and on at least one of its offshore islands, Tarut, these include the island of Umm an-Nar,[27] and inland sites such as Hili in what is now the Emirate of Abu Dhabi and at Hafit in the Sultanate of Oman;[28] slightly later than these are settlements at Ibri and Bat, also in the Sultanate. Such settlements, dating from early in the third millennium, were associated with the extraction of copper ore and its distribution.[29] In one case at least, that of Umm an-Nar, a highly individual culture flourished there, c.3000 BC, with a well-developed funerary cult demonstrated by handsome stone-built tombs.[30]

There is some evidence that the Bahrain islands may originally have been colonised by voyagers from Umm an-Nar. If Petrie were right about voyagers from the Gulf sailing up the Red Sea coast to make their eventual entry into the Valley, then the inhabitants of the island of Umm an-Nar could have represented an important point of contact on the journey. However, to associate such sites with the formative influences which triggered the development of a high culture in Egypt would require a considerable imaginative leap.

Some scholars have followed Petrie's suggestion about the transfer of civilisation from the Arabian Gulf to Egypt but there is simply no evidence of an invasion or even of the incursion of a dominant alien group in the Valley at this time.[31] There have been attempts to identify some skeletal remains from Egypt in late predynastic times as representing a non-indigenous population but such evidence is notoriously unreliable.

The one 'document' which has been advanced as evidence of some sort of conflict between native Egyptians and foreign 'invaders' is the Jebel El-Arak knife. This is a very splendid object, (if indeed it is genuine; its authenticity has been questioned) a finely crafted, probably votive offering, with a beautifully prepared blade and an ivory hilt which is richly and most skilfully carved. On one side of the hilt groups of sea-borne warriors are shown in combat; they are identified with two quite distinct types of sailing craft. One is known to be Egyptian. The other type of vessel has high prows decorated with animal heads which are well known from Mesopotamian seals of the Archaic period (in Mesopotamian chronology, late Uruk, Jamdet Nasr) which corresponds with the likely date of the knife's manufacture. From the scene depicted on the knife it appears that the Mesopotamian 'invaders', if that is what they are, have won.

On the other face of the knife's hilt a powerful male figure is shown standing on a hill or mountain top dominating two heavily-maned lions. He is dressed in a long robe and wears a form of turban; neither item of apparel is remotely Egyptian but both are well known from southern Mesopotamia. Excavations of late predynastic tombs at Abydos have produced more knives the designs of whose hilts appear to show Elamite influences.

A small, though not unimportant, piece of evidence which does suggest that the Egyptians were influenced in the arts of war was their adoption, in late predynastic times, of a form of mace-head which has its origin in Western Asia. This is a bulbous-shaped stone mace-head, which is that with which the Kings of Egypt, from the earliest times, are shown 'smiting' their enemies. The Egyptian mace used in the Naqada I and II periods was discoid and was rejected in favour of the Western Asiatic model, which clearly was more effective in close engagements.

None of the borrowings from Western Asia which can with reasonable confidence be accepted could be the result of chance or the response of two emergent cultures producing identical solutions to the comparable situations which they faced at a similar point in their development, a phenomenon which is otherwise well documented. They are too particular for this explanation alone to be convincing and, whilst any one of them might be duplicated by chance, the probability of so many identical and specific elements appearing is simply too unlikely.

It must therefore be assumed that there was some form of actual contact between the people of the Nile Valley and the inhabitants of the headlands of the Arabian Gulf at the end of the fourth millennium. The mechanisms by which that contact could have been effected, however, are very far from clear, though it appears that they flowed only in one direction, from the Gulf to Egypt; there is no evidence of influences moving from Egypt to Sumer or Elam, though Naqada II pottery has been found at Habuba Kabira in north Syria. This is likely to have reached its destination there through Palestine.

In the eastern desert of Egypt there is an ancient route, the Wadi Hammamat, which links the Nile near Coptos (and, more suggestively, near Naqada where many of the basic components of late predynastic culture were first recognised) and the Red Sea coast near Quesir. The route through the desert is remarkable for the extensive repertory of rock carvings, many of which seem to be of the late predynastic period and feature the high-prowed 'Mesopotamian' type of boat.[32]

The association of boats and the Red Sea access has encouraged a number of commentators, led by Petrie, to postulate a maritime connection between the Valley and Western Asia. There is nothing inherently impossible in this, though the idea of early Western Asiatic peoples undertaking a sea voyage (presumably *many* sea voyages) of such an extent over five thousand years ago must stretch credulity somewhat.

Yet something of the kind would seem to have happened. At the right time of year the conditions for travelling westwards from the Gulf to Egypt would be much enhanced, for once the voyagers came out of the Gulf, to sail through the straits protected by Ras Musandam into the Arabian Sea, they would be carried by the monsoon winds along the southern Arabian coast through the Bab Al Mandab into the Red Sea.[33] The monsoon's force would carry them some half-way up the Red Sea's western shore. This would be in the area of the modern port of Quesir which, in late pre-dynastic as in historic times, was the principal eastern point of entry into Egypt, leading through the wadis of the eastern desert, including the Wadi Hammamat, to Coptos in the Valley itself.

Two other routes connecting the Gulf headlands and the Nile Valley are possible. Both are by land; the first moves westwards across what are now the northern reaches of the Arabian desert into Palestine and then south-wards through Gaza or Sinai into northern Egypt. There were certainly contacts between Palestine and Lower Egypt in predynastic times which continued into the historic period. Recently excavations at the ancient Egyptian city of Buto, in the north-western Delta,[34] have revealed what appears to be architecture of a Western Asiatic inspiration there. This is shown by the use, in a public building of the late fourth millennium, of decorated clay cones which were fixed into the plaster coatings of the building's walls and pillars. This practice originated in Uruk in southern Mesopotamia and could not have reached Egypt other than by the presence, either of Sumerian builders, or of people of influence who were concerned to build their own style of temple and were powerful enough to do so in so distant an environment.

However, this evidence in the Delta is actually easier to explain than that which has come from the south, where the influences are far more important to the development of royal Egypt's culture. In the case of the builders of the Buto structure a route westwards across the Syro-Arabian desert is the most likely, taking the travellers eventually into the Delta. This does not of itself explain how their status was such that they were able to build what was evidently a temple in their own tradition once they got there.

The second alternative also postulates a land route, but this time it would run directly across the Arabian peninsula, moving in a south-westerly direction from the head of the Gulf and hence anticipating somewhat the pilgrim route established in the early years of Islam, which linked the Holy Cities of western Arabia with Iraq and the northern Gulf.[35] Equally, a route east to west straight across Arabia, perhaps beginning in the region of Tarut island, close to the eastern Arabian shore almost opposite the Bahrain islands, is also feasible.

In the latter part of the fourth millennium the climate of Arabia was marginally more benign than it is today. It has always been possible for desert people to criss-cross the peninsula to an extent which seems miraculous to those who do not know their skilful exploitation of so apparently inhospitable an environment. The essential precondition for travel in the desert is access to water; provided the traveller moves from well to well, he will survive. Since the timbers of the boats which are depicted on the rocks of the Wadi Hammamet, which it may be presumed were used to cross the Red Sea, were probably sewn rather than nailed or dowelled together, it is possible that they were dismantled for the land crossing, and reassembled when they reached the coast. Sewn boats were made in the Arabian Gulf until modern times; the boat which was found dismantled beside the pyramid of Khufu of the Fourth Dynasty was made in the same way.

It is most probable that the travellers who undertook this long and, as it must have been, hazardous journey were, initially at least, traders. Even in Upper Palaeolithic times, millennia before the period with which we are dealing, artifacts, stone or shells, were traded over great distances, handed on from one community to another. In the fourth millennium the most remarkable evidence of the distances over which a coveted product might travel is provided by the trade in lapis lazuli, the rich, brilliant blue stone much admired by the ancients, the only ancient sources of which lay very far away, to the east. Lapis was widely used in Iran, where it is found on sites which were evidently important points in its distribution, in Mesopotamia, the Gulf, Syria and, most distant of all, in Egypt.

Lapis was exported to Egypt in the late predynastic period until the early dynastic period. It ceases suddenly in the reign of Den, the third king of the First Dynasty, *c.*2900 BC . Its trade is not resumed until the latter part of the Old Kingdom. Clearly some development far away to the east from which the lapis came, or on the route of its journey, interrupted the traffic. What this might have been we can only guess at, but there is one likely possibility.

In the early third millennium a culture developed in eastern Arabia which was based on trade and the search for raw materials. This culture was known as Dilmun; the earliest recorded references to Dilmun and its international contacts date from early written sources from Sumerian sites, *c.* 3000 BC .[36]

Some time later, in the latter half of the third millennium, Dilmun's epicentre shifted from eastern Arabia, where it seems originally to have been established, to the Bahrain islands in the centre of the Gulf. There it was to flourish exceedingly, becoming effectively the centre of the world's trade as it then was, for the next seven hundred years. It was especially concerned with the distribution of copper, ore and ingot.

Why Dilmun migrated from eastern Arabia to Bahrain is not at all clear. One possible explanation may be that the inhabitants of the Arabian desert who, if it is too early to call them *Badu*, may yet have been rootless nomads who preyed on more settled communities, making life and commerce intolerable for the traders living in the settlements in eastern Arabia, lying close to the Gulf's western shore. The Bahrain islands, lying some twenty miles offshore, would be more easily defensible; indeed the waterway separating them from the mainland would probably be enough to deter people who had not yet fully mastered the sea and sailing craft. At this time only the Sumerians, the people of south-western Iran and the Egyptians possessed the technology to make sea-going journeys.

If the mainland in Arabia became unsettled at this time it is a fair assumption that something similar happened in southern Iran, through which the lapis was carried to the Gulf. By this time also, the Gulf's international trade, which was particularly concerned with the mining, smelting and distribution of copper, was developing very satisfactorily, with its strongest trading links to the north and the south-east; a distant market such as Egypt, particularly for a product which required a substantial investment in recovering it from its source, may have perhaps seemed less appealing than the more ready markets in Mesopotamia and the Indus Valley which were already closely associated with the Gulf trade. The disruption of the lapis trade to Egypt, though it is an intriguing phenomenon, may be nothing more than a shift in trading patterns, in which economic factors are influenced by political considerations.

There is evidence that the Egyptians acquired some of their domesticated animals and their cultivated cereals from the east. Strains of sheep and goat which appear in Egypt in late predynastic and early dynastic times are known in earlier contexts in Western Asia. The presence of a particular breed or strain of animals would require a significant number of individuals to have been brought to Egypt to establish a viable population.[37] There is no evidence of how such a migration might have been effected.

The Egyptians were skilled stockmen and very early on began the domestication of species which were native to the Valley and East Africa. They were herdsmen of great experience and were accustomed to the management of large herds; they had hunted and probably otherwise exploited the great numbers of *bos primigenius* which were present in North Africa and the Sahara. These great wild cattle exercised a considerable influence on the collective psyche of the Nile people.[38]

The influences on commerce and animal and plant husbandry in these early times which were derived from Western Asia are surpassed by the presence of south-western Asiatic elements in the iconography and possibly the regalia of the Egyptian Kingship. This is an altogether more remarkable phenomenon than any of the other apparent borrowings which have so far been described.

The Kingship is the most important and the most enduring concept to which the Nile civilisation gave birth. There is one aspect of its symbolism, the presentation of the king's most sacred name which is of special importance and of what, in an Egyptological context, may for once be genuinely described as a mystery.

In later times the king had five names; in the earliest reigns he made do with three. His most important name, that by which he was proclaimed the Horus, revealed him as the reincarnate divine ruler of the cosmos. In the later dynasties the king's name was displayed in the cartouche, a hieroglyph of a coiled rope. In the earliest periods, however, when the technique of writing first appears in Egypt, the king's name is presented in a format which adapts the architecture of the temples which are depicted on early Elamite seals. This is the deeply recessed niche which decorated the exterior of monumental buildings such as Mesopotamian temples, and in later times in Egypt appeared on the walls of important tombs; it is also to be found on the enclosures which surrounded especially important building complexes. This design is customarily referred to as the 'palace facade'.[39]

This technique of enriching the exterior walls of public buildings with recessed panelling was first developed in southern Mesopotamia in the middle of the fourth millennium; it was then apparently transmitted to Elam where it is particularly identified with the decoration of temples.[40] Somehow it reached the Nile Valley and obviously made a deep impression on the communities there, which certainly had no comparable architectural tradition. It appears rapidly to have been adopted as an architectural form, particularly employed in constructions associated either with the Kingship or with powerful figures in the society. Further and even more dramatically it became a crucial part of royal image-making through its use as the badge on which the king's most sacred name was displayed. In this form the niched and buttressed facade, its high pilasters surmounted by battlements, was known as the *serekh*, which perhaps means something like 'the proclaimer'.

The king's name was displayed in a panel above the 'palace facade' and the whole device was surmounted by the Falcon who, in this context, perched upon the battlements of him whose name was proclaimed. The falcon was the manifestation of Horus, the divine power incarnate in every king. It is surely very remarkable that so alien a form should have been employed over many hundreds of years to protect the king's name in its

Figure 1   The stela of King Djer of the early First Dynasty, *c.*3000 BC. The tablet records the king's most sacred name whilst the Falcon surmounting it identifies him as the reincarnated god Horus and thus the true King of Egypt. The elegance and austerity of the design are very remarkable at so early a point in Egypt's history.

The king's name, Djer, is indicated by the serpent in the sky. It sails above the battlements of a fortified palace, the recessed panelling of its towers forming a recurring element in the monumental architecture of the earliest periods which were to be retained for many centuries in the proclamation of the divinity of the king.

The whole design is the *serekh*, which conveys the meaning 'to proclaim'. The fortified palace facade first appears on seals which originate in south-western Iran. How the connection with archaic Egypt came about is still obscure.

most magically charged manifestation. It is especially notable that what seems to be the oldest record of a royal name in Egypt is already contained in the *serekh*.[41]

The King of Egypt's most important name was conferred at his coronation. At this event, the most important in his entire life, the king rose from his throne a god, not, indeed, merely one god of many but in the early centuries of Egyptian history the supreme divinity of the entire universe.

The singularly bold concept of the divinity of the king is deeply rooted in African belief systems; there can be little doubt that it is the product of the African psyche. The more remarkable therefore is it that the *serekh*, a very specific and distinct design, is neither Egyptian nor African in origin, but comes from so far away to the east.

We have therefore the singular situation that an architectural form, developed in southern Mesopotamia and adapted in south-western Iran, is exported right across or around the Arabian peninsula to the southern Egyptian principalities and becomes a symbol of the Divine Kingship at the very point when the process to bring about the unification of the Valley was begun. Some at least of the principalities were already edging their way towards the idea of Kingship, in which they were ahead both of the Sumerians and the Iranians. The fledgling kings of Egypt, gods as it were in embryo, for some reason at which we cannot guess, adopted an architectural detail from buildings several thousand miles away to proclaim their reincarnation as the living god, the Horus.

The articulated or recessed and buttressed panelling which is the dominant motif of the palace facade on the *serekh* was also adopted by the Egyptians of the earliest dynastic periods in the architecture of the immense mud-brick tombs in which the great magnates were buried.[42] Perhaps more significant still, the recessed panels articulate the huge walls which surround the funerary temples built for the kings of the first two dynasties, of which examples survive at Abydos. In this case the panelling surrounds and protects the body of the dead king, not alone his name.

There is another intriguing similarity between an Elamite design and the early Kingship. This is the form of headdress worn by figures on early Elamite seals from Susa,[43] a high, conical cap which is virtually identical with the White Crown which the later kings (and gods) wore to symbolise their rule over southern Egypt. This very distinctive form of headgear is replicated in the high cap worn by the enigmatic hooded figure from Amra, who may be a predynastic chieftain or perhaps the Egyptian equivalent of a shaman. Who or whatever he is, he is a disturbing, almost sinister figure.

These perplexing evidences of the distant origins of the *serekh* and of contact with Western Asia are too many to disregard. None of the other elements, however, has quite the same resonance as the adoption of the Uruk style of recessed panelling, which reaches its highest manifestation in the high limestone wall which encloses the Step Pyramid and the complex of the monumental buildings dedicated to King Djoser Netjerykhet of the Third Dynasty, several hundred years after its first appearance in the Nile Valley. The walls of Djoser's funerary domain run for approximately one and a half miles in length; it is an immense *serekh* enclosing all of Egypt and thus proclaims the king's supreme divinity.

Were there people from south-western Asia in the Nile Valley at this crucial time of the emergence of what was to become the Unified Kingdom? It is quite likely that traders, particularly those who carried lapis lazuli to the Egyptian courts and perhaps sought gold from the Egyptian princes who had access to the gold mines, were present, possibly in significant numbers, in late predynastic times. This is plausible, but how did the Egyptians come to know of the style of Sumerian temple architecture and why would they wish to adapt it into such monumental and sacred usages? Why, in any case, should traders, rarely a particularly charismatic class of person, have been able to persuade the putative kings of Egypt to identify themselves by so alien a form? Could it be that the travellers, whoever or whatever they were, actually became kings in the southern Nile Valley? Surely not, yet the figure on the obverse of the Jebel El-Arak knife, if he is not entirely mythological, looms formidably and uncomfortably large.

There is a glimmer of what might be the evidence for an alternative medium through which the influences from Western Asia passed into predynastic Egypt. This suggests the intervention of a 'third party', mediating between the seafaring people of the Arabian Gulf and those of the larger peninsula, and the communities in the Nile valley which were moving towards the creation of royal Egypt.

In recent years one of the most significant developments in the history of the ancient Near East has been the revelation of the early history of Arabia, not only of its eastern limits in the coastal regions bordering the Gulf, but throughout the entire peninsula. The conventional image of Arabia has tended to be of a wasteland, supporting life only on its peripheries and in the occasional oasis. This is far from the reality of the situation.

The acute climatic changes which overtook the Near East and which culminated at the end of the third millennium sealed the peninsula in a regime of extreme aridity which had not prevailed throughout the preceding period; the climate in Arabia had in fact oscillated fairly dramatically between wet and dry phases over the previous 17,000 years.[44] Recent studies have shown that, *c.*6000 BC, there was a large body of standing waterway, a lake in fact, in the area of Jubba, in the north of Arabia.[45] At this time also there is evidence of large herds of wild cattle present in the peninsula which were the prey of hunters who left an immense repertory of reliefs and carvings engraved and pecked on the rocks which bestrew the deserts.[46] Wild cattle require large amounts of water to survive,[47] and are the most convincing witnesses to a climatic regime in Arabia eight thousand years ago very different to that which prevails today.

Arabian rock art, some of the images of which are extremely powerful, has been extensively studied.[48] It has been suggested that the techniques of representing the cattle, the equids which were their companions and the hunters who followed the herds, can be traced moving down the

peninsula as the process of desertification spread from north to south.[49]
This process seems to have taken about four thousand years, from c.6000
BC around Jubba to c.2000 BC on the edge of the great waste of Ar-Rub
al-Khali, the 'Empty Quarter', in the south.

Archaeological survey on the northern limits of Ar-Rub al-Khali has
revealed considerable evidence of the presence of advanced Neolithic
hunting communities who camped along its perimeter.[50] They lived on the
herds of cattle and on large game, including hippopotamus, which watered
from the extensive, brackish lakes which ran deep into the Empty Quarter
from the southern limits of the Arabian Gulf. Although not a great deal is
known about the lives of these communities, it is clear that the people were
not simple savages: the flint and stone tools which they made are exceptionally fine, the equal of the very best Egyptian tools, of which the Jebel
El-Arak knife is an outstanding example. The Arabian neolithic tools are
approximately contemporary with the Jebel El-Arak knife: the technique
of manufacture of both type of tools is comparable.

The desiccation which the region experienced in the fifth, fourth and
third millennia resulted in a drop of as much as two metres in the level of
the Gulf, which had the eventual effect of draining the Ar-Rub al-Khali
'lakes'. The inevitable consequence was that the sites hitherto occupied by
the hunters became uninhabitable.

The decline in the viability of the environment in the south of Arabia
did not, so far as we can tell, occur catastrophically; it was evidently a
gradual process, a phenomenon which has been repeated frequently in
Arabia and elsewhere on much more limited scales. The people would have
had ample warning of the impending destruction of their living space, and
would have moved away, probably over several, even many, generations.[51]

There are hints, no more, of where some at least of the proto-Arabians
may have gone. Some probably moved eastwards, to the southern islands
and coastlands of the Gulf, some to settle in what today is the Oman peninsula. Others would have moved west, along the desert rim towards the
highlands of western Arabia which remained rich and fertile; some of these
migrants, who already may have had something of the sort of social organisation which is customarily found amongst neolithic hunting communities, could well have moved up the shores of the Red Sea. There is intriguing
evidence of the presence of warriors or hunters depicted on the rocks,
whose weapons, clothing, hairstyles and accoutrements are identical with
those of armed men who appear on the 'Hunters Palette' of late predynastic Egypt.[52]

Rock carvings, in Egypt, Arabia and Oman, display a number of
common themes in their repertory which can hardly be the consequence
of anything other than contact or a mutually inherited tradition.[53] In addition to the feathered headdress of the hunters which is found in Egypt,
western Arabia, Oman (and, incidentally, in south-western Iran) there is

also a shield or buckler with prominent projections at each corner. This is also found on seals in the Arabian Gulf island of Bahrain,[54] and again in Omani rock carvings. A still more striking form is a dagger with a lunate pommel, found in Egypt, western Arabia and Oman. Finally a five- or seven-stringed lyre is also depicted in all the lands mentioned; the lyre also appears on Arabian Gulf seals.[55]

It is not necessary to assume that any or all of these influences were the result of any one process or series of related events; indeed, it can probably be confidently asserted that they were not. However, it is surely significant that all of the elements appear, *together*, in Oman and the Gulf. One possible explanation for this may be the curious fact that the Sumerians, from very early times, seem to have known of the presence of copper in Oman. It is not impossible, if the thesis expressed here can be accepted, that the Sumerians (or their ancestors) were amongst the people who migrated from the region of Ar-Rub Al-Khali and by returning to the wadis of Oman in search of copper, maintained contact with their 'cousins', some of whom migrated westwards.

This much is sheer speculation but we tend to forget the great distances over which the peoples of early times travelled, especially in the early days of domestication. Given the possibility that such movements occurred away from the southern regions of the peninsula, the many common elements in their culture between apparently widely disparate peoples, may seem less radical and mysterious.

The Egyptians seem to have retained a distant memory of a mystical land far away to the east, on 'the edge of the world'.[56] This land, which is never named other than 'God's Land', was associated with the journey of the Falcon, the eponym of the first royal house and his companion, the very ancient god Ta-Tanen. The record of their journey from the archetypal island which is the place of origins and the birthplace of the first generation of gods is contained in the Pyramid Texts and in later temple records, which may also descend from very early times. The distant land to the east was associated with the ancestors and also with the spirits of the dead. It was a land of magic from which the divine powers who were immanent in Egypt in historic time were said to derive their strength. The king, the reincarnated Horus, was so potent that he was said to consume the older gods, his mothers and fathers, thus adding their powers to his own. The island which was the birthplace of the gods was forever commemorated in the primeval mound which was concealed in every monumental tomb and pyramid.

CHAPTER V

KINGSHIP AND THE
ARCHAIC KINGS

—— •◆• ——

The nature of the Egyptian Kingship is so extraordinary that no study of the many centuries in which it was discharged by the three hundred or so men (and a handful of women) who held the office can hope to achieve any sort of balance which does not place it firmly in the very centre of the foreground. In a quite inescapable sense the king was the reason for the existence of Egypt, just as he was the culminating product of the genius which produced the Egyptian state and all its multifarious and brilliant apparatus. All that apparatus was constellated around the figure of the king, in whose person the essential *idea* of Egypt as much as its actuality was realised.

The Egyptians, though they may have sometimes seemed to be in tune with a reality beyond the natural world and to move with ease from the mystical to the matter-of-fact, were a supremely down-to-earth people. They viewed the world optimistically, certainly, but they viewed it as it is. This view of the world even applied, with qualifications, to their attitude to the Kingship.

According to Egyptian belief the Kingship had existed since before the creation of the world.[1] It was thus recognised as the first and greatest of the archetypes at its appearance, the most definitive statement of the essential order of the cosmos. All the divine powers found their ultimate expression in the king and in the office of which he was the personification.

The Kingship and the Egyptian state were inseparable. The state is integrated by the existence of the king and all its multi-faceted nature is brought together into a whole, an entity, around him.

The elevation of the king to this unprecedented level of existence was a necessary step in the formulation of the state itself. It is in this respect that Jung's understanding of the king as the 'self' of Egypt is so profound. To fix for all time the nature of the Kingship and its relationship to the emerging state the Egyptians took a decision as audacious as it was characteristic: they brought the concept of the Kingship and of the godhead into a precise conjunction.

The accession to the Kingship in Egypt, attended by all the proper ceremonies and conducted in the presence of the divine powers, at once conferred divinity on the holder of the office. 'You rise a god', the coronation rubric went.[2] The king was no longer simply a man with the fallibility and insecurities of humanity: he was a god and hence immutable, infallible and entirely assured.

The decision thus to present the king was an inspired one. At once it made sense of the absurd and conferred on the institution of the Kingship the qualities most prized by all Egyptians, order, regulation and continuity. The king was god because he was king.

It is not known when the momentous decision was taken to bring Kingship and divinity into such exact conjunction. In the earliest representations of the king, in the scenes depicted on the Narmer palette, or on the great votive mace-head on which King Scorpion cuts a new canal, he is shown as superhuman, towering over his companions and attendants. On the Scorpion mace-head the king's name is indicated by the glyph 'Scorpion' and it is also linked with an eight-petalled rosette or star. This is highly suggestive, for in Sumerian epigraphy the star was the determinative which indicated that the name which followed it was that of a divinity; at this particular time, the very end of the predynastic period, as we have seen, Egypt appears to have absorbed a number of influences from its distant Mesopotamian contemporary. At this time both peoples pursued star-cults; was Scorpion, one wonders, a Sumerian or an Egyptian who understood the value of propaganda and adopted the glyph for divinity to which a Sumerian introduced him?

Throughout the First Dynasty the king is separated from ordinary mortals by every device. His name is contained within the sacred badge, the *serekh*, which, as we have also seen, has a particular and powerful significance. His costume and regalia are quite different from anything that his companions wear. He is personified as Horus, the Falcon who was symbolic of the Kingship; he is also portrayed as the divine bull, destroying his enemies, a form which he was often to adopt, particularly throughout the predynastic, Archaic and Old Kingdom periods. In the titles which he assumed at his coronation 'Bull' was one of the most frequent epithets applied to him throughout the centuries that the Kingship endured.

From the earliest times elaborate rituals attended the waking life of the king, as much as they were planned to preserve him after death. Despite the fact that the very idea of the Kingship was so entirely innovative, by the lifetime of only the third man to hold the office the Egyptian Kingship had evolved complex ceremonies and a system of royal names and epithets.

At the outset the king had three great names which he assumed on his coronation: the very act of crowning is Egyptian and deeply symbolic, for the crowns themselves were gods. In early times the first title was the king's Horus name, by which he was proclaimed the reincarnation of the eternal king, Horus the Falcon. This was the name contained in the *serekh*. Then there was the *nesu byt*, by which he was acknowledged as king of Upper and Lower Egypt, literally 'he of the sedge and bee', the two entities which symbolised the southern and the northern Kingdoms. His next title was 'The Two Ladies' *neb-ty*, by which he was identified with the two divinities Nekhbet the vulture and Uadjet the cobra, who protected his royal divinity. In the reign of King Den (*c.*2900 BC) a fourth title was added, that of Horus of Gold. The final entry in the full recital of the king's titles was the birth-name of the king which, when added to the others, became the final element in his titulary.

The sonority of the king's titles as they were proclaimed on occasions of great state, or as set out in the sacred inscriptions, is well conveyed by this recital of the names and titles of Ramesses V (*c.*1146–1142). That the quality of royal power was effectively at an end does not diminish the sonorities of the king's titulary. It comes from a stela set up in a fort, built by the king, at Semna.

> Living Horus: Mighty Bull, Great in Victory, Sustaining Alive the Two Lands; Favourite of the Two Goddesses: Mighty in Strength, Repulser of Millions; Golden Horus: Rich in Years, like Tatenen, Soverign, Lord of Jubilees, Protector of Egypt, Filling every Land with Great Monuments in His Name; King of Upper and Lower Egypt, Lord of the Two Lands: Nibmare-Meriamon; Son of Ra, of His Body, His Beloved, Lord of Diadems: Amenhirkhepesher-Ramesses (V)-Neterhekon, given life, like Ra, forever.[3]

The Egyptians themselves referred to the king either by his *nesu-byt* name, the *neb-ty* name or, in a circumlocution, as 'the Good God'. However, since the latter centuries of Egyptian history it has been customary to speak of the King of Egypt as 'Pharaoh' and to adopt the same word in an adjectival form to describe ancient Egyptian civilisation. Such usages are anachronistic.

The term derives from a hieroglyphic compound which is usually transliterated *per-o*. This means 'Great House' and was used to describe the place of the royal administration, in other words, the palace: 'Whitehall' or 'the White House' have precisely similar meanings. The term 'Pharaoh', applied to the king, does not appear until the New Kingdom (*c.*1550–1070 BC); by this time it had achieved particular currency in the Near Eastern courts with which the Egyptian administration was in correspondence. Later the Egyptians, uncharacteristically, themselves came to adopt it as one of the terms by which the king was described.

'Pharaoh' has gained general currency as a consequence of the Christian world having absorbed the books of the Old Testament into its sacred texts. The editors of the Old Testament identified the King of Egypt, usually unfavourably, by the term Pharaoh and hence it has gained universal currency. It is nonetheless incorrect to use a term such as 'the Pharaohs of the Old Kingdom' or to apply the word 'Pharaonic' to Egyptian civilisation as a whole.

The divinity of the king was early on revealed in the art which derived from him and from his office. By the end of the Second Dynasty royal portrait sculpture shows the king enthroned, exuding something considerably more than merely human majesty: the statues of the enigmatic Khasekhem (Khasekhemui), which are the most ancient three-dimensional representations of a king on his throne, demonstrate this convincingly. The sense of distance, between the merely human and the patently divine, achieves its most superb realisation in the serdab statue of the Third Dynasty King Djoser Netjerykhet (c.2670 BC) with its sternly African features, found in his monumental funerary complex at Saqqara.

The concept of the divinity of the king is evidently one of Egypt's particularly African elements. A related, not dissimilar African belief that is present in the earliest days of the Kingship relates to the king's placenta, which was honoured as a god and was believed to have a separate existence, awaiting reunion with the king after death.[4]

A representation of the royal placenta was carried in procession before the king even in the first days of the Kingship, in much the same way as the ostrich feather fans which survived into modern times as part of the panoply of the Roman pontiffs. The king's regalia were also very ancient; on ceremonial occasions he is shown wearing a bull's tail, for example and the bull as a royal symbol, like the lion, dates to predynastic times.

The King's crowns were particularly powerful supporters of his royal and divine status: they were proclaimed 'Great of Magic'. As divine powers themselves the crowns extended their protection over the king. Each kingdom, South and North, had its own crown. In Upper Egypt the king wore the white crown, a high mitre-like hat which may be connected with the hood worn by the strange figure carved in schist from El Amra and the headdresses of the figures on early Elamite seals. To symbolise his rule over the north the king wore a red crown, a flat-topped cap, originally made perhaps from wicker with a tall projection, like a plume, at the back. By a brilliant piece of synthesis, when the two Kingdoms were unified the two crowns also were united, so that by wearing the composite crown all the world could recognise the holder of the dual Kingship. Other crowns appeared in later times. A blue crown was worn by the king as war leader and a high crown surmounted with feathers identified him as a god.

The royal power, human and divine, reached its height in the Old Kingdom. From the Third Dynasty, when the first Pyramid was built by Imhotep at Saqqara, the great stepped monument for Djoser, through the Fourth Dynasty (c.2575–2465 BC) and the building of the Giza Pyramids and on through the placid Fifth (2465–2323 BC) and Sixth Dynasties (2323–2150 BC), the king's power and dignity were supreme. In the Pyramid Age he could summon the help of men of immense talent, like the builder-princes Hemionu and Ankhaf, who raised the stupendous monuments which bear the names of their masters. The psychological effect on the Egyptian state of the corporate effort involved in the creation of these great enterprises requiring the coming together of the whole society was profound. Such works were designed to proclaim the king's divinity, to ensure his life through eternity and to express the selfhood of the Egyptian state. They were declarations in stone of the stellar destiny to which the king was heir.

Figure 2 King Narmer, shown here wearing the crown of Lower Egypt as he walks in procession, was one of the last kings of the predynastic period, *c*.3150 BC. It is possible that he was the immediate predecessor of King Aha, the first king of the First Dynasty.

Before the king and his chief retainer, a standard-bearer carries a representation of the king's placenta, which was invested with great mystical significance. Its appearance as part of the royal panoply is a remarkable demonstration of the sophistication of the Egyptians' attitude to the divinity of the king at the very beginning of the monarchy.

In the pyramid of the last king of the Fifth Dynasty, Unas, there is engraved on the walls, in superb hieroglyphs, the earliest recension of the Pyramid Texts.[5] Some of these spells, incantations, prayers and dialogues are of very great antiquity, probably descending from predynastic times. These echoes from an earlier time make it clear that the king is not merely divine, but the greatest of the gods. He is a star and on his death he returns to the transfigured world to rule over the divine powers who are his companions.

But change, generally a distinctly un-Egyptian phenomenon, was impending. In the Fifth Dynasty (*c*.2465 BC) the king became no less a god – except that he was no longer supreme; he was one of the gods in the company of Ra, the sun-god. The ominous rise of the priests, always a potentially cancerous element in Egyptian society, had begun. Their rise was perhaps halted in the Sixth Dynasty, but by that dynasty's end, *c*.2150 BC, the Kingship was greatly diminished, the consequence of having to buy the support of the provincial magnates by more and more lavish grants of land, over succeeding generations.

When order in the form of the royal and centralised autocracy was restored by the founders of the Middle Kingdom, the nature of the Kingship had undergone a subtle change. A family of Theban princes reimposed unity on the Valley and broke the power of the magnates, at least to the extent that now they acknowledged the authority and the notional divinity of the king.

The men who were kings of the Middle Kingdom (c.2040–c.1650 BC) (the Eleventh, Twelfth and early Thirteenth Dynasties) are amongst the most gifted and remarkable of the rulers of antiquity. The material evidences of the Middle Kingdom, in art and to the extent that their buildings survive, in architecture, represent a profound change from the tranquillity and sense of the sublime which distinguishes the products of the Old Kingdom. In the same way funerary practices changed, quite subtly but equally profoundly; now it was no longer only the king and his close associates who would be given sumptuous obsequies. Less elevated officials, even women, might presume to the rights of immortality, to be laid in the tomb in finely painted coffins, embellished with funerary texts to guide them to the afterlife, a form of passport previously reserved only for the very great. Thus the *numen* of the Kingship gradually drifted down through the society, like a wise ruler distributing his treasure to his subjects.

The founder of the Eleventh Dynasty and the kings of the Twelfth were formidable men, as formidable in their determination to ensure the integrity of the Nile Valley as the earlier rulers of the Archaic period had been. The problems which they faced, however, were more complex. Not only did they need to contain the ambitions of the great provincial magnates, who had benefited greatly by the decline of the central authority at the end of the Old Kingdom, they had to do so with discretion, to conciliate them and ensure their support whilst at the same time attending to the threat of incursions into the Valley by powers outside Egypt. Eventually they were able to break the power of the provincial nobles and to centralise authority in their own hands.

The existence of external threats was very largely a new experience for the Two Lands. Hitherto such disturbances as might occur on Egypt's frontiers could very largely be put down, with a firm and decisive action. Such had been the way even of the archaic kings, if the propaganda which they displayed in a variety of media – on finely carved palettes, on the rock walls of Sinai or engraved on ivory labels – is to be taken literally. 'Smiting' foreigners, easterners, the Libyans from the west or the blacks from the south, had become a cliché of the earliest royal publicists. But the sovereigns of the Middle Kingdom faced a more serious threat to their authority.

By the beginning of the second millennium, around the year 2000 BC, the world outside Egypt was changing. Kings were beginning to be relatively commonplace in the organisation of Near Eastern states. With the popularisation of the institution of Kingship came ambition and its twin, greed; even little kings, sitting uneasily on makeshift thrones, attended by a few bedraggled retainers, could be drawn into larger alliances and manipulated to feed a greater prince's plans. In the north in Syria and Palestine, increased commercial prosperity led to political adventurism and the record begins to tell of the King of Egypt sending (indeed sometimes himself leading), expeditions to put down recalcitrant and obstreperous foreigners.

The king, though still titularly a god, now becomes still more a chief executive, managing the Kingdom and directing its affairs. Because from the beginning the King of Egypt was very largely able to concentrate on the business of being king, amplified by his role as the mightiest of all immanent divinities, and because in the early centuries he was able to do so largely within the secure confines of the Valley, the institution itself developed in a way which was both subtle and very powerful. The king was always the focus of affairs and even the greatest of his officers was merely a favoured assistant. The complexities of the situation at the end of the Old Kingdom and the pressures, quite unknown hitherto, to which the Kingship was then exposed, began to change its essential nature. The executive role now began to supervene and to become dominant.

The Middle Kingdom kings did not bother too much about concealing their humanity, nor their origins as mortal men. The convention might require that they would accept the myth that the accession to the Kingship brought with it the gift of divinity but it is difficult to believe other than that this was a sceptical adoption of a form which no longer carried with it the tremendous sense of paramountcy which seems to touch the earliest kings.

There is a sombre magnificence about the Middle Kingdom Kingship. That the kings have about them a melancholy nobility, powerfully expressed in their portraits, has long been recognised. Magnificent they certainly were, richly robed, throned majestically in halls of great elegance and splendour. The Middle Kingdom is one of the high points of the Egyptian historical experience and nowhere is it expressed more potently than in the trappings and paraphernalia of the Kingship. But the kings, unmistakably, are men.

It may be that this recognition of the king's essential humanity contributed to the next decline in Egypt's fortunes, when internal dissent and a monarchy weakened by the very tranquillity which the long, untroubled reigns of the Middle Kingdom produced, allowed the unthinkable to happen and for foreigners to establish themselves, however uneasily, on the throne of Egypt. This was during a period of uncertainty and confusion, with the Valley splitting once more into competing principalities, which followed the collapse of the Middle Kingdom's central authority. Once more it was the south which had to provide a line of kings who reimposed order over the Valley, but again the nature of the Kingship changed. Now the effects of invasion had been experienced in their most drastic form with the divine Kingship itself being usurped by, of all deplorable creatures, 'Asiatics'. When they were driven out and the frontiers made secure, the preoccupation of the King of Egypt now became, not so much ensuring the eternal order of the cosmos, as keeping the foreigners out of Egypt. Increasingly, with the rise of more and more sophisticated societies beyond the Valley, with new weapons and powerful means of transportation, this meant facing Egypt's enemies before they became Egypt's masters, cutting them off at source. In effect this required extending the frontiers of Egypt, far beyond the immemorial confines of the god-given Valley, to more and more distant regions.

The king now became an Emperor, leading armies into remote and distant lands, imposing the fear of Egypt, where once there had been reverence and wonder, on subject peoples. 'Smiting', always one of the king's prerogatives, now became in effect the royal way of life. The King of Egypt was to be feared, as a mortal and terrible force, destroying his enemies far from his own lands. The effect of this policy was to create an immense empire, to which tribute flowed into the Valley in an apparently limitless flood of treasure, slaves, animals and all the riches of the burgeoning societies which were awakening beyond Egypt's frontiers.

The Kingship in Egypt can thus be recognised as undergoing three distinct phases in its development, with the king to be seen as divinity, as ruler and as imperial warrior, the products of the stages through which Egyptian society progressed from the end of the fourth millennium to the middle of the second. Whether the idea of the Kingship spread outwards to other lands from Egypt, in these forms, is not important: the truly remarkable fact is that the most powerful and enduring device for the management of human societies first received its definition in this small tract of land, in the north-eastern corner of Africa.

At the time of the campaigns to effect the Unification of the Two Kingdoms (as we have seen, more probably several chiefdoms) the princes from Hierakonpolis (Nekhen) appear to have moved their base from that city some 180 miles to the north, to This, near the ancient sacred centre of Abydos. The First Dynasty was always to be associated with This, though Hierakonpolis, too, retained its special importance as a shrine sacred to the Kingship.

All of these centres, Hierakonpolis-Nekhen, This and Abydos, were invested with a powerfully numinous character throughout the ensuing centuries. Hierakonpolis declined, though its status was from time to time revived; Abydos grew in importance, the consequence of an early First Dynasty tomb, in all probability that of King Den, being identified as the burial place of Osiris. He was associated with the idea of the king in death and, as we have seen, appears in the Egyptian pantheon at a relatively late point in its history, around the end of the third millennium.

The first king of the First Dynasty, Aha, continued his progress northwards, to set the pivotal point of his new domains at an appropriate point to manage their destiny. According to legend – and it is probably correct in fact – he established his capital in the region of what was to become the city of Memphis, to the south of the modern capital city, Cairo. He is also reputed to have undertaken large-scale engineering works for the establishment of his new city, including the diversion of the Nile itself.

For the next three thousand years, though the capital of the country might shift from time to time to new locations, the area around Memphis was always to be of great importance. It is close to what was always considered to be Egypt's fulcrum, the point at which the northern and southern Kingdoms met. Its choice was thus symbolic of the union on which the early kings were set; it was also politically a wholly apt location for the centre of the royal administration. From time to time a dynasty might favour another place for the capital, but Memphis always retained its position of special importance.

Memphis is actually a Greek corruption of the name of the pyramid of King Pepi II, *Men-nefer*. The city's proper, Egyptian name was *Ankh-tardy*, 'that which binds the Two Lands', a clear expression of the city's origins. It was also called *Ineb-hefj*, 'the White Wall'.[6]

The corruption of Men-Nefer to Memphis was repeated, even more enduringly, by the Greeks when they contrived to misunderstand the name of the great temple of Ptah at Memphis, which was called *Hikuptah*,[7] 'The House of the Ka of Ptah'. This they apparently heard as 'Aegyptos', which became 'Egypt'.

From the moment, probably in the first or second decade of the thirtieth century BC when the Falcon house started on its programme of consolidating the Valley, tremendous changes began to erupt throughout the region over which they and their allies exerted control. These affected every aspect of Egyptian life and every department of the society. For the first time it is even appropriate to speak in such terms for already it is now possible to detect the origins of a formalised and compartmented society emerging in the Valley.

Although such changes touched so many different parts of Egypt, from the appearance of writing to radical developments in art, architecture and the organisation of the state, it is the person and office of the king around which the most important of them begin to constellate. The Kingship was a unique historical phenomenon and its invention (or, more precisely, its recognition) in the early historic period produced a force around which the movements to create the unified kingdom could converge.

The most important development, other than the creation of the Kingship itself, was the imposition of a centralised authority over the country, at first tentatively, later with the full assurance of an organised, coherent system running from one end of the country to the other. In the First Dynasty we begin to detect the presence of the great officers of state who were always to attend the king and to act as his coadjutors; almost certainly some at least of the great offices were present in the late predynastic period. Already a bureaucracy is born; the order of the kingdoms is ensured by the delegation of royal power into the hands of trusted magnates, drawn, principally, from the family of the king. By the First Dynasty, many of the orotund titles, which were to identify the offices which the great magnates held, can be recognised.[8]

Although only a relatively small part of the Valley was habitable, comprising the cultivable lands on both banks of the river and some parts of the Delta, it was nonetheless a large country to administer as a unitary state, the more so as it was at first the only one in existence. From the earliest times, the kings recognised the importance of creating a reliable bureaucratic system, with an increasingly large body of officials, great and small, whose duties were clearly defined and controlled, with each level of official reporting to the next in seniority. The concept of the Two Lands was retained by the duplication of the great offices of state and their dependent bureaucracies; the dualism which the system demanded was in any case wholly consonant with the duality which was so deeply rooted in the Egyptian psyche.

From very early times the great offices were identified by titles, the complexity and invention of which suggest that they were already of considerable antiquity. The greatest office was 'the Controller of the Two Thrones'; then there was 'He who is at the Head of the King'. Collectively the administration was spoken of as 'the King's House'. The king was directly assisted by 'the Master of the Secrets of the Royal Decrees'.[9]

By the reign of Djoser in the Third Dynasty, we encounter 'He of the Curtain' as a title borne by the Chief Minister; he was also a judge, emphasising the importance of the delegation of this aspect of the royal powers. There were two chancellors, the treasurers of the kingdoms, which were spoken of as 'the White House' and 'the Red House' respectively. Amongst their other duties the chancellors were responsible for receiving wine from the royal vineyards. Labels indicating the delivery of wines, with comments on their quality, are known from the First Dynasty.[10]

The distribution of resources, particularly important in times of shortage or famine, was also the concern of high officials. 'The Master of Largesse' had his own offices from which he would distribute both gifts to favoured courtiers or foodstuffs to the needy.[11] In later times it is notable how often the discharge of these responsibilities are made the occasion for self-congratulation by the holders of the offices, in their tomb inscriptions.

In the Second Dynasty the king was served by an official who seems to have had some degree of responsibility for foreign affairs. In the far south of the country a viceroy was appointed who often stood in a very close relation to the king. In early days the viceroy was 'The Keeper of Nekhen', recalling the ancient significance of Hierakonpolis.[12]

The king's principal officers bore hereditary titles of nobility; thus, 'Hereditary Prince' and a title rendered as 'Count' are often encountered amongst the king's closest assistants. Interestingly, there is some indication of the existence of a council of the southern part of the kingdom known as 'the Tens of Upper Egypt', suggesting perhaps a survival of what may have been an ancient system of chiefly assembly.[13]

The creation of monumental buildings is inseparable from the first appearance of the Kingship and all the multitude of artifacts, rituals, ceremonies and offices to which it gave existence. The very rapid development of architecture, to a degree quite unparalleled either in Egypt or anywhere else at this time, is a feature of the First Dynasty. Much of the evidence which survives is drawn from funerary buildings, the tombs and 'funerary palaces' in which the kings and their immediate associates were buried. However, it is clear that many of these reflected the buildings in which their lives were passed.

Late in the fourth millennium we find the first evidence of elaborate funerary architecture specifically identified with high status and the authority of rulership in the making of the decorated tomb at Hierakonpolis, known as Tomb 100. This is divided into two compartments, floored with timber, and its walls are plastered. On the walls were painted vivid if enigmatic scenes of ritual, hunting and the lives of men and animals; these seem to have connections with the iconography of south-western Asia.

At the very beginning of the First Dynasty (*c*.3000 BC), however, a further most significant change begins to overtake the royal tombs of the leading figures of Egyptian society, who were dependants of the king. The tomb now is built above ground, with no attempt to conceal it. It is made of brick and, as the Dynasty goes on, becomes larger and more elaborate. One of the earliest, associated with the reign of King Narmer, was built at Naqada. Examples are to be found at Abydos, Abu Roash and various other sites. A very extensive cemetery, largely containing the burials of officials other than those of the highest rank, has been excavated at Helwan, south of Cairo. The burials date mainly from the First Dynasty and provide evidence both of the extent of the bureaucracy already existing and the richness of their possessions – at least of those which they were disposed to take with them to the next world.[14]

The actual burial chambers of the early tombs are often sunk, deep below ground. Around the burial chamber are a large number of rooms for the storage of goods and treasure for the use of the tomb owner. The interior of the tomb is frequently decorated with what are evidently painted simulacra of the hangings of a palace of the living. In the richest of the tombs, fine woods and gold leaf are used to decorate the walls. Sometimes a lavatory is thoughtfully provided.[15]

The exteriors of the finest of the tombs are punctuated with the recess panelling and buttressing which are to become their enduringly distinctive feature. In two cases of the First Dynasty burials at Saqqara the base of the tomb walls, standing on a brick platform, are decorated with a massive display of life-size wild bulls' heads, modelled in clay, with actual horns mounted on them.[16]

The earliest royal tombs appear to follow the brick-built mock-palace form, known by the Arabic term 'mastaba'. Later in the Dynasty the mastaba became the customary monument in which the great magnates were buried, whilst the kings themselves were interred in what are now generally described as 'funerary palaces', large brick-walled compounds in which the actual burials were made, with chapels and other subsidiary buildings to be used for the practice of the rituals which would be conducted, theoretically at least, for all eternity to honour the dead king. The finest survivals of the funerary palaces are to be found in the royal burial grounds of Abydos, in the area known as 'Umm al-Qab'. These huge structures have, in the past, been described as forts.[17]

Around both types of structure, the mastaba as well as the funerary palace for the king, were ranged subsidiary graves in which courtiers and servants of the owner of the tomb were buried, having been sacrificed at his death. These subsidiary burials were predominantly of women, sometimes of dwarfs and in the funerary palaces ascribed to Narmer and Aha at Abydos a number of young males had evidently been sent to their deaths, to join their masters. This is unusual in that the majority of such sacrifices tended to be of female servitors, though sometimes craftsmen would be included in the slaughter. In Aha's case he also took with him seven young lions; they and the young men were probably intended to serve the king in hunting in the afterlife which the presence of the lions in particular indicates that it was his intention to pursue.[18] Sometimes these immolations would be counted in hundreds; it was, it might be thought, a distinctly un-Egyptian practice, since the whole purpose of the funerary cults was to prolong life beyond death, not to curtail the lives of the living. The practice had disappeared by the end of the Second Dynasty (2770–2649 BC). It is, however, a curious and rather disturbing fact that, despite the reverence which the Egyptians always showed to the persons and – sometimes – to the burials of the kings, these early burials were, virtually without exception, destroyed, apparently deliberately, by intense conflagrations. To burn the body or the mummy of a dead Egyptian was to destroy the hope of immortality.[19]

The origin of Egyptian writing dates back to this time, even, indeed, somewhat before it; it is also the consequence of the newly emerging state being centred around the person of the king. In late predynastic times there seems to have been a system of identifying property and perhaps the contents of stone or pottery vessels by means of sealings and signs engraved or impressed on the containers. From the very earliest appearance of the kings their names were recorded ceremonially, using a primitive hieroglyphic form which was both ideographic (conveying its meaning by the appearance of the glyph) and vocalised. Quite rapidly the process was developed to permit the recording of more extensive texts: these often took the form of ivory 'labels' which were evidently attached to other, more perishable objects. These give details of the high points of a king's reign and are the first truly historiographical documents in the experience of the world. Seals are also used, sometimes in the form of engraved cylinders, a shape clearly borrowed from Mesopotamia and Elam. The cylinder seal became a particular mark of honour and one of the principal titles bestowed by the kings on favoured nobles was 'Seal-bearer'.

The arts in this period, associated with the Kingship's increasing state, are especially vibrant. We know that textiles were exceptionally finely made and often of brilliant design. One of the glories of Egyptian craftsmanship, the carving of stone vessels, achieves heights which were never to be approached in later times.[20] All over Egypt there appear to have been production centres, ateliers where craftsmen spent their lives producing these magnificent vessels, some of which show an ingenuity of manufacture and an elegance and restraint of design which is breathtaking.

By the middle of the First Dynasty, *c.*2850 BC, the style of the court was sumptuous; the king was surrounded by a panoply of ceremonial and elaborate ritual. He was clearly recognised as the most powerful divine presence incarnate in human form. What is generally but loosely called the religion of Egypt was also being codified and established in what were to become its canonical forms, varied and sometimes apparently contradictory though these might appear to be. Great gods like Ptah, Min, Horus, Anubis and Apis, all of whom were to exist throughout Egyptian history, are visible in the First Dynasty; most interestingly there appears actually to be the recording of the beginnings of certain cults, as, for example, in the case of the Apis Bull, in this period: the 'First Running of the Apis' is noted as an important event, identifying a significant year in the king's reign.[21] Likewise the birth of gods such as Anubis are recorded, presumably signifying the first practice of their special cult.

Shrines and temples are depicted on the ivory and some very ancient symbols, like the arrows associated with the northern Goddess Neith, are already in evidence. The king's particular protectors who, like Horus, were always to be associated with his office, such as the Two Goddess, Uadjet and Nekhbet, are powerful influences even in the earliest period. However, as will be the case for several hundred years to come, the cults and sacred

Figure 3 The Horus and Set Khasekhem enthroned (*see opposite*), the first example of a king thus portrayed. Under the name Khasekhemui he adopted the dual form of proclaiming his divine succession to the kingship by incorporating the names of the two gods, whose conflict was reconciled in him; their symbolic animals, the Falcon and the Hound, surmount his *serekh*.

A SEATED STATUE OF KING KHASEKHEM

places are the concern only of the king and his immediate entourage and had little impact on the life of the ordinary people.

The establishment of the unified control of the country did not happen without opposition. There is evidence that some of the southern peoples, loyal to their very ancient god Set, rebelled against what they may have seen as the pretensions of the Thinite house.[22] Set was an equivocal divinity, associated with the desert and with storm; much later he was to become the embodiment of evil, a sort of precursor of Satan, though this was clearly not his original nature.

The Second Dynasty of Egyptian kings seems generally to have been less distinguished than the First. However it ended, around 2650 BC, in the person of one of the most influential and remarkable of Egyptian sovereigns, Khasekhemui. He had been preceded on the throne by a king who assumed the title 'The Set Peribsen' in contrast to the more usual ascription 'The Horus . . .' Peribsen surmounted the *serekh* which proclaimed his name not with Horus the Falcon but with Set the Hound, the only occasion when this divinity was said to be solely incarnate in the king's person. This suggests that, at least for the time, the supporters of Set achieved some sort of predominance in the society. Khasekhemui (originally he was called 'Khasekhem') succeeded to the throne; his name means 'In him the Two Powers are reconciled'. This, in a particularly telling way, suggests that he was a conciliating figure, who brought together the two otherwise inimical factions represented by the conflicting gods. He confirmed his nature as a force for reconciliation by surmounting the *serekh* which proclaimed his name by the animals symbolic both of Horus and of Set – the Falcon and the Hound respectively. From this time onwards the king was the medium through whom the two otherwise antithetical powers were brought peaceably together. The Egyptian genius for the production of symbols which at a stroke encompass a complex and diverse series of meanings is nowhere more dramatically realised than in the *serekh* of King Khasekhemui.

Khasekhemui was remembered throughout Egyptian history as a wise and compassionate ruler. He was said to be of gigantic stature; certainly his reputation and the benign shadow which he cast over subsequent generations of kings suggests a man of more than ordinary powers. He was revered as the ancestor of the remarkable Third Dynasty of kings, which was to succeed him, probably the consequence of the marriage of his daughter to the first king of the dynasty. From this alliance was to stem the flowering of the richest period of Egypt's history.

The Archaic kings ruled Egypt for nearly five hundred years. In the two dynasties which comprise the Archaic period, altogether seventeen kings are known. From the work of so limited a number of men the whole splendid history of Egypt was to unfold.

CHAPTER VI

EGYPT'S GLORY: THE OLD KINGDOM

—— •◆• ——

The high point of the ancient Egyptian contribution to the civilisation of the world and one of the highest points of human experience thus far achieved by our peculiar species, is to be found in the period known as 'the Old Kingdom,' which lasted from c.2650 to c.2130 BC. This was a time of almost unremitting achievement, in the arts, architecture, in the management of the society, in the definition and promotion of religious belief, in the formulation and conduct of elaborate rituals and state ceremonies. It was also, at least as far as the inhabitants of the Nile Valley were concerned, a tranquil time, generally untroubled by the threat of invasion or of the dislocation of a world which ran, untrammelled, along a course determined by the essential order of the universe. At the centre of this immense mechanism the King of Egypt presided, not only over the Valley, but over the entire universe, which, according to the best available belief, ran at his behest and will.

The great achievements of the kings of the Archaic period had laid the ground well for what was to come, a sequence of extraordinary creative fulfilment which was to occupy most of the third millennium before the present era. By the end of the Second Dynasty, under the rule of the ultimate unifier of the Valley, Khasekhemui, the great enterprise on which the Thinite princes had set out half a millennium earlier had been realised and the entire Valley, and all its human and material resources, could be brought to the enrichment of life of those, admittedly the more favoured ones, who lived in it, and, at least as important, to the prolongation of life beyond death.

By the conventions of Egyptology the Old Kingdom begins with the Third Dynasty (c.2649–2575 BC). It is at this point that Egypt's historic destiny begins to be fulfilled, as the first King of the dynasty, Sa-nakhte (whose name is also rendered Nebka) ascends the throne.

The Third Dynasty, though it lasted only some seventy years, was exceptionally important in setting the future course of Egyptian history. First, the names of individual men, not only of kings or gods, begin to be known: the idea of the individual begins to emerge from the group identity derived from Egypt's neolithic inheritance. This had been only marginally affected by the appearance of the king as the Great Individual, who, in his person, expressed the identity of the entire community. Below him, high and low, were shadowy figures, only taking their existence from him. Now, in the new dynasty, new men appear, not necessarily drawn from the king's immediate family but ones chosen by him, by reason of their talent and, no doubt, by their zeal to serve his divine will. Though ordinary men now appear on the stage, often enacting the most important roles in the state, the king's divinity is enhanced and he becomes the very embodiment of the god in living form. The Third Dynasty thus represents a most important stage not only in the development of Egypt's techniques and social and political structures but also in the increasing growth of the Egyptian psyche as expressed in the Kingship and its relationship to the society at large. The Third Dynasty presages the great advances which will come about in the later centuries of the Old Kingdom.

At this time, too, there was a great flowering of the arts and in the respect for the craftsman and the work of his hands. The royal designers could now experiment, even producing wonderful free representations of the king himself.[1] The opulence in materials which had been one of the glories of the Archaic period now assumed its richest forms, though these were not extravagant but always carefully disciplined. In particular rich glazes were used in decoration, making the walls of temples and tombs brilliant and shining.

The dominant cult of most ancient Egypt, related to the observation of the stars, reached its zenith during the Third Dynasty before being supplanted, very largely, by solar cults in the next dynasty. It seems likely that in the Third Dynasty the stars and planets were skilfully observed and charted, the knowledge gained thereby being available to the builders when the immense projects of the Fourth Dynasty came to be undertaken. It is not at all clear, however, why the change from stellar to solar cults occurred. There seems to be no particular disruption in the succession when the Fourth Dynasty came to power, so change does not seem to have been, in any real sense, revolutionary. But the change was profound and was probably the consequence of some astronomical event which has been lost to us. The stars did not, of course, disappear entirely from the Egyptians' consciousness at this point, as witness their crucial importance in both the planning and construction of the pyramids and also their central role in the liturgy of the Pyramid Texts.

The special triumph of the Third Dynasty was the creation of an entirely new dimension of human experience: the building of monumental structures in stone. This innovation, amongst the most important advances ever achieved in technology, will forever be associated with the second king of the Third Dynasty, Djoser Netjerykhet (2630–2611 BC) and his minister and Master Builder, Imhotep son of Ka-Nefer who, according to tradition, was an Upper Egyptian.

Imhotep, it is not an exaggeration to suggest, was one of the greatest creative geniuses the human species has yet produced. His achievement dwarfs those of Praxiteles, Michelangelo and Leonardo, for what he did no man before him had attempted, nor perhaps had even conceived.

Throughout the first two dynasties the practice of tomb-building had developed greatly, the massive rectangular mastabas growing larger and more richly decorated. When Djoser Netjerykhet came to the throne, probably in succession to his brother, it was natural enough that work should begin on his tomb and that responsibility for it should be entrusted to his minister, Imhotep, who was, even in his own lifetime, recognised as a man of exceptional and varied genius.

Imhotep began by designing a large if otherwise conventional mastaba for the king on an escarpment at the ancient funerary ground of Saqqara, looking down on to the capital, Memphis. Here the kings of the Second Dynasty had been buried and, earlier still, some of the great magnates of the First Dynasty. Djoser Netjerykhet's tomb was built a mile or so from these, on gently rising ground.

Then Imhotep's, or the king's, ambition and, more important still, creative imagination, began to assert themselves. The original mastaba was enlarged, time and again, until it had become an immense structure, with some 10,000 tons of stone being quarried for its construction. The use of stone on this scale was entirely unprecedented and it may be that extracting such great quantities from Tura, where it was excavated, allowed Imhotep to ponder on its properties and to decide to set course into a wholly uncharted region. Whatever the cause his imagination took flight and Djoser's monument began to rise towards the stars which were to be his eventual eternal home.[2]

With superb audacity Imhotep began to build upwards, raising the monument step by step, enclosing the original mastaba and opening a complex of chambers below the structure in which Djoser would be laid. The monument, when complete, consisted of six gigantic steps, each diminishing in size as the monument rose towards the sky. It was the centre of a great shrine, a complex of buildings of varied purpose and diversity of design, all executed in finely cut and polished limestone. The king, lying in his subterranean chamber, would be at the heart of the entire complex.

Eventually this first of all pyramids stood 60 metres high. It contained 850,000 tons of stone excavated for its construction and cut into small blocks: the sheer quantity of stone quarried for the purpose is without precedent. Altogether around one million tons of stone was required for the complex all, so far as we know, quarried in the king's lifetime. The whole immense structure was cased in fine white limestone; nothing like it had ever before been seen anywhere upon the earth.

It was not only the Pyramid which was so extraordinary: Imhotep created an entire complex, a microcosm of the Egyptian state designed for the eternity of Djoser, on the ridge above Memphis. The Pyramid stood in the centre, surrounded by a great wall, its sides measuring 536 metres in length by 272 metres in breadth. The wall is recessed, panelled and buttressed, like the sides of the archaic mastaba tombs; there are thirteen dummy entrances. Only one is real, in the south-eastern corner of the complex, which then gives entry to the area enclosed by the wall, which symbolises the land of Egypt. Surrounding the huge courtyards to the north and south of the Pyramid are dummy buildings, exquisitely built in polished limestone; in one corner are what may be chapels for the daughters of Djoser or halls used in the ceremonies intended to perpetuate the king's divinity.[3]

Altars were placed in the courtyards in which a perpetual round of Heb-Sed festivals could be celebrated, to ensure the eternal life of Djoser and of the lands over which he ruled. Beneath one of the altars, close to the Pyramid itself, a wild bull's skull was buried in a small, stone-lined chamber.[4]

The most miraculous survival of all in Djoser's funerary complex, however, was found close to the southern face of the Pyramid. Here, enthroned and robed for the Heb-Sed festival, designed to ensure the renewal of life for the king, sat Djoser himself, in the form of a statue only slightly less than life-size, painted and splendidly carved.

The statue of Djoser Netjerykhet is one of the world's supreme master-pieces: this is not merely the exaggerated claim of an enthusiast but an objective assessment of a work of art. The statue radiates power: even seen from behind, with the king's head made mountainous by his huge wig and its cover, the effect is formidable. It is the very prototype of the king throned in majesty. But this king is also a god and it is not possible to mistake his more than mortal quality.[5]

It is difficult, perhaps even impossible, to comprehend how Imhotep was able to manage a project of so vast a scale as the building of this huge complex. How did he calculate the stresses, train his workers, select the stone, ensure the efficiency of the mining operations, design all the exquisite details of the complex decoration, like the half-opened doors to the dummy store room, the curtains hanging over the false doors, the superb line of cobra-heads which crowns one of the walls? These are only the fragments which survive, from a vast and intricate design, yet they are so full of power that it is only possible to marvel at the achievement which they represent.

It is customary to describe the Step Pyramid complex as the first monu-mental arrangement of buildings to be constructed entirely in stone. This it undoubtedly is, though behind it must linger the recollection of the great limestone platform which was laid down in the Sumerian city of Uruk a thousand years before Imhotep created his funerary palace for Djoser. There is no evidence, anywhere, of a stone structure of such proportions as the platform of the Limestone Temple being built before Imhotep's enterprise. Yet, given the other evidence of contact between Western Asia and late predynastic Egypt it is difficult not to believe that some knowledge at least of the properties of stone must have passed, by whatever means, from Mesopotamia to Egypt. The hiatus of about a thousand years, however, is very difficult to explain.

In the Djoser enclosure there are several indications that Imhotep was still experimenting, as if he were not entirely certain of the effects which stone might be relied upon to achieve. The limestone blocks from which the Pyramid's casing were made are still quite small, reminiscent of the mud-bricks with which Imhotep's workmen would have been much more familiar. In the colonnaded hall that leads from the entrance to the great courtyard the columns are engaged to the walls as if Imhotep were unwilling to let them stand unaided.

Apart from the unique achievement of the building of the Step Pyramid complex much of the history of the Third Dynasty is obscure; nonetheless it was perhaps the most important single period in all the centuries of Egypt's history. It was at this point that Egypt began to consolidate the many diverse components of the society which would survive for so long.

The advances in construction technique which allowed the building of stone monuments on the scale of the Step Pyramid and those which followed it represent the single most important achievement of the dynasty, but it was not the only one. The subtlety and potential diversity of Egyptian as a written language became fully apparent at this time, as did the refinements in the manner of inscribing the hieroglyphs; it is arguable that the most beautiful of all hieroglyphs are to be found in the Third Dynasty. The use of glazed tiles and the elegance with which wall reliefs were carved are the more remarkable when it is recalled that, at least in the case of the latter process, it had, apparently, only been learned during the early decades of the Dynasty when the Step Pyramid was being built.

The practice of raising up large and impressive monuments in the king's name in different parts of the Valley were also undertaken on a considerable scale during the Third Dynasty. Temples and large tombs were built in places far removed from the long-established centres which were identified with the Kingship from the beginning of Egyptian history. Imhotep was believed to have lived on into the reign of the last king of the Third Dynasty, Huni (c.2599–2575 BC); he must by then have been a great age, or have carried out his stupendous project at Saqqara as a very young man. Other Third Dynasty kings built stepped monuments, in evident emulation of Djoser. These included Sekhemhet at Saqqara and Kha'ba at Zawyet el-Aryan.[6] Sekhemhet's ruined, unfinished pyramid contained an apparently intact, polished limestone sarcophagus, with the remains of the flowers which had been placed on it, still intact. Very strangely, however, when the sarcophagus was opened it was found to be empty; it had never contained the body of the king.[7] Other stepped pyramids from the Third Dynasty are probably not the tombs of kings.

Figure 4 King Djoser Netjerykhet of the Third Dynasty, *c.*2650 BC, for whom the Step Pyramid complex at Saqqara was built. Djoser's monument was the first pyramid built above ground and is generally acknowledged to be the first large-scale monument constructed entirely in stone anywhere in the world.

Figure 5 Hesy-Ra was a high official in the reign of King Djoser Netjerykhet. His tomb at Saqqara contained carved wood panelling of superlative quality, indicating how fine was the work of Egyptian craftsmen even in the early centuries, before the building of the Giza Pyramids.

The hieroglyphs of the inscriptions on Hesy-Ra's panels are also exceptionally finely executed. Having in mind the fact that only in the Second Dynasty did hieroglyphic writing achieve a developed form, the elegance and assurance of the epigraphy of the early Third Dynasty is the more remarkable.

The relationship between Huni and the line which succeeded him, the Fourth Dynasty of kings, is unclear. Again it was probably one of his daughters, Hetepheres, who brought the Kingship with her; indeed, the succession was always theoretically through the female line, though only rarely did women themselves rule.

Pyramid-building was by now well established as an activity appropriate for the posterity of the monarchy. Huni built a handsome monument at Meidum, which, unfortunately, partly collapsed, probably after its completion by his successor, Snofru, the founder of the Fourth Dynasty (*c.*2613–2589 BC). Snofru appears to have built two pyramids for himself at Dahshur; he reigned *c.*2575–2551 BC. One of the Dahshur pyramids was built to a plan entirely different either to the stepped structures of the Third Dynasty or the later, purely pyramidal form. This was the 'Bent Pyramid', built to a rhomboidal design which was not repeated. Snofru was remembered throughout Egyptian history as a just and noble king, a god who was invested in legend with something approaching what we might recognise as saintliness. His buiding operations were carried out on an astonishing scale. It is estimated that, for the pyramids built in his lifetime, some *nine million tons* of stone was quarried, dressed and erected in the monuments which have been attributed to him. The implications of managing engineering and construction projects on this scale so very early are overwhelming. From the death of Djoser to the accession of Snofru is a mere thirty-six years. Somehow, in that brief time, the Egyptians developed skills which allowed Snofru to extract more than ten times as much stone for his pyramids as was used in Djoser's entire monument.

His son, Khnum-Khufu (*c.*2551–2528 BC), known more generally by the Greek rendering of his name, Cheops, was to attain immortality as the king for whom the first and largest pyramid on the plateau at Giza was built; in the process his memory was also vilified throughout Egyptian history. The only likely image of Khufu to survive, ironically for one who build so vast a monument, is a tiny figure in ivory and shows a rather portly little man, with an expression of dyspeptic disaffection. However, Khufu's apparent petulance may be the consequence of the restoration which has been done to the face of the little ivory figure since its discovery by Petrie at the end of the nineteenth century; the original illustrations of the piece suggest an altogether more agreeable personality, with a slight, almost quizzical smile on his admittedly rather podgy features.[8]

There is really little to be said about the Great Pyramid, and its immediate successors which stand with it, which has not been said a hundred times before. It is in the nature of the passing of time that we today see only the ruins of a most audacious concept: when the Giza Pyramids were new they must have seemed magical, clad in pure white limestone which reflected the brilliant light of the sun by day and at night would have thrown back the light of the moon into space. We know, too, that the building of the Pyramids may not have been only the indulgence of despots seeking eternal aggrandisement but also served as important corporate enterprises, by which the people who worked on them, and who evidently delighted in competing amongst themselves (for so their graffiti make clear) could share and so participate in the life of the state. In the process of moving towards a fully realised maturity of the state's potential, the participation of its members, not only its élites, was necessary; this participation the building of the Pyramids dramatically provided. Even the Pyramids, as befits wholly Egyptian artifacts, are more subtle than they may at first appear.

The subtlety of the Pyramids' conception and their ultimate use is explicable – perhaps – by the recognition of the influences which, evolving over the centuries of the Archaic period, resulted in their eventual shape and the mystical significance which they represented. It is reasonable enough to view with sceptical reserve some of the more arcane explanations of the Pyramids' origins and purpose. What cannot be gainsaid, however, is the extraordinary quality of their engineering.

It is this aspect of the Pyramids' very existence which is so astonishing. Djoser died around 2610 BC, by which time it may be assumed that his monument was completed, or very largely so. The reigns of his successors were fairly brief, amounting in all to little more than thirty years. Yet in that time the art of pyramid-building, based on Imhotep's great prototype, advanced to such an extent that, by the death of Snofru, barely sixty years after Djoser's, immense monuments amounting to millions of tons of excavated and finely worked stone were set up in the Pyramid fields in the vicinity of Memphis. Less than a century after Djoser's death Khnum-Khufu could cause to be built the greatest of all the Pyramids which, despite its colossal size and the majesty of its proportions, is the heir to the work of the previous decades which even taken together would represent only the lifetime of a man as old as Pepi II, who is reputed to have lived until he was around 100 years old.

Whilst it is the Pyramids' exteriors and the perfection of their proportions which have induced the wonder of the ages which have followed their construction, their interior mathematics and the assurance of the engineering techniques which they reveal are still more remarkable. Imhotep realised, when he came to build the stages of Djoser's monument, that the internal pressures would be so great that if they were unchecked they would cause the pyramid to collapse. He introduced internal buttressing, therefore, which spread the load-bearing of the pyramid's mass. This technique was refined still further by the builders of the Pyramids which succeeded Djoser's, particularly the true Pyramids of the Fourth Dynasty where the internal pressures were even greater. Even as early as Snofru's Pyramids the interior contains corbelling which is both elegant and an important aid to the pyramid's stability.[9]

Within the Great Pyramid even more complex devices were employed to maintain the stability of a structure which was some three times heavier than the Step Pyramid. Despite the colossal forces which are present in Khnum-Khufu's Pyramid and its immediate successors, many of the internal structures, including the exquisitely cut and polished granite and other hard stones often weighing as much as 200 tons, are laid in place with the precision of the watchmaker's craft.

It really is these aspects of the Pyramids' construction which should provoke wonder, not speculation about their occult purpose. How the Egyptians were capable, after so short a time for the evolution of the complex techniques involved, without, so far as we can judge, the benefit of access to any other centre from which prior experience might be gained, of the feats of engineering skill, lifting masses of superbly dressed stone and setting them into place with such precision, is still the greatest enigma.

Beside Khufu's Pyramid were stone-lined pits which contained full-size royal boats, of which one has so far been recovered. This is a wonderful artifact in its own right, over 40 metres long with a displacement of about 40 tons, made of finely selected timbers with all its details, exquisitely crafted, intact.[10] Khufu's lovely craft, in which his mummy may have been carried on the river before his burial, is a sewn boat, the finest example of an ancient technique of shipbuilding, which survived into the twentieth century in parts of the Middle East.

To the Egyptians the idea of the journey of the soul and of the sun's journey through the darkness of the night were powerful images. In the Pyramid Texts there are constant references to such journeys and to travel by boat, across the stars, to the sun, or into the underworld.

From time to time large boats, or models of them, were buried alongside important tombs. At Saqqara, in the First Dynasty, a remarkable tomb of the time of King Aha, perhaps the first ruler of the Dynasty, has adjacent to it a model estate, containing granaries and store rooms in miniature, and the outline of a great boat. An entire fleet of twelve large model boats has been found in the desert at Abydos, near the funerary palace associated with King Khasekhemui of the Second Dynasty. In the burial of Senwosret III of the Twelfth Dynasty (1878–1841 BC) several large Nile boats were set in the ground alongside his pyramid at Dahshur.

It is hardly to be wondered that a river people like the Egyptians should attach a special symbolic importance to boats, as much as they valued them for their practical use. It is likely that the boat represented another primordial form to the Egyptians, providing a connecting point between the visible and invisible worlds. The boat beside Khufu's Pyramid was by far the largest ever built in ancient Egypt and must be seen as analogous to the Pyramid itself, in whose shadow it lay undisturbed for four and a half thousand years.

What is certain is that the Pyramids were the product of a regime which cultivated not only symbols of the power and authority of the state conceived on the largest scale but which also produced some of the most sumptuous artifacts ever made, to grace the lives of the élite of the society. The furniture and toilet equipment of Queen Hetepheres, the mother of Khufu, well illustrates the point. Her carrying chair and the furniture which accompanied her as she moved about the royal estates are prodigies of elegant, restrained design, highlighted by gold. Even the razors in her toilet box are gold and of a purity of shape which is wonderful.[11]

Figure 6 The funerary boat, of an unsurpassed elegance of design, of King Khufu (Cheops), to whom is attributed the Great Pyramid at Giza, was buried beside the pyramid, in a stone-lined chamber which preserved the timbers and rigging until the present day. The boat is 145 feet long and was the largest ship known to have sailed on the Nile until the twentieth century.

So it was with all the products of the finest of Egypt's craftsmen, working for the court or for the state's highest officers. Statuary, even that made for quite humble officials who now begin to emerge more and more into the sunlight, is refined but strongly delineated, its lines firm and confident. Painting, to be seen in its highest level of achievement in the early Fourth Dynasty at Meidum, is highly accomplished and, by its simplicity of line, suggests an assured and long-standing tradition.[12]

The immediate successors of Khufu, Djedefre (*c.*2528–2520 BC), Khafra (*c.*2520–2494 BC) and Menkaura (*c.*2490–2472 BC) were great patrons of the arts. The statuary which is associated with them, like the colossal head of Djedefre and the temple statues of Khafra and Menkaura, are acknowledged masterpieces which reveal Egyptian artists at the highest level of achievement; Djedefre, though he was Khnum-Khufu's immediate successor, was evidently disputed in his right to the succession yet he could still command in the eight years of his reign, a sculptor who could produce one of the noblest portraits ever made. Egyptian sculptors of this time were the first to sense the presence of the statue in the stone. This is revealed in the preparatory work, 'roughing out', which they undertook when first approaching the making of the most monumental figures.

The later years of the Fourth Dynasty seem to have been marked by divisions in the royal family, with perhaps one branch of the family asserting its claims to the Kingship above the other, older line. The last king, Shepseskaf (*c.*2472–2467 BC), departed from the tradition of pyramid-building and instead built at Saqqara a huge mastaba in stone, in the shape of a sarcophagus. Eventually the succession to the throne devolved upon a new line, which seems to have had a particular connection with Heliopolis.

This was to be significant for the remaining centuries of Egypt's history. Heliopolis, Iwnw to the Egyptians, was the centre of the sun-cults; these had begun to come to prominence even in the reign of one of Khufu's sons, who first assumed the title 'Sa Ra', 'Son of Ra', the god of the sun who was to dominate the pantheon for centuries to come.

The rise of the priests of the sun to power marked the decline, perhaps the final eclipse, of the protagonists of the older stellar cults. The High Priest of Heliopolis was always regarded as the most skilled observer of the celestial bodies and the reputation of the temples in the city for knowledge based on these observations long endured. Heliopolis was also the centre of one of the most important recensions of Egyptian cosmology and theology. Its High Priest bore the title 'Greatest of Seers'.

By the beginning of the Fifth Dynasty the power of the sun-god and his adherents was well established. One of the early kings of the new line, Sahura (2458–2466 BC), built a magnificent sun temple at Abu Gurob; thereafter the kings vied with their predecessors to honour Ra and to increase the power of his priesthood. The rise of the priests to this degree

Figure 7 King Djedefre, son and successor of King Khufu. This head of the king, carved in hard diorite, is one of the masterpieces of the art of the Old Kingdom.

of power was ultimately to have lamentable consequences for the entire fabric of Egypt, the first but certainly not the last time that religious bureaucracies were to have destroyed the state on which they lived.

This, however, was in the distant future, and could hardly have been apparent to those living in the golden glow of later Old Kingdom Egypt. The prosperity which Egypt enjoyed had never been greater; at home the Two Lands were at peace and there were no signs of external threats to menace them or to disturb the tranquillity which is so much the determining characteristic of this time.

This assured tranquillity of Egyptian life is well demonstrated by the vigorous and engaging scenes of daily life which were portrayed on the walls of the tombs of the great nobles. High officials such as

Figure 8 (a) The interior of the Valley Temple of King Khafra at Giza. The style of architecture is quite unlike that customarily associated with the Old Kingdom; it is only paralled by the so-called Tomb of Osiris at Abydos, which probably dates from the reign of King Den of the First Dynasty and which comprises the same massive cyclopean granite columns and lintels.

(b) The treatment of the exterior walls of Khafra's Valley Temple is perplexing in that a granite skin, using the same stone as appears in the temple's interior, has been laid on the limestone blocks from which the walls were originally built. The walls appear to be excessively weathered, a condition which is also apparent in the body of the nearby Sphinx.

Figure 9 One of the triads, showing King Menkaura in the company of fellow divinities, which were found in his mortuary temple at Giza. The triad is carved in greywacke and is finished to an exceptional smoothness, which gives the work a remarkable appearance of plasticity.

Ptahshepses, Ti, Mereruka and Neferhotep, all men close to the king, with great possessions of their own, reckoned to enjoy their earthly existence, suitably transfigured and translated to the dimensions of eternity. The Egyptians believed resolutely in the principle that the possessions of this world could be reinvested in the next. The representation of such aspects of life in their palaces and on their estates, showed how close to the ideal the life of an Egyptian magnate had become: or, at least, so he would have posterity believe, for if he did not surround himself with the good things of this life, he would be the poorer in the life hereafter. No ancient people, at least until the appearance of the Greeks some two thousand years later, left so detailed and meticulous a picture of what daily life was like than those who lived in the Nile Valley in the third millennium BC.

It was not only the greatest officials who so depicted their lives and their hopes for its perpetuation. One of the most engaging tombs at Saqqara is that of Nefer, buried with his family beside the route of the Causeway which, a few decades after his death, was built for the Pyramid of King Unas (2356–2323 BC). In building the Causeway, up which the king's sarcophagus would be drawn for its entombment in the Pyramid's burial chambers, Nefer's modest tomb and those of other Fifth Dynasty courtiers were buried under the rubble thrown up by the builders hastening to make the way clear for the king's last journey. This chance obliteration of Nefer's and the others' tombs had the consequence of saving them for posterity, until indeed our own day when they were found and brought again to the light in the 1960s.[13]

Nefer came from a family of professional musicians: he was fortunate that his father attracted the notice of the king, who allowed young Nefer to be educated with his own sons. As a result a career far more distinguished than his father's opened before him and he became one of the trusted confidants of the young prince who eventually would become King Ne-user-ra (2416–2392 BC), who was the owner of the splendid solar temple at Abu Gurob. Nefer died around 2400 BC.

Nefer's biography shows what could happen to an able and intelligent man in Egypt, even one of relatively modest origins. Nefer rose high in the civil service; as a result he was given estates, servants and all the appurtenances of the Egyptian good life. His tomb, though it is quite small and its decoration a little provincial, is full of life and the joy of living. The tomb also contains one of the oldest and best-preserved of all Egyptian mummies.[14] The scenes of life on Nefer's estates, the antics of the family's pet baboon and the services of a small orchestra, appropriate for the eternity of one of Nefer's background, are all recorded.[15]

All, however, was not really well in Egypt as the Old Kingdom drew on. The rise of the priests of the sun-cult was a symptom of a larger malaise which was affecting the fabric of Egypt and bringing with it a decline in the absolute power of the king. To ensure, generation after generation, the loyalty of families like Nefer's and more particularly those of the great provincial magnates who provided the governors of the districts, the nomes into which Egypt was divided, the king had conferred substantial privileges and still greater grants of land on his principal officers. In time, these grants, once made at the will of the king, became accepted fact, the patrimony of the families so endowed. Offices once conferred by the grace of the king, became hereditary benefices, passing through the generations as did the fiefdoms on which the magnates' territorial power was based.

This is not to say that such matters would have been apparent in late Old Kingdom Egypt. The Fifth Dynasty flowed into the Sixth (*c*.2323 BC), the kings of which maintained their customary state, going to war when necessary against marauders (now becoming something of a problem, compared with the past) and conducting the great ceremonies. They were still buried with all the funerary pomp which now had the best part of a thousand years of tradition behind it and still huge tombs were built to ensure the survival of the Great Individual around whom, theoretically at least, Egypt and all the world revolved.

The royal mortuary cults continued to develop. Following their appearance in the Pyramid of Unas, the last king of the Fifth Dynasty (c.2356–2323 BC), the kings of the Sixth Dynasty were buried in chambers below their pyramids on the walls of which are inscribed the immense sequence of prayers, incantations and spells known as the Pyramid Texts. These were intended to serve as a sort of eternal aide-mémoire for the king, to ensure that his transition from this world to the next was effected smoothly and without risk of attack by the forces of evil which awaited the spirit after life. The Pyramid Texts are the oldest corpus of sacred texts in the world. Though they are, in our terminology, religious, they are also manuals for the enactment of the ceremonies associated with the king's burial. They are also the oldest dramatic works, for many of them are antiphonal, with several characters participating. They provide a unique insight into the minds of men living more than four thousand years ago.

The depletion of the Royal Treasury and of the lands on which the king's power to reward was based, continued, gaining pace in the exceptionally long reign of King Pepi II (c.2246–2152 BC). He came to the throne at about 6 years old and was reputed to be around 100 years old when he died. Although the state was already being eroded, Pepi's reign enjoyed much new building and a considerable amount of activity beyond Egypt's frontiers. Pepi's reputation, despite his remarkable antiquity and a generous number of queens who were attached to him, was somewhat equivocal. A story, written down in the Middle Kingdom, apparently records his amorous pursuit of one of his generals.[16]

The end of the Old Kingdom, which is customarily dated to the end of Pepi's reign, was invariably described by historians as a 'collapse', with the country supposedly falling into a state of near-anarchy. The evidence for this harsh view of the state of affairs in Egypt in the late third millennium was principally provided by literary exercises which became popular at around this time and which were characterised by their deep pessimism; one such, the so-called Admonitions of Ipuwer appeared to be a first-hand account of the chaos which swept over the lands at this time.

It is now less certain that this was quite the situation, though there was a degree of social and political upheaval in the country and there is some evidence of incursions by foreigners. However, the essential institutions of Egypt seem to have survived, but effectively for the first time in its history the world beyond Egypt's frontiers was beginning to have an impact on life in the Valley – and the world outside itself was changing.

For the remaining two thousand years of Egypt's history, the first six dynasties were remembered as a veritable Golden Age. The names of the great kings, Djoser, Snofru, Khufu and the rest, were remembered and entered into legend. The art of the Old Kingdom remained the model for succeeding generations, though with few exceptions, the artists of later times did not find it easy to invoke that quality of the transcendental which is characteristic of Old Kingdom art at its finest.

The third millennium was a time of exceptional achievement for our species, much of which occurred in the Nile Valley. Thereafter, very often quite consciously, the Egyptians sought to regain contact with this time, recognising that it was especially favoured, and to bring back some of its splendour. Remarkably, very occasionally they seemed to come near to achieving this aspiration.

CHAPTER VII

HIATUS: THE FIRST
INTERMEDIATE PERIOD

—— •◦• ——

The otherwise stately procession of the dynasties of ancient Egypt is punctuated by three principal periods of intermission, when radical change is thrust into the seemingly unchanging Egyptian landscape. Known to Egyptologists as 'Intermediate Periods' they are amongst the least understood and the least defined of the Egyptian historical sequences. They are generally regarded as small Dark Ages when the steady rhythms of the Egyptian state become discordant, strife becomes widespread and foreign influences begin to disrupt the confident order of the true Egyptian genius.

The chief importance of the first of these periods to the future course of Egyptian history is that it marks the beginning of a real change in the status of the king. Something of this had been discernible even in the later Old Kingdom when, from being identified as the incarnation of the universal divinity, existing for ever as a star, the king became one god of many, serving in the barque of the sun-god, Ra. As the Old Kingdom flowed on, with its achievements in the arts in particular growing ever more remarkable, the king's position became, imperceptibly, weakened, a consequence of his need to reward, generation by generation, his senior servants and ministers, to bind them to the throne. The king's material wealth inevitably declined: the office, however, was still useful, even in a period of relative poverty, as a device for confirming the pretensions of a provincial noble or giving substance to an ancient title of honour.

Other changes which affected Egypt during this time were yet more subtle, though, for the vast majority of those living in the Valley life continued as it had always done and such changes were probably quite imperceptible. There is evidence at the end of the Old Kingdom of a succession of Low Niles, always feared as the greatest catastrophe which could afflict Egypt.[1] The climate of Egypt seems to have changed at this point, just prior to 2000 BC, becoming notably more arid, with a drastically reduced precipitation. Similar conditions were experienced in other parts of the ancient Near East, at much the same time. The exceptional levels of desiccation which characterise the Arabian peninsula today, for example, appear to have been consolidated at this time, whilst the level of the Arabian Gulf fell by some two metres. The final extinction of the Sumerian city-states was probably hastened by the same deterioration in the climate.[2]

After the Sixth Dynasty sputtered to its end a Seventh Dynasty was recorded by Manetho, the Hellenistic Egyptian historian, consisting of 'seventy kings, who reigned seventy days',[3] a compelling image of a disintegrating authority, for which there is no actual historical evidence. But after the centenarian Pepi there does seem to have been a line of shadowy and transitory kings and one rather mysterious queen, Nitrocris, but little is known of any of them for certain.

An Eighth Dynasty now came to something like power: the throne names of its kings incorporate the principal name of Pepi. These successors were either his descendants or, less likely, sought to give legitimacy to their title to the throne by associating themselves with him. The turnover in kings, however, remained high; the Seventh and Eighth Dynasties occupied the years *c.*2150–2134 BC.

A new dynasty of rulers, the Ninth, emerged around 2134 BC, more determined and with some prospects of survival. Its founder was a prince from Middle Egypt and Herakleopolis became its capital. This city was significantly situated for it commanded one of the key trade routes, running south to north. This is of interest, for despite the uncertainty of the times the First Intermediate Period shows quite a considerable increase in foreign trading activity in Egypt. This was to accelerate in the next period of Egyptian history, but it is already apparent and foreigners, particularly the 'Asiatics' about whom the Egyptians were generally most disparaging, began to be found in considerable colonies in some of the Delta towns. These trading colonies were to be of much greater importance in later times.

Away to the east trading activity at this time developed very considerably with caravans by land and argosies by sea being transported over great distances; similarly there were important developments in what might reasonably be called 'business practice'. It is possible to trace the ancestry of many modern business techniques, such as the role of the banker, the concept of credit and the establishment of networks of import–export businesses, to this time, particularly in Mesopotamia where the Old Babylonian merchants inherited many of the Sumerians' attention to business and the management of capital.

Given the much earlier connections between south-western Asia and the Nile Valley in late predynastic times, it is a little surprising that there is no evidence of trading contact between the Mesopotamians and the Egyptians at this time, despite the considerably increased volume and range of Western Asiatic trade.[4] The staple of that trade was copper and Egypt had its own sources of supply: it may be that this limited the incentives for Asiatic traders to make the long journey to the Valley.

The Ninth Dynasty seems to have given some attention to the ancient royal capital of Memphis. The kings adopted names which purported to link them with the Memphite kings of the late Old Kingdom. Again, there is no means of knowing whether such claims were justified by any familial connection with the earlier dynasty.

After these two rather shadowy dynasties, the Tenth arrives with somewhat more substance. Its founder took the name Neferkare, a popular throne name of Old Kingdom monarchs. His dynasty was to last for the best part of a century, until c.2040 BC.

However, to the south, events were in train which would eventually change the history of Egypt once again and, in the process, sweep away the Herakleopolitan kings. For the first time Thebes enters the historical record, as the seat of a line of princes who resented the pretensions of the Herakleopolitans to the Kingship and who eventually were to overthrow them.

One of the provincial magnates who originally supported the Tenth Dynasty kings was a certain Ankhtify, who was nomarch of no less a centre than Hierakonpolis, the source of Egypt's founding dynasty of kings a thousand years earlier but now much diminished in all but reputation. His seat was at Moalla and he seems to have exercised some degree of control over much of the south.

Ankhtify was not lacking in confidence. He left behind him, in his rather graceful tomb at Moalla,[5] a long autobiographical statement, recording his many virtuous deeds and the splendid achievements of his life. With becoming diffidence he describes himself as 'the beginning and the end of mankind, for my equal has not and will not come into being'. In addition to his responsibilities as a provincial governor he was also a military commander and he fought several engagements with Inyotef I, the prince of Thebes who proclaimed himself king of all Egypt. It was from Inyotef's line that the kings of the Eleventh Dynasty, the founders of the Middle Kingdom, were to come.

The First Intermediate Period is perhaps better to be thought of as the Old Kingdom in terminal decline, rather than a time of rabid anarchy. The officials and nobles of the time obviously saw themselves as still participating in the unchanging sequences of the Egyptian Kingdoms as they had always been. There is however some evidence of diminished standards in the art which followed the Sixth Dynasty. It is not lacking in charm; it often demonstrates in an appealing way that humanity which always was one of the glories of Egyptian art. The paintings and especially the woodcarvings of this period, have a directness and often a simplicity which is most engaging. The art of the First Intermediate Period is never grand; it suggests a people bravely sustaining their traditions in circumstances which, at best, were challenging. Painting, in particular, seems to have flourished at this time, perhaps because the opportunity for the grander architectural enterprises of earlier days was lacking. Some of the tomb paintings of the period anticipate the high quality of such art in the Middle Kingdom and, later, in the New Kingdom's painted tombs in the Valleys of the Kings and of the Nobles, outside Thebes.

There is increasing evidence of foreign contact during the First Intermediate Period. The Egyptians were never easy with foreigners but nonetheless their influence on the Valley at this time is unmistakable. Such relatively minor art forms as that of the seals used to mark merchandise show foreign influences in their designs; indeed, the Egyptians originally borrowed the idea of the seal from Western Asia, though eventually they transmuted it into one of their own distinctive forms, the scarab, the industrious dung-beetle which, to the Egyptians, signified 'becoming'. The seals of the First Intermediate Period are generally round stamp seals. Their form may well have been influenced by those used by Western Asiatic sea-traders.

No form of creative expression was alien to the Egyptians; if some, like architecture and portrait sculpture, have gained especial recognition, this is the consequence of their scale, quality and the immediacy of their ability to communicate. Egyptian literature is perhaps a less familiar art form, other than to specialists, by reason of its essentially second-hand transmission.[6] In the nature of things anyone wishing to appreciate Egyptian writings will almost certainly need to approach them both in translation and transliteration. This last is especially important since the visual aspect and impact of Egyptian inscriptions are often as important as the meaning of the words which the hieroglyphs or the more cursive scripts of less formal writings convey. There is still considerable uncertainty about Egyptian language: what is accessible to us is only a shadow of its real substance.

Literature became a more widely employed form of expression in this period before the beginning of the Middle Kingdom. An entire genre of funerary autobiography grew up, of which Ankhtify's essay in self-adulation is a particular and idiosyncratic example. There are many examples too of what seem to be folk-tales, which are for the first time recorded and assume the character of literature. Among these are the celebrated story of 'The Eloquent Peasant', the 'Dialogue of a Man with his Soul', which presents an almost Sumerian, very un-Egyptian and deeply pessimistic view of the world, 'Bata and his Brothers' and a conventional genre, which goes under the general term 'Admonitions' and which are cast as advice or instructions for a king, minister or governor, handed down by a predecessor.[7] These are especially interesting, given the rather uncertain times from which they come, for the concern which they continue to show for justice, fair-dealing and for the welfare of the poor or disadvantaged is remarkable.

Although there were clearly no longer the great corporate projects of the Old Kingdom to keep large sections of the community gainfully employed during this troubled time, life for the majority of people was probably largely unchanged. What is clear, however, is that the process which some have seen as a sort of religious democratisation, whereby people of relatively modest social origins began to claim the benefits of an immortal life, emerges ever more strongly. It was, of course, apparent in the Old Kingdom that people of quite humble origins could attain high office, under the benevolent interest of the king. By the time of the intermission before the re-establishment of the unified Kingdom under the founders of the Eleventh Dynasty, this process had gained momentum and we are able to read the life-stories of quite modest men, officials or priests though they may be. Herein lay one of the most crucial changes in the character of Egypt in antiquity. It was probably inevitable, given the forces which were released in the Old Kingdom, but it was eventually to lead to the decline of the ancient, god-king directed polity which had so marvellously created the civilisation of ancient Egypt. It was also to produce a host of individuals, great and small, who now throng the ancient Egyptian stage.

CHAPTER VIII

RESTORATION: THE MIDDLE KINGDOM

—— •◆• ——

Time after time, whenever Egypt felt the need to reinvigorate itself or to attempt to re-establish its pristine character, it would return to the origins of the Kingship from which the state had grown, in the south of the Valley, in the region above Abydos which ran on to Hierakonpolis. From this area seemed always to come the initiatives which promoted the interests of the Kingship and the idea of the unified, centralised state. It can be argued that the very idea of unification, so protractedly sought by successive charismatic leaders, was not natural to the Valley. The ebb and flow of politics in Egypt from early dynastic times onward seems as often to be striving for a return to the fragmented structure of little principalities into which, it is presumed, though without any hard or formal evidence, the river lands were divided before the First Dynasty. The forty-two nomes (twenty-two in Upper Egypt, twenty in the north),[1] which comprised the administrative departments of Egypt in historic times are frequently cited as the probable successors of the predynastic chieftaincies which may once have been the political configuration of Egypt before the establishment of the Kingship. During the First Intermediate Period it is clear that some of the leading families in the nomes, and others who saw the opportunity to better themselves, attempted to assert their independence of the much weakened central authority.

After the collapse of that central authority at the end of the Sixth Dynasty, none of the contenders for sovereignty seems to have had either the military power or the political muscle to impose control over anything other than a limited stretch of the Nile's banks and the hinterland. It was from the south that eventually the drive was to come which would bring all the Valley once again under the rule of a single master.

The rise of the house of Inyotef, prince of Thebes, has already been mentioned, in the later years of the uncertain period which followed the end of the Old Kingdom. The family of Inyotef does not seem originally to have had a direct connection with any of the dynasties before them; rather, they were nobles of a considerable lineage and were probably powerful in the Pyramid Age. They were high priests and senior administrators who rose to something like local paramountcy during the time of the weakening of the central or royal authority. They then consolidated their status, ruling as sovereign princes over an increasingly extensive area of the south, centred on Thebes. Prior to this time, c.2134 BC, Thebes does not appear to have been a particularly significant town. Some late Old Kingdom tombs have been found there,[2] but it owes its prominence in Egypt's history to the Inyotef family; thereafter it was never to lose its importance and indeed, for hundreds of years, especially during the New Kingdom, it was the richest and most important city in the ancient world.

The elder Inyotef, 'Inyotef the Great', fought a number of engagements in the Valley to bring under his authority the provincial nobles who had become accustomed to life as independent rulers. One of his opponents was the superb Ankhtify whom ultimately he defeated in battle. This did not, however, prevent Ankhtify from inhabiting his elegant tomb at Moalla, some thirty miles south of Thebes, where, for at least as long as he was able to occupy it before it was pillaged, he could enjoy the assurance of his splendid life and achievements.

One of the Inyotefs decorated his tomb with a handsome portrayal of his favourite dogs, who are shown, seated proudly, with their names blazoned beside them and with their own attendants.[3] The family of Inyotef seem to have assumed the royal power in the lifetime of the first Inyotef's grandson.

The House of Inyotef continued the process of consolidating its authority over the Valley until, in the person of Nebhetepre Montuhotpe II, the fourth generation from Inyotef the Great, a new King of Upper and Lower Egypt could be proclaimed (*c.*2060 BC). He would lay claim to the rule of the Two Kingdoms and be proclaimed a god, inheritor of the divinity of those kings who had ruled a unified Egypt before him and who would, by convention, be considered his ancestors.

Nebhetepre Montuhotpe II was one of the greatest of Egypt's kings, confident, determined, clear of purpose and swift in action. He reigned long, for more than fifty years; he was thus able to direct the reunification of the Valley and to see it very largely achieved in his lifetime. Unusually he changed his Horus name three times. Finally he proclaimed himself the Horus Sematowy, 'the Uniter of the Two Lands'. Thus he associated himself with the other two great unifiers, Menes–Narmer (Aha) and Khasekhemui.

His surviving portrait statues are many. They are often massive, still showing something of a naïveté of execution which is more typical of the past First Intermediate period than the elegance of the approaching Middle Kingdom; Nebhetepre Montuhotpe was, in real terms, its founder though dynastic piety attributed the foundation of the Eleventh Dynasty to Inyotef the Great. Like Inyotef, Nebhetepre Montuhotpe II, having come from that stratum of Egyptian society himself, was not prepared to be balked by the other provincial magnates who had exercised quasi-royal status and privileges in their domains. They were vigorously cut down to size by the Theban princes, though some evidently accommodated themselves to the new order and were confirmed in their offices; they were, however, definitely to be subordinate to the Theban autocracy.

In the early years of the Eleventh Dynasty the great provincial nobles, like the successive Khnumhoteps in Middle Egypt who ruled a large domain around Beni Hasan, living and dying in something like royal state, built themselves splendid and handsomely decorated tombs. This practice ceases in the later years of the dynasty when such ostentation was evidently considered unsuitable in a subject, no matter how great his status or ancient his lineage.

In many of his surviving statues Nebhetepre Montuhotpe II sits, enthroned, massive and rather fierce. His face is painted black; this may be artistic convention for he is portrayed as the dead king, Osiris, whose face was also painted black. However, the colour and the rather negroid cast to his features and those of some of his successors have suggested that the Theban family was originally from further south. Whether this was so is not certain, but the ability of the founder of the Theban house to rule is undoubted. Nebhetepre Montuhotpe II and his successors set about the reorganisation of the administration of Egypt and restored the absolute royal domination of Egyptian society which was to last for the next two centuries.

Their rule, however, was subtly different from that which had persisted during the Old Kingdom. Then the kings were unquestioned gods, the very raisons d'etre of Egypt's existence, but they were not the executive functionaries who actually powered the Kingdom's administration. Everything was enacted in the king's name and he was the focus of all the great ceremonies of state. But the business of Egypt's government was usually placed in the hands of officials, rigidly graded though with opportunity for all talented individuals to gain access even to the highest levels of the bureaucracy. The great officers of state, the king's ministers, regional governors and the high priests of the various temple congregations, ran the country; it was this fact that led to their assumption of hereditary privileges which contributed to the collapse (if that is what it was) which occurred at the end of the Sixth Dynasty.

The kings of the Eleventh Dynasty, who were separated from the later Sixth Dynasty kings by little more than a century in fact, had learned the lesson not to allow a subject, no matter how great, to overreach himself. In the following Twelfth Dynasty one of the kings, Amenemhet, who as will be seen had occasion to know what he was talking about, spelt out the need for the ruler to be aloof from human relationships and trust, expressing a rather un-Egyptian pessimism and a distinctly ungodlike cynicism. His admonitions, however, seem to be particularly apt for the Middle Kingdom whose kings, great men though several of them were, seemed distinctly more steely-eyed and earthily purposeful than many of their predecessors.

Nebhetepre Montuhotpe II was inclined to keep the reins of power firmly in his own hands. He set out on a programme of building which recalled the great days of his Old Kingdom predecessors: he was also an active military campaigner and carried out important punitive campaigns, especially in the south, to secure Egypt's frontiers against incursions by the tribes who from time to time menaced its integrity. He seems to have felt an obligation to his soldiers who fought and died in his cause: some sixty young soldiers who were killed in battle were buried close to his own splendid tomb, so that they might share in his immortality.[4] He built important fortresses in the far south, designed to prevent the Nubians and other Africans from entering Egypt. He led punitive campaigns against the Nubians who at this time were ruled, as an independent kingdom, by a dynasty of renegade Egyptians.

His most enduring monument, however, was to be the immense and graceful tomb which he made for himself north of Thebes at Deir el-Bahri, a great natural bay on the western side of the Valley, backed by towering curtain rocks. Here Nebhetepre Montuhotpe II created (it is so highly individual a building it is difficult to believe that it is anyone's invention other than the king's) a unique monument, a square platform, approached by a high ramp and probably surmounted by a pyramid. The approach to the tomb was laid out with gardens, with trees and shrubs suggesting that the king appreciated nature tamed. Trees were also planted on the upper terrace of the platform.

The king's tomb was carefully hidden, approached by a long, subterranean corridor. When the site was excavated it was found to have been plundered, though a cache of the king's portrait sculptures was recovered from it. Provision had been made in it for the burials of his queens and also for several of his daughters.

Nebhetepre Montuhotpe II's tomb at Deir el-Bahri is a fair monument for the Middle Kingdom itself: preserving the most potent symbolism of the past, but transmuting it subtly, with great elegance and sense of form into something new. The pyramid which it is supposed rose above Montuhotpe's burial place links it with the monuments of the Old Kingdom. The immense brick terraced platform on which it stood was a microcosm of Egypt, as much as the space enclosed by the walls of Djoser's monument at Saqqara, yet less assertive, more integrated with the landscape in which it was set.

As with architecture, so the Middle Kingdom developed and changed the age-old canons of belief, bringing to the fore other of the many forms of expression which Egyptian belief systems permitted. The splendid texts carved on the walls of pyramids were no longer only the perquisite of the kings. Instead, great nobles, courtiers and, increasingly, lesser figures – officials, priests, landowners – were buried in handsome painted coffins, moulded in the form of the once-living. With them they took the comfort of the guide to the afterlife which the kings had once alone enjoyed, for on the interior of the coffins were painted the essential texts which would ensure the owner of the coffin an untroubled journey to the eternal life.[5]

The Eleventh Dynasty would be remarkable enough by virtue of the life of Nebhetepre Montuhotpe II alone. His genius lay in reimposing the central authority of the Kingship which, when it was skilfully and forcefully managed, produced Egypt's greatest triumphs. But he did so in ways which very exactly met the requirements of the times in which he lived, adapting it to a degree of accommodation with the world which lay beyond Egypt's frontiers. This was a world which was changing drastically, which Egypt could no longer disregard.

For a political system that paid so much respect to symbol and the expression of truth through images, it is not altogether surprising to find the new Theban family adopting an evocative device to mark the beginning of a new age, in the terrestrial sphere where the immemorial Kingship ruled as much as it was presumed to do in the celestial dimension. There, the changing of the epochs was signalled by a new constellation which could be seen to be rising before the appearance of the sun on the horizon at dawn at the time of the equinox.

Whilst the matter is not supported by most orthodox historians and archaeologists, the period around 2000 BC is thought by some to mark the transition from the sign of the Bull to that of the Ram, in the cycle of the so-called Universal Zodiac, the expression of the astronomical phenomenon known as the Precession of the Equinoxes.[6] Since the end of the fifth millennium, *c.*4000 BC, the constellation which appeared on the horizon immediately prior to sunrise at the vernal equinox had been Taurus, from very ancient times, and for no very evident reason, identified with the Bull. This had been the dominant constellation, in a very real sense, the archetypal visible sign, of the entire period of Egyptian history thus far, from its modest beginnings in Badarian and Naqada I times, to the heights of the Old Kingdom and now the more austere splendours of the Middle Kingdom monarchs. Around 2000 BC, the vernal equinox was marked by the heliacal rising of Aries, the Ram, in the light of dawn.

Whether or not the ancients knew of the mechanics of the Precession before its definition by Hipparchos the Bithynian in the second century BC is uncertain, but as dedicated watchers of the night sky they could not fail to be aware of its effects. This awareness is demonstrated unmistakably during the 'epoch of Taurus', by what is effectively a universal preoccupation with bulls. This enthusiasm for bulls, originally the wild strain, later the domesticated, is of great antiquity. It is a preoccupation not confined to Egypt but is found throughout the ancient Near East, raised to the proportions of a universal cult. This preoccupation is demonstrated in art, particularly that associated with ritual, Kingship and the gods.

In Egypt, even before the beginning of the First Dynasty, the king is identified with the Bull, more openly than he is with the Falcon, though the hawk was always to personify the living king in his incarnation as Horus. Throughout the Old Kingdom this identification persists. When the family of Inyotef assumed the Kingship they took as the throne name of the kings which the line produced 'Montuhotpe', 'Montu is content'. Montu was a god of the Theban region who is represented both as a bull and as a falcon, a combination unique in Egyptian iconography. The Theban princes thus neatly encapsulated the *two* images of the royal state, bull and falcon, in the warlike god Montu who was manifest in both forms. In doing so the Montuhotpes also anticipated symbolically the end of the reign of the Bull, represented in more than the millennium which had passed from the first kings to their own time. The kings of the Eleventh Dynasty, by this elegant use of symbol, confirmed their own status as true kings, the heirs of the original unifiers of the Kingdoms, whose function they were themselves to assume.

This was particularly the case in the lifetime of Nebhetepre Montuhotpe II, who reigned so long and so effectively. Powerful and able a monarch that he was, he himself carried into effect most of the reforms which he judged necessary to restore the status and vigour of the Kingship. But long reigns usually resulted in periods of less certain authority in the time which followed them: the melancholy example of Pepi II's near century of Kingship must still have been alive in the recollections of thoughtful Egyptians. The problem was that an elderly king tended either to be succeeded by an elderly son or by a more distant descendant, often young and not fully in the confidence of his predecessor. Equally, an aged king might leave many descendants, any or all of whom would jostle for the succession.

Nebhetepre Montuhotpe II was succeeded by his son, already elderly, who assumed the style Sankhkare Montuhotpe (2010–1998 BC). He, too, planned a tomb at Deir el-Bahri but it was not completed. He evidently was aware of a continued growing threat from the peoples to the north and east of Egypt, and built substantial defences against them in the Delta.

Sankhkare Montuhotpe was succeeded in turn by the last of the line, who took the prenomen Nebtawyre (1998–1991 BC), which proclaimed the Lordship of the Two Lands as the prerogative of Ra, the sun-god, still the supreme divinity in the Egyptian pantheon. His reign, apparently seven or ten years in duration, was undistinguished. The Eleventh Dynasty which had begun so auspiciously in the assumption of the Kingship by Nebhetepre Montuhotpe II sank into exhaustion less than a century later.

The house of Inyotef was succeeded by another family which, though evidently noble, was seemingly not connected with any of the ancient royal lines. In the Middle Kingdom it does not appear that there was any attempt to invent a royal genealogy, in any literal sense, as had always been the custom in the Old Kingdom, by which the founder of a new dynasty would be at pains to demonstrate a blood line or familial connection with his predecessors. The accession of a new dynasty in the Middle Kingdom marked, in something like the formula adopted in much later times by the Emperors of China, the descent of the 'mandate of Heaven' or much earlier when the rulers of Sumer spoke of the Kingship being 'handed down' from heaven. Sometimes continuity between the dynasties was ensured by the newly enthroned king taking the daughter of the previous ruler as his wife; throughout the history of Egypt the succession was actually through the female line for it was the daughter-sister-wife of the king who would be impregnated by the god in his human form and she would therefore bear the divinely conceived heir, who would one day succeed in the same manner as his earthly father. The Middle Kingdom kings, particularly in the Twelfth Dynasty, often took the extra precaution of associating a son with their rule, often as co-regent.

The assumption of the royal power by the founder of the Twelfth Dynasty marked a significant departure in Egyptian royal history. The last king of the preceding dynasty, Montuhotpe IV was succeeded by his vizier or Chief Minister, a southerner, the son of a woman from Elephantine, from whom he may have inherited Nubian connections, and a priest, Senwosret. His name was Amenemhet (1991–1962 BC) and, like Nebhetepre Montuhotpe II, he was a powerful and determined ruler. His accession evidently did not pass unchallenged but he secured the throne and, after some initial discontent represented by rival contenders, he ruled successfully, leaving in place much of the previous reign's administration, for which, in any case, he had presumably largely been responsible.

Amenemhet was, unsurprisingly, aware of the sort of manipulation of the central administration which could be perpetrated by an unscrupulous official. He tightened the administration over all Egypt, but he left a number of senior officers, including provincial governors, in their offices though their loyalty would now be directed to him alone. Although he was a southerner he felt no special ties with Thebes; indeed, as it was the capital of the previous dynasty which he had replaced, he may have felt uneasy there. For whatever reason, he moved the capital to an entirely new location, at el-Lisht, in Middle Egypt, south of Memphis; it was called Itj-tawy, 'The Seizer of the Two Lands'.

Amenemhet was a warrior as much as he was an administrator, conducting campaigns deep into Nubia, and he deputed one of his generals to put down the Bedu in Sinai, to the north-east of Egypt. He was a keen builder, with that enthusiasm for construction projects which always was a mark of a great Egyptian monarch. He is represented in many statues with a rather watchful expression, suggesting that he was not an easy man, an impression confirmed by the possibly apocryphal but deeply pessimistic series of admonitions which he is represented as having left to his heir. In the advice which he gives his son he emphasises the ruler's isolation, urging him not to trust anyone, not even a brother, to hold no man his friend, to make no intimates.[7] Despite his conscientious discharge of his responsibilities as king Amenemhet reveals that he feels ill repaid by his subjects and his associates alike. His legacy to his son is bitter.

Like many of Egypt's kings Amenhotep was a skilled propagandist. Early in his reign one of his adherents, Neferty, a priest from Bubastis, invented a prophecy alleged to have been pronounced during the Old Kingdom, which foretold, in suitably obscure and arcane terms, the coming of a southerner who would restore the glory of Egypt and of the Kingship after a period of decline and disorder. This Messianic figure is, unsurprisingly, revealed as Amenemhet, who clearly felt the need for some mystical support for his assumption of the Kingship.[8]

Amenemhet's distrust of those around him seems to have been justified: he was assassinated in a harem conspiracy, one of the few important kings of Egypt to experience this fate. He was succeeded by his son, Senwosret I (1971–1928 BC), who had reigned with his father for the last ten years of his life and who moved swiftly to contain any dangers which might have threatened his dynasty as a result of his father's murder. Interestingly, Senwosret also used the device of a voice speaking from the past, not unlike the prophecy announcing his father's rights to the succession, when he himself succeeded. The 'Instructions', which purported to be the testament of Amenemhet to his son, were clearly designed to give authority to his own accession and to warn off any in the court who might have ideas of seizing the throne for themselves or of promoting an alternative candidate to Senwosret. In the event, his assumption of the Kingship seems to have been unopposed.

From this time, the occasion of the death of the first Amenemhet and the succession of the first Senwosret, there descends a story which was to delight and instruct generations of Egyptian children for many centuries afterwards. This was the tale of Sinuhe, an official at the court who was in some way implicated in or privy to the plans to assassinate Amenemhet.[9] Fearful of the knowledge which he possessed, he fled from Egypt and sought sanctuary among the Bedu, the 'sand dwellers' in the north-east, probably in Sinai. Here he married the daughter of one of the great shaikhs and eventually became a rich and respected shaikh himself. However, the lure of Egypt for its children always proved irresistible and at length he sought the permission of the king to return. He was welcomed home with great rejoicing, even the king's children shouting and leaping with delight. Sinuhe is able at last to die and be buried in his homeland and not outside the Valley, for an Egyptian always a miserable fate most earnestly to be avoided.

Senwosret followed Amenemhet in a generally tranquil sequence. Senwosret was, it will be recalled, the name of the dynasty's ancestor; indeed in the later mythology of the Kingship this first Senwosret was credited as the founder, presumably to give still greater credibility to the assumption of the royal power by the first Amenemhet. However, the king who is known as Senwosret I, who reigned from 1971 to 1926 BC, was revered as a god, certainly down to the time of the New Kingdom.

Figure 10 King Senwosret I of the Twelfth Dynasty. Senwosret succeeded his murdered father, Amenemhet I and was one of the Egyptian kings who contributed to the legend of the magician-king Sesostris.

Figure 11 Serenput, governor of Elephantine in the Twelfth Dynasty. Attended by his dog, Serenput displays the dignity and assurance of a high official in Egypt during the height of its civilisation.

Figure 12 King Senwosret III commissioned a series of highly naturalistic portraits of himself, some of the later of which show him as apparently deeply melancholic. This larger than life-size head in granite shows the king in early middle age.

The Twelfth Dynasty produced one of the most remarkable of all the Kings of Egypt, whose name was never to be forgotten, was indeed to be known in lands unknown to the people of the Valley. He was the third to bear the name Senwosret; he succeeded to the throne in 1878 BC and reigned for nearly forty years. In this he was similar to many of his house, for their reigns were all of them remarkable for their length, a testimony both to the strength of the family's genes and to the tranquillity and prosperity of Egypt.

Senwosret III was the great-grandson of Senwosret I. They were both charismatic kings and their reputations became conflated in later times, producing, as will be seen, a particularly powerful legend.

To succeeding generations Senwosret III personified the magician-king, whose power is derived from beyond the visible world; the magus was always a figure closely associated with the Kingship. The potently endowed, more than human figure was not far from the Egyptians' customary concept of their kings' divine nature, but in Senwosret's case it is something more. He was honoured as a god far beyond Egypt's frontiers and the cults associated with him lasted through the second millennium into late antiquity. To the Greeks he was the wonder worker Sesostris, for whom an entire repertory of marvellous stories was created.[10] His fame lived on into Renaissance times and, in the eighteenth century he became Sarastro, the noble high priest of Mozart's *Die Zauberflöte*, where, from the heart of his great temple, he opposes the darker magic of the Queen of the Night. In the twentieth century, undergoing a change of gender, he becomes 'Madame Sesostris, famous clairvoyant, / Had a bad cold, nevertheless, / Is known to be the wisest woman in Europe, / With a wicked pack of cards', in T. S. Eliot's *The Waste Land*.[11]

The extraordinary persistence of Senwosret's reputation over something like four thousand years goes some way towards revealing the nature of the mysterious appeal which Egypt itself always so potently exercised. The survival of Senwosret's name and legend recalls one of Egypt's most golden periods, of which he became the archetype, standing for the magnificence of a king who is something more than mortal and who has access to powers beyond those of the natural world. He became the king who is at the heart of a thousand stories, of the quest for the lost prince, of the mysterious king waiting in his palace of gold for a return to the world of the living.

Like most of Egypt's greatest monarchs Senwosret was a warrior whose campaigns took him far from the Valley. One campaign, far to the north, went beyond the hill which was to become Jerusalem.[12] He built an important series of forts at Semna, at the Second Cataract, to keep safe the southern access to Egypt.[13]

The later Middle Kingdom was a time of great artistic achievement. Such buildings as survive are very beautiful, often of a splendidly balanced austerity which recalls, but does not emulate, the best of Old Kingdom architecture. Of surviving buildings of this period the most accomplished is the so-called Senwosret Kiosk at Karnak,[14] an exquisitely proportioned enclosure which served as a 'way-station' in which the image of the god (and the priests who carried it) might rest as it progressed around the temple. The Kiosk is built in golden polished limestone, adorned with high relief carvings of Senwosret I in the company of the ithyphallic Amun-Min Kamutef, the patron both of Karnak and of the royal house, who displays potently his most memorable attribute as the king adores him. In other episodes on the beautifully carved reliefs the king is shown in company with other gods including Atum, Ptah and Amun-Ra in scenes of great and rather touching intimacy.

Funerary architecture also reached great heights of construction and decoration. The immense tomb complex of Amenemhet III (1844–1797 BC) at Hawara excited Herodotus and was preserved until Greco-Roman times. It gave rise to the stories of the Labyrinth, by which term it was described by the geographer Strabo.

Middle Kingdom statuary is immediately recognisable. It has a formality and solidity which are deeply impressive; it is also entirely human in scale, no matter that royal portraits still defer to the convention of the king as god.

The harsh, almost brutalist statuary of Nebhetepre Montuhotep II has already been described. These seated figures are powerful representations of a formidable ruler, which make no concessions to the idea of the king as the shepherd of his people: here he is indisputably master. The statuary of the Twelfth Dynasty, by contrast, is more sophisticated in execution, elegant and formal; the king is human in scale and in the manner of his portrayal. Occasionally a work of great power, comparable with the inspired works of the Old Kingdom, appears. Such a work is the extraordinary statue, of which only the bust and head survives, of Amenemhet III, as a high priest, found in the Fayum, an area of great importance to the kings of the Dynasty. Similar, but even more remarkable, is the double statue of the king as a Nile-god, found at Tanis. Both of these productions suggest powerful African influences: the Fayum bust could very reasonably be seen as a representation of the king as an African paramount chief, though it may be doubted whether any African chiefs, other than the king of Egypt, would have been thus accoutered, early in the second millennium BC. The monarchs of the Middle Kingdom were also given to having themselves portrayed in the form of massively powerful sphinxes.

Some of the most remarkable of all Egyptian royal portraits come from the lifetime of the great Senwosret III. These are drawn from a series of portraits of the king showing him, alternately, as a young and an old man. The latter are quite extraordinary, showing the king as weary, careworn and with something like an expression of disillusion in his heavily hooded eyes, suggestive of a degree of dejection as profound as that put into the mouth of Amenemhet I.

The Middle Kingdom is rich in portraits of lesser people as much as it is of the kings. There is a large quantity of standing figures of officials and priests, all clearly individualised, usually mature in years and often dressed in a long, enveloping cloak, leaning on a staff, a form of representation popular in the Old Kingdom too. Women are frequently portrayed and, occasionally, children.

Although the later years of the Old Kingdom reveal to an increasing extent the role of the individual in Egyptian society, the individuals who are named tend still to be the favoured servants of a great prince or people who by birth or opportunity are close to the king. There are exceptions, but they are few. Those lesser people who were named owed their identification most commonly to the generosity or affection of someone to whom access to immortality was available. The great mass of the Egyptian people in the time of the Old Kingdom are anonymous, living out their lives in the shadow of the Great Ones.

In the Middle Kingdom this anonymous mass begins to separate and to take on individual identities. Lesser officials, priests in the lower ranks of the temple administrations and soldiers are named, as are the stewards of estates and the upper servants of the magnates. Often they are actually portrayed, the result on the one hand of increasing levels of prosperity seeping down through the society and, on the other, of the skills of artists and craftsmen becoming available to patrons other than the king and his immediate circle. Now the elaborate techniques evolved to preserve the living form of the individual after death, once so exclusive a privilege, began to shared by more and more Egyptians, many of them really quite humble people.

One aspect of this access to immortality is to be found in a new development in Egypt's long-established funerary industry. As more people became eligible for access to the rituals which ensured life after death, a means less costly than the large, sumptuous burial mansions, inscribed with the Pyramid Texts, had to be found. The solution was the manufacture of richly painted anthropoid coffins, moulded into a similacrum of the deceased, ever beautiful, ever young, protected for eternity by a version of the elaborate incantations and liturgies which were inscribed on the interior walls of the tombs of the later kings of the Old Kingdom.[15]

These have become known as 'the Coffin Texts'. They were inscribed on the interior of the coffins in which the mummy of the deceased lay, so that they were forever before his (or her) eyes. Since the Egyptians rarely discarded any idea when they were convinced of its efficacy, the coffins often displayed the recessed and buttressed walls of the ancient tombs, but now in paint rather than brickwork or stone.[16]

For those for whom even a coffin was out of reach, other means of ensuring eternal life were available. It is some of these, the funeral stelae of the ordinary people, which reveal the Egyptians of the Middle Kingdom most appealingly.

From the vast quantity of such *mementi mori* which survive, one instance will be cited here both to demonstrate the practice and to show that the history of Egypt is not exclusively to be seen as a recital of the triumphs and disasters of the Great Ones. Occasionally apparently quite insignificant people appear, clutching their small immortality.

Neferhotep was a musician but, unlike his near namesake of several hundred years earlier, he was never to achieve any sort of greatness, never to be noticed by an indulgent king.[17] He was in the employ of the Overseer of Prophets, Iki, an official in the temple. Neferhotep was a harpist; he was also grossly overweight. The reason is recorded for eternity: Neferhotep is revealed on one of his surviving stela reaching out, with an expression of ineffably greedy anticipation, for the funerary repast which is laid out before him, thus ensuring that he will never go hungry in the afterlife.

But it is not Neferhotep's greed or his skill as a harpist which make his memorials so appealing. On another stela Neferhotep is playing his harp. The inscription records that it was set up to Neferhotep's memory (and to ensure for him an ample and perpetual supply of the good things of life) by 'his friend whom he loved, the Carrier of Bricks, Nebsemenu who has made this for him'. He begs the gods, 'Alas, give him love'.[18]

This stela is one of the few to be signed. Below the relief is the signature 'The Draughtsman Rensonb's son Sonbau'. It is not very skilfully done but we can see that it is done with affection. Neferhotep is shown as he really was, not idealised and ever youthful but as his friends knew and evidently loved him: we must assume that since he apparently had neither wife nor son it was they who performed his obsequies.

All three, the harpist, the beloved friend the Carrier of Bricks, and the Draughtsman's son, must be assumed to have achieved by the survival of their names the immortality which they sought. This is accordingly ensured, allowing them to live happily together in the Duat, the idyllic land to which justified spirits were translated to pass eternity in a glorified version of the Valley or, in Neferhotep's case, in the perpetual consumption of vast amounts of beer, bread, beef, fowl and all his favourite dishes.

The minor arts flourished in the Middle Kingdom. Some of the finest and most resplendent jewellery made in Egypt has been recovered from burials of Middle Kingdom princesses, works of great beauty and exceptional craftsmanship. As was the case of the Hetepheres' furniture and toilet equipment of the early Fourth Dynasty, the treasure of Lahun, the property of the princess Sit-Hathor-Yunet,[19] and of Dahshur, from the tomb of the princess Khunmet,[20] shows how sumptuous must have been the appointments of the court of the Middle Kingdom rulers. Many splendid pectorals, with exquisite workmanship married to rich materials, were part of the royal regalia. The exceptional ability of Egyptian craftsmen to achieve a resplendent effect combined with understatement in their designs and the most exact control of their materials is brilliantly demonstrated in a suite of black stone cups, decorated with a single fine gold line round their rims bearing Amenemhat II's cartouche and found in the Lebanon.[21] They were evidently a gift to a local ruler from the Egyptian king.

Formal relations with other states in the Near East were established during the Middle Kingdom, virtually for the first time. Similarly the kings, evidently concerned at both the emergence and the influence of other states on Egypt's security, waged punitive campaigns in distant places. Even in times of evident prosperity, most of the kings kept a wary eye on conditions at the frontiers and beyond. Their influence was very far-reaching: a cult of Senwosret III was evidently maintained as far away from Egypt as Ankara in Turkey.[22] This was a testimony both to the extent of Egyptian concern with foreign lands and the already growing reputation of Senwosret, which was eventually to assume such immense proportions.

The concern with foreign influences was a matter of policy the necessity for which was imposed on Egypt's administration by the increasing unrest beyond the frontiers and the threat which previously despised and little regarded peoples now posed to the tranquillity of the Valley. As the Twelfth Dynasty cruised placidly on its course, a familiar Egyptian problem recurred: the very peacefulness and prosperity of the Two Kingdoms led to long reigns with sovereigns who, as they grew older, were perhaps less innovative and enterprising than the times demanded. In consequence the pressure on the frontiers increased, as foreign influences saw the opportunity to take advantage of Egypt's deep-rooted sense of security, which could sometimes shade into complacency.

The last king of the Twelfth Dynasty, Amenemhet IV, (1799–1787 BC) enjoyed also one of its shortest reigns. He was succeeded, remarkably, by Egypt's first acknowledged female king, a condition which reflects the titulary adopted by the Egyptian scribes who reported this singular occurrence. Sobekneferu was the sister and probably also the wife of Amenemhet IV. Sadly, she reigned only for about four years (1787–1783) and then she disappears, though the circumstances of her disappearance are obscure. Once more Egypt was to enter a period of uncertainty, this time, to the deep and abiding distress of scribes yet unborn, with an alien people ruling the sacred land.

CHAPTER IX

INVASION: THE SECOND INTERMEDIATE PERIOD

—— •◆• ——

The Twelfth Dynasty, once so vital and assured, declined into oblivion with the short-reigned Queen Sobekneferu. The Thirteenth, a number of whose rulers also bore the name 'Sobek', a crocodile-god to whom they paid particular devotion, may have had a familial connection with its pre-decessor. This line of kings is relatively little known though there is evidence that some degree of prosperity still was maintained and the arts, always a barometer for the times, flourished with fine architecture and some stone-carving of the highest quality being produced. Some of the carving is executed in the hardest of stones, including a wonderful polished yellow quartzite. From this uncertain period derives a rather strange creation, the so-called *ka*-statue of King Awibre-Hor (*c*.1750 BC).[1] He is represented as a naked boy, (though originally he may have worn a gilded kilt) almost life-size, stepping forward from an enclosed wooden niche. On the king's head the two raised arms represent the hieroglyph *ka*, the etheric double of the individual, fashioned at the moment of conception. Awibre-Hor was a very short-lived ruler; his expression of apprehension as he steps out of his shrine was probably well justified.

The events which followed the demise of the Middle Kingdom were, in part, the consequence of its most successful sovereigns' own policies. Egypt, having become much more conscious of the world beyond its frontiers, partly because of the increase in trading activity with much more sophisti-cated systems and networks in place and representing very extensive trading interconnections, was increasingly opening up to foreign influences and to foreigners themselves. The Levant and the eastern Mediterranean generally shared in the rapid growth of trading activity and Egypt, by far the richest country in the world of the time, represented the most appealing market for traders of all nations. To a degree which it had never before experienced Egypt opened itself to foreigners; caravans of exotic traders were depicted in Middle Kingdom tomb reliefs and products from the eastern Mediterranean and the Aegean became familiar in the courts and households of Egypt.

The Twelfth Dynasty kings, in particular, had been adventurous in their overseas campaigning. From these excursions, especially those to the north and east, they returned with booty, captives and hangers-on. These last began to form communities within the Egyptian state which, with the merchants and traders and their entourages moving in and out of the country, began to represent a significant alien component in the society.

Figure 13 The '*ka* statue' of King Awibre-Hor of the Thirteenth Dynasty shows the young king, who reigned only briefly, stepping from his shrine. His inlaid eyes and appearance of apprehension have given this figure, carved from acacia-wood, a very lifelike quality which is almost disturbing.

When the strong central authority of the Twelfth Dynasty kings began to falter it would not have taken long for word to have reached the watchful rulers of neighbouring countries, from agents close to Egypt's own centre of government. Egypt was a prize whose acquisition it would be difficult to resist, nor were the rulers to the north and east, in particular, who had long sustained links with the Delta, inclined to resist it. Invasion was inevitable, the foreign forces being drawn irresistibly as if by a vacuum, into the Valley.

The Thirteenth Dynasty (c.1783–1640 BC), though it continued for a time some of the traditions and policies of those who had gone before it, petered out in a welter of short-lived reigns. The weakness of the dynasty clearly encouraged the ambitions of the watching foreign princes, who seized the opportunity and swept down into the Valley, penetrating it from the north, across the Sinai peninsula and into the Delta.

It is probable that the invaders came from Syro-Palestine; certainly, their names were predominantly Semitic, indicating that they were members of the various tribal groups which occupied the eastern Mediterranean littoral and which had maintained contacts with the Egyptian court for long past. The term generally used to describe the invaders is 'Hyksos' derived from the Egyptian term *Hikau-Khoswet*, meaning 'rulers of foreign lands'.

To the Egyptians in later times the invasion by the despised 'Asiatics', as the peoples from the north and east were dismissively categorised, was the ultimate disgrace and an affront to all that Egypt represented. The foreign princes who established the Fifteenth and Sixteenth Dynasties (c.1640–1532 BC) thrust aside the Fourteenth, a transitory native Egyptian dynasty ruling for a short time from the eastern Delta. They were the first foreigners to rule Egypt; as a result their memory was execrated throughout the remaining centuries of Egyptian history.

During the period when they provided the kings of Egypt, the foreigners seem to have been anxious to conform to Egyptian practice in all matters and to adopt, so far as they were able, Egyptian ways. There was a degree of syncretism promoted between their gods and those of the Egyptian theogonies; this was to have enduring results in bringing changes to the religious practices which came to predominate in later periods of Egyptian history. They were diligent restorers of the great temples and played their part in the eternal round of ceremonies.

There is no evidence of widespread disaffection among either the nobles or the ordinary people of Egypt during most of the time that the foreigners ruled it. On balance, collaboration with an occupying power that seemed disposed to maintain Egyptian traditions and institutions was evidently seen as more sensible than fruitless resistance. That this was evidently the most productive policy was reinforced by the fact that the Hyksos kings confined themselves very largely to the north of the country.

However, the memory of this period bit deeply into the Egyptian collective consciousness, to manifest itself, once Egyptian rule was restored, in the most bitter recriminations against the foreigners. This reaction is the more notable when it is set against recent scholarly views which consider the much later stories of the captivity of the Hebrews in Egypt to be the products of imperfectly recollected memories of the Hyksos occupation of much of northern Egypt during this period.[2] There is no archaeological evidence to support the stories of the captivity in Egypt of a large number of Semitic-language speakers, stories which in any case were not set down in the form in which they have survived until after the Babylonian captivity of the Jews, more than a thousand years later than the invasion of Egypt in the mid-second millennium.

It is profoundly ironic that the myths of the Egyptian captivity, the Exodus and the life of Moses the Lawgiver, should all derive from a period, not of slavery but of sovereignty over at least a part of Egypt by Semitic-speaking invaders. At the time of the Palestinian incursions into Egypt it is not of course possible to speak of the Hebrews, let alone of the Jews; such distinctions simply did not exist. It is possible, even likely, however, that amongst the Syro-Palestinian hordes who came into Egypt at this time were the ancestors of some of those who were to become the Hebrews of the first millennium. After the return from the Babylonian captivity it was these people who conflated the memories of their recent misfortunes with the much more remote memories, distilled from a millennium of storytelling around the campfires of the nomads and the hearths of the more settled people.

There is no episode in Egyptian history which has had so lasting – and, some might say, so malign – an influence on the history of the Western, Judeo-Christian world, than the two centuries in which Semitic-speaking peoples ruled northern Egypt. The foreign princes did indeed leave a bitter legacy behind them.

At another level the presence of the Palestinian invaders from the Syro-Palestinian deserts left a less corrosive but nonetheless enduring influence. Recent excavations at Tell Ed-Daba'a in the eastern Delta have confirmed that it was the capital of the invaders, known in ancient times as Avaris.[3] Amongst the remains on a large and complex site has been found a substantial building, set in a garden, on the walls of which are painted scenes of bull-games, including bull-leaping sequences which are very similar to those which appear in the Cretan palaces, whose discovery made so profound an impact on European art and culture at the beginning of the twentieth century.[4]

Not only are the Ed-Daba'a frescos remarkable for their subject matter and the high quality of the paintings themselves, they are also very significant in that they antedate the earliest Cretan paintings of similar scenes by at least a hundred years. It has been plausibly suggested that the Ed-Daba'a paintings are part of an eastern Mediterranean tradition which was founded on the taste of the many small courts which flourished in the Levant in the second quarter of the second millennium BC.[5] These little courts kept contact, both diplomatically and by way of trade, with Egypt; it has been suggested that the Ed-Daba'a frescos may have been produced for a princess from one of the Levantine states who was married to the then King of Egypt.

There is much evidence for the pursuit of bull-games and for the existence of a long-standing bull-cult in Egypt from early predynastic times. It is very possible that because the foreign centre of influence in Egypt was always in the north, where the bull-cult and bull-games had been established for a very long time, the bull-games were in origin Egyptian, and were exported to the Aegean, later to flourish so remarkably in the island of Crete and later still in Mycenae.

The generally pacific character of the foreign rule of Egypt at this time can be demonstrated by the presence of a native Egyptian Dynasty in southern Egypt which existed quite amicably with the invaders in the north. The Hyksos kings were not, in any case, very much interested in the southern Kingdom, preferring to remain in the north where they could maintain contact with their own ancestral lands in the Levant.

The Seventeenth Dynasty (c.1640–1550 BC) came from the south, from lands around the city of Thebes. Its founders sought to connect themselves with the great kings of the Twelfth Dynasty: one of its earliest princes, who bore the ancient Theban name of Inyotef, adopted the royal style Nebkheperrure. The Seventeenth Dynasty had control of much of the southlands, throughout the Hyksos period: many of the princes were warriors whose memory was long venerated. One of them, Seqenenre Tao, was killed in battle, as the gruesome wounds on his mummy reveal dramatically.

Eventually a native Egyptian prince from this same family brought about the reunification of the Two Lands. Ahmose, son of Kamose, drove out the invaders and, in a very short time brought the Valley again under the unified authority of an Egyptian royal line, the Eighteenth Dynasty (c.1550–1307 BC), one of the longest-lasting and most luxurious in Egyptian history. Thus was inaugurated the last great period of Egyptian history, half a millennium of unexampled splendour in the royal courts and in the power of the temples. This period, known collectively as the New Kingdom (c.1570–1070 BC), was to be remarkable not least for the creation of that contradictory concept, an Egyptian Empire.

CHAPTER X

IMPERIAL EGYPT: THE NEW KINGDOM

———— ·◆· ————

Invasion and the incursion of foreign rulers into Egypt had once again changed the Egyptians' perception of their place in the world. Clearly the episode in which the north of the land was ruled by foreigners was deeply traumatic to the people of the Valley. To the kings of the Fifteenth and Sixteenth Dynasties were attributed all manner of cruelties, blasphemies and general wrongdoing, though these are not apparent from either the archaeological or the documentary records of the times.

Nonetheless, Egypt was now obliged to recognise, beyond a peradventure, that it was part of a larger world. In the New Kingdom Egypt became a world power: as such it was compelled to admit the existence of other, perhaps lesser but nonetheless competing states. For much of the next five hundred years Egypt was unequivocally the greatest power in the ancient world but that greatness and power began to be judged on a human scale, expressed in the proportions of empire.

This period of Egypt's history began most auspiciously with Theban princes once more bringing about the Valley's consolidation. The beginning of the Eighteenth Dynasty was also notable in that three great queens were associated with its foundation and were long to be honoured as patrons of the Kingship and of the Two Lands. In a country which tended to be male-dominated, the place of women was nonetheless acknowledged and clearly important, in rank, status and responsibility. However, during the New Kingdom women come to be seen much more as equal partners with men in the business of government, and the wives of the kings emerge often as influential, even formidable proponents of the royal power.

The presence of the three queens at the outset of what was to prove one of the most luxurious and graceful periods of Egyptian history is particularly telling. In this, as in many other ways which will become evident, the New Kingdom marked a departure for Egypt from its previously established procedures. The three queens stood at the threshold of the new dynasty. Each was the wife, sometimes also the sister and the mother of kings; as such they were revered as ancestresses of the dynasty and long-lasting cults were established to their memory.

The eldest of the three was Tetisheri, the wife of Senakhtenre Ta'a I, one of the later kings of the Seventeenth Dynasty. In many ways the most remarkable of the three, Tetisheri was of humble, not of royal, birth. She lived long, into the lifetime of her grandsons, both rulers of Egypt.

She was the mother of Seqenenre Ta'o II (*c*.1560 BC), who was to be killed in battle. He married his sister, Ahhotpe I and they produced Kamose, the Theban prince who laid the foundations for the reconquest of the Valley. When Kamose died he was succeeded by his brother Ahmose, who was acknowledged as the first king of the Eighteenth Dynasty (*c*.1550 BC). He was evidently a child at his accession and his mother Ahhotpe acted as regent.

The third queen of the line whose memory was long honoured was Ahmose-Nefertari, the sister-wife of Ahmose whose son, Amenhotep I (*c*.1526–1506 BC) was also too young to rule at his accession. At her death she was venerated throughout Egypt and her cult remained popular for long afterwards.

The influence of these women and of the others who were to be dominant at other times in the Eighteenth Dynasty is not inconsistent with the Egyptian view of the world. Although there is no evidence of an all-powerful Mother Goddess cult in Egypt at any time, in the mythology of the Kingship the role of Hathor, the mother of Horus (later assimilated with Isis, the sister-wife of Osiris) is crucial. The succession to the throne in fact went through the female line, hence the practice of brother marrying sister, or, in later times, father daughter. The royal blood, since the kings were incarnate gods, was sacred. The marriage of close blood relations obviously can have considerable physiological and psychological consequences but these do not seem to have affected the Dynasty very noticeably, except perhaps at its very end. Though the rate of infant and child mortality was inevitably very high, there is no independent evidence of significant genetic malfunction. In any case the marriage of close blood relatives was not especially significant in a society which practised polygamy on the generous scale of the kings of Egypt. It is perhaps not accidental that many of the most influential women in the dynasty were not of royal birth.

Frequently, where only an heiress was left, her marriage would convey the Kingship to her consort. The myth of the young prince or even the young commoner who marries the King's daughter and succeeds to the Kingdom has its origins here.

The act of the king seating himself on the throne at his coronation was the moment at which he was invested, not only with the Kingship, but with divinity. The throne was personified as Isis (the hieroglyph of her name actually pictured the throne) and by his contact with her lap the king became a god. This event was iconographically represented in somewhat later times by the statues of Isis holding Horus, the divinely reincarnated king, seated on her lap, an icon which was to have an enduring influence long after Egypt's decline.

This open acknowledgment of the power of the feminine is significant in the later development of the Egyptian psyche and is virtually unique in the ancient world. The Egyptian experience of the feminine principle is altogether more benign than that of societies which had acknowledged a supreme Mother Goddess. The recognition of the female principle effectively as equal with the male may account for the exceptional balance of tensions in the Egyptian society throughout most of its history. Its origins possibly lie in the African strain which was of great importance in forming the historic Egyptian personality, where queens, and especially queens mother, have exercised a powerful influence in the society and, even in the present day, will often determine the succession to the Kingship or chieftaincy; this process may still be observed in some African chiefly societies where the queens mother have the right of naming the successor to a dead paramount chief.

It may not be entirely fanciful to suggest that the New Kingdom is somehow more feminine in character than its predecessors. Not only do women appear in much more significant roles in the society than hitherto, but even the art of the New Kingdom displays a softer, lighter, more delicate character (except perhaps in architecture) than had ever been the case before. If these qualities can be defined as feminine, then their influence can be seen strikingly over the next five hundred years.

Life in New Kingdom Egypt reveals sharp differences in virtually every department, compared with the millennium and a half which had gone before it. The administration itself, always one of the most highly developed aspects of Egyptian life, became even more pervasive, a massive bureaucracy usually organised under two powerful viziers, with parallel organisations for each of the Two Kingdoms and an administration which increasingly affected the lives of all the people. The temples developed their own religious bureaucracies still further and exercised a far from benign influence on the political economy. For the first time a standing army became a feature of the society, with predictable and far-reaching consequences.

At the top of the pyramid of administration the king continued his life apart, though now he was engaged in every phase of the Kingdom's management. He was still honoured as a god, though his divinity was certainly less unreserved than had been the case in the not so distant past. However, when the king was a powerful and determined ruler he was able to influence events very substantially.

Egypt now entered a phase of its history where it became the archetype of the oriental despotism, with the all-powerful ruler surrounded less by reverential awe than by the deference to which absolute power, absolutely manifested, gives occasion. Throughout the ancient Near East for the next fifteen hundred years and more, empires and powerful kingdoms would rise and fall which to a greater or a lesser degree drew their inspiration and certainly their trappings of authority from the Egyptian model.

But once again Egypt itself was changing. Whilst many of the New Kingdom's works of art were delicate, finely crafted, elaborately decorated, and highly naturalistic, the architecture which began to predominate in the mid-second millennium was massive in scale, with special value being placed upon the use of brilliant colour and the effects of mass, heightened with an extraordinarily skilful use of natural light and shadow. The abilities of the artisan, sometimes at the expense of the innovating and creative artist, were especially to the fore. The sculpture of the period, especially royal sculpture, is superbly executed, vigorous and clearly the result of skilful observation and immensely refined technique. It lacks, however, that quality of transcendence which the finest works of both the Old and Middle Kingdoms so movingly display.

During the New Kingdom unparalleled riches flowed into Egypt, the product of conquest, tribute from client kings and princes, and trade. Egypt, it might be said, invented luxury and the court and the magnates enjoyed it to the uttermost. No other nation on earth approached Egypt's opulence, splendour and extravagance. The deference of client kings, revealed by their correspondence with the King of Egypt, reflects an acute awareness of the wealth which he was known to possess and the power which he was expected to wield.

Much of the accepted image of ancient Egypt in the Western world derives from this time. The immense temples built at Thebes by the kings of the Eighteenth Dynasty, and maintained and extended by later dynasties, are the hallmark of Egypt at the high point of its political influence and have come to be recognised as the archetypal buildings in which it is appropriate to honour divinities.

The kings of the Eighteenth Dynasty were amongst the most prolific builders in Egypt's long history. With the memory of the two periods of the disintegration of the royal administration of Egypt behind them, they were concerned to give a visible and enduring dimension to their rule of the Two Kingdoms. The panoply of the royal state was one way in which this could be effected; another device, which stimulated the building of the great temples at Thebes and at other centres throughout the Two Lands, was the consequence of a deliberate policy to forge an indissoluble alliance between the royal house and the powerful temple administrations.

A flood of riches was also directed towards the temples and their very receptive priesthoods. The estates managed for the benefit of the temples grew vastly; by the Ramesside Dynasty (early twelfth century BC) one-third of the land of Egypt was owned by the temples.[1] This policy was part of the reason for the survival of the New Kingdom over five centuries but it also sowed the seeds of the destruction of Egypt's immemorial civilisation and the final, persistent violation of the Valley by foreigners.

The Theban family which provided the Eighteenth Dynasty sovereigns, like their predecessors, tended to recycle a limited number of names which they adopted at their coronations. In the early years of the dynasty Thutmoses ('Born of Thoth') was the preferred name, followed by Amenhotep ('Amun is Satisfied').

One of the reasons for the considerable political power enjoyed by women during the Eighteenth Dynasty was the consequence of the frequent minority of the king at his accession. The first Thutmoses (c.1504–1492 BC) was another such youthful king whose mother acted as his regent.

After the death of Thutmoses II (c.1479 BC) a similar situation arose, when the succession was in some doubt and the choice fell on the young son of the late king by a minor wife, who became Thutmoses III. Thutmoses I had a son and a daughter by an earlier, royal wife. This son, for whatever reason, was not considered for the succession or was not available. Thutmoses I's daughter married her half-brother, who succeeded as Thutmoses II; when he died his sister-wife was still very much in evidence and seized the opportunity to have herself proclaimed, first, regent to the young Thutmoses III who now succeeded and then, not queen-regnant, but king. This was the formidable Hashshepsowe, known also by the name Hatshepsut (c.1473–1458 BC).

She was another of the dominant women which the Theban family seemed to have produced with such frequency, the most assertive indeed of all of them. Her insistence on being portrayed always as a king was statement enough and she ruled with vigour and a sure hand, at least for most of her reign of twenty-one years.

She seems to have maintained some sort of intimate relationship with her architect Senenmut, who may have been the father of her daughter Neferure; perhaps he played Potemkin to her Catharine, whom she considerably resembled. He is famously portrayed holding the little princess in his arms or between his legs, in an unusually tender and intimate representation.

According to Hashepsowe's portraits she was slight and graceful; her insistence on the myth of her Kingship did not extend to have herself portrayed as in any way masculine, except for the presence of the sacred beard which, incongruously, she wore beneath her lightly boned chin. The contrast between the delicate-featured Egyptian queen, with the strongly sculpted nose which seems to have been an inherited characteristic of the Theban family, and her most famous state visitor, the gross, steatopygous queen of Punt, shown in the reliefs in Hashepsowe's mortuary temple, must have been remarkable.

Hashepsowe was, in the tradition of her family, a diligent builder. She renewed the temples of the gods in generous measure and many of her works, such as the lovely rose-granite temple at Karnak, with its elegant hieroglyphs and inscriptions, at once look back to the grace of the Middle Kingdom and forward to the approaching Amarnan age.

The most splendid survival from Hashepsowe's reign is undoubtedly the tomb which she built for herself, at Deir el-Bahri, where, long before, Nebhetepre Montuhotpe II had built his great monument. Hashepsowe laid out another immense terraced structure, in the process cheerfully burying (and thus preserving) a large part of Nebhetepre Montuhotpe's tomb. Much of Hashepsowe's survives, somewhat surprisingly given the depredations which were to be wrought on all her monuments by her successor. In the context of her temple the queen had no reservations about asserting her femininity, identifying herself with the goddess Hathor. She had the episode of the Queen of Punt's visit carved on the walls; she even permitted Senenmut, probably the architect of Deir el-Bahri, a small place in one of the side chapels. He enjoyed the title, amongst others, of 'Chief Steward of Amun', not an especially exalted appointment. Before the end of her reign, he seems to have fallen into disfavour and nothing is heard of him after the queen's nineteenth year.

All the while that Hashepsowe was ruling Egypt the young Thutmoses, who had been proclaimed king as a boy, was kept in obscurity whilst the Queen held the reins of government of the Two Lands firmly in her hands. At some point, however, Thutmoses and his partisans revolted against what they could with reason regard as Hashshepsowe's usurpation of the Kingship. Hashepsowe disappears and Thutmoses III, like a new sun, rises over Egypt (1479–1425 BC).

Thutmoses was another of Egypt's great kings. His reign was long and he was a man of exceptional administrative ability who imposed his control over all the departments of government swiftly and firmly. He was also a warrior and he extended the boundaries of Egypt to an extent greater than they had ever been. He imposed Egyptian suzerainty over great swathes of the Near East, with client kings as far away as north Syria paying tribute to him. He was as remarkable a commander as Senwosret I, whom he most closely resembles.

Once Thutmoses became the unchallenged sovereign he set out, with a sort of grim determination, to obliterate the memory of Hashepsowe. All the monuments which bore her name on which he could lay his hands he destroyed. So thorough was the process of his elimination of all traces of the queen, the wonder is that anything survives at all. His evident dislike of Hashepsowe did not however, inhibit him from marrying her daughter, the same Neferure who was portrayed as a little girl, in the arms of Senenmut.

But Thutmoses was not only a great destroyer; he was also a great builder. Some of the greatest monuments in Egypt which survive are from his time. His tomb, as befitting so great a king, is one of the wonders of the Valley of the Kings which, by the time of his reign had become the principal burial place of the Theban monarchs.

In its record of foreign conquest, the flood of riches into Egypt, the extent of royal building programmes and the splendour of the king and the royal court, the reign of Thutmoses represents one of the peaks of the history of the kings of Egypt. What came after was, with a few exceptions, something of a decline from the qualities which had made Egypt great.

Figure 14 King Thutmoses III of the Eighteenth Dynasty, one of the greatest kings of the New Kingdom, a warrior and a man of sensitivity and culture.

The long reign of Thutmoses ended tranquilly; he died knowing that he had raised Egypt to unexampled heights of power and prestige. He was succeeded by his son, Amenhotep II (1427–1401 BC), who followed the example of his father worthily; he, too, was a forceful soldier, evidently with a streak of cruelty which does not seem to have been typical of Thutmoses. He is known to have hung the bodies of defeated princes from the prows of his ships, no doubt to discourage others who might be inclined to resist Egyptian rule. He was a keen hunter and, like all his house, a determined builder. His tomb, in the Valley of the Kings, was not especially notable but for the fact that when it was excavated it was found to contain the mummies of several important kings in addition to his own, of whom the most distinguished was none other than that of his father, Thutmoses III himself. The other mummies, of some of Egypt's greatest kings and queens, had been hidden in the tomb by order of one of the High Priests of the Twenty-First Dynasty, at a time when there was a serious outbreak of tomb-robbing in the Valley.[2]

The fourth king to bear the name Thutmoses followed Amenhotep II. He is best remembered, in a fairly uneventful reign (c.1401–1391 BC), for his clearing away of the sand which obscured the Sphinx. He recounted a dream which he had when, as a young prince with no expectations of the succession, he slept between the Sphinx's paws, after a day's hunting. The god, in the form Harakte with whom the Sphinx was identified in the New Kingdom, promised him the crowns of Egypt if he would clear away the sand. He did so and, naturally enough became king, though he reigned barely for a decade.

Amenhotep III was a boy of 12 when he succeeded to the throne, which he was to occupy with singular magnificence for many years (c.1391–1353 BC).[3] His mother, though technically a concubine, acted as regent during his minority, thus repeating a pattern made familiar by other occasions in the Dynasty. Amenhotep married young and, when he did so, married for what some have thought to have been love. His wife was a commoner or at any rate not royal. Queen Tiy joins the lengthening line of powerful women who are so much a feature of this dynasty.

Tiy was the daughter of an influential couple, prominent at the court, Yuya and Tuya. It may indeed have been policy as much as inclination which linked Amenhotep with such leading people; throughout his life he was to use marriage as a tactic to develop or cement alliances. The association with Yuya's family was to have long-term consequences. Tiy's influence on the course of Egyptian history effected through her son who was to reign as Amenhotep IV–Akhenaten, was to be very great. Her portraits suggest that there was an African strain in her ancestry.

Amenhotep III presided over a period of the greatest opulence which opulent Egypt had ever enjoyed. The quality of craftsmanship developed in his service is superlative and the use of materials never less than sumptuous.

Figure 15   King Amenhotep III, of the Eighteenth Dynasty, in the company of the crocodile-headed god Sobek. To judge by his appearance, looking little more than a boy, this pair-statue was produced early in the king's reign.

His portraits show him ageing, from a handsome young king, apparently to a bloated and dissolute voluptuary. This may, however, be unfair for the king, despite his wealth and power, suffered very poor health for much of the latter part of his reign.

Though Amenhotep III's reign was deeply peaceful, a time for Egypt to renew itself after the preceding centuries which had seen extended periods of uncertainty, even sometimes of turmoil, there were nonetheless increasing indications that all was not well with the Empire. The world outside Egypt was developing rapidly and, in Anatolia, the northern Levant and in Mesopotamia were states with powerful military capabilities which were ready to disengage themselves from the subservience which they had endured, to a greater or a lesser extent, since the conquests of Thutmoses III. This situation was to deteriorate further until it reached a crisis point in the reign of Amenhotep IV.

Like all the great kings Amenhotep III was a prodigious builder. His works ranged from Nubia to the Delta; many survive to the present day. He built an immense funerary temple for himself at Malkata, near Thebes, of which only two huge seated figures remain today, 'the Colossi of Memnon'. He particularly promoted the cult of the goddess Sekhmet, whose lioness-headed statues were made in great quantity and are to be found in many of the most important Egyptological collections through-out the world. His devotion to Sekhmet may have been the consequence of his own ill-health, for she was a goddess especially identified with healing.

Amenhotep III died after nearly forty years as king. His mummy, too, was eventually to be hidden away with the others, packed into Amenhotep II's tomb. Like them, this most magnificent of Egypt's kings finds his present resting place in the Egyptian Museum in Cairo.

With the possible exception of Tutankhamun, whose brief life, briefer reign and extraordinary resurrection are described in Chapter XI, no king of Egypt has excited more extravagant and often over-excited speculation than Amenhotep IV who, in the fourth year of his reign, assumed the name Akhenaten. He has been claimed as a revolutionary, a monotheist, a creative innovator of genius, a precursor of Moses. With the possible exception of the third of these he was none of them.[4]

Akhenaten was the second son of Amenhotep III and Queen Tiy. His elder brother, the heir, did not succeed and presumably predeceased his father. The younger brother succeeded as Amenhotep IV (c.1353–1335 BC).

The Great Event of Akhenaten's reign was his uprooting of the royal capital from Thebes down-river to a virgin location, at the site known today as Tel el-Amarna where he founded the city of Akhetaten, 'the Horizon of the Aten'.[5] At the same time he deposed Amun from his Kingship of the gods and proclaimed the Aten, the personification of the sun's rays, as the supreme divinity to whom worship was to be paid.

Figure 16   King Amenhotep IV-Akhenaten had himself portrayed in a distinctive fashion, exemplified by this head. He was responsible for the introduction of a new, naturalistic but at the same time highly mannered style of Egyptian art, as part of his promotion of the worship of the Aten as the supreme god of Egypt.

Or so it is usually alleged. In fact the old gods of Egypt remained in place, though somewhat subdued, and the divinity of the king was in no way diminished. If Akhenaten was a religious revolutionary, it was within very conservative bounds.

But it is clear that Akhenaten had a vision of the relationship of the divine principle to Egypt, its people and its king, which was at odds with the conventional religion of the Two Lands. Already the power of the priesthood was increasing dramatically, as a result of the generous bene-factions of earlier rulers in the Eighteenth Dynasty. Something like a parallel, temple-based bureaucracy had arisen which at times clearly conflicted with the priorities of the royal administration.

The power of the priests and the rising influence of the Aten were already to be seen in the reign of Akhenaten's father. There is some evidence that Queen Tiy, who lived on well into Akhenaten's reign, was an enthusiastic supporter of the new cult, if to call it that is somewhat to overstate its character and importance. She insisted on moving to Akhetaten when her son transferred his capital there; clearly, she exercised a powerful influence on him whilst he lived.

Akhenaten's name is forever linked with the evidently quite stupen-dously beautiful Nefertiti, whose enigmatic bust, with its barely visible smile and the disconcerting blank eye, has become an icon both of feminine beauty and of the Amarnan period as a whole. She bore Akhenaten six daughters; she, too, was translated to Akhetaten but there seems to have been a rift between the king and herself and nothing is heard of her after his twelfth year.

There is no doubt a deal of truth in the frequently projected image of Akhenaten as a religious zealot, caught up wholly in his particular view of the world, cut off from reality but inspiring a group of followers who shared his vision. During the Amarnan period the king neglected many of the affairs of state which normally absorbed the holders of his office; this was notably true of Egypt's relations with the world outside, where the needs of its garrisons, and the client kings who depended upon them, were ignored.

Other than within the carefully demarcated precincts of Akhetaten,[6] the great traditions of royal munificence in building for the gods went unful-filled. The most diligent attention, however, was given to acts of destruction, the excision of the name of Amun, or of any compound which contained it, from the monuments of the past.

All this is all too familiarly redolent of the religious fanatic, locked in the darkness of his own obsessions. The unbalanced insistence on a theo-centric system of government has too many precedents to make Akhenaten an easy companion.

It is in the realm of the arts that Akhenaten deserves more than a foot-note in the long history of Egypt. If contemporary inscriptions are to be believed (and there is no reason, *prima facie*, why they should not be) the king himself instructed his artists and craftsmen carefully in the effects which he wanted to achieve. This may be nothing more than the type of propaganda which makes Stalin or Mao the source of all creative inspiration. In the case of the Amarnan style, however, the effects are so distinctive that it is highly probable that they emerged from one, deeply neurotic but powerful source.

This said, it must be acknowledged that much Amarnan art is delightful, highly naturalistic, sometimes perhaps a little sentimentalised: occasionally it is Mabel Lucie Atwell who seems to be in charge rather than Leonardo. It is certainly profoundly different, in respect of its portrayal of the king and his family, from anything which had gone before. The royal portraiture now has an unbuttoned quality, literally so since the king and his children are sometimes shown nude, the king disturbingly sexless and the Queen wrapped only in a diaphanous robe, the depiction of which was one of the artistic triumphs which the previous reign of Amenhotep III had achieved.

It is of particular interest, in the context of the artistic production of the Amarnan period, that the name of one of Akhenaten's principal creative assistants is known. This was Bak, the chief sculptor, a man evidently of modest origins who caught the attention of the king who made him responsible for carrying his ideas into sculpted form. The names of few artists of Bak's relatively modest status have survived, in contrast to the officials who had more opportunity to provide for their own immortality. Bak's funerary stela survives, where he is shown, as pot-bellied as a nineteenth-century alderman, with his wife.[6] The series of events by which the stela of Bak was lost to the British Museum and reached its present home in Berlin is one of the more farcical episodes in twentieth-century Egyptology.[7]

Another of the artists who was of importance during Akhenaten's time was Thutmose, in the ruins of whose workshop the bust of Nefertiti was found. She too now resides in Berlin (having been taken there, the Egyptians maintain, illegally) where she was admired, in a peculiarly surrealist episode at the height of National Socialist rule, by Hitler: another episode in the footnotes of Egyptology which deserves perhaps to be better known.[8]

It is, however, the personality of the king which posterity has cherished. To Siegmund Freud he was the first monotheist;[8] this he patently was not for there are plenty of contenders earlier than him for such a title, for behind all the many gods of Egypt there always lay the One unnamed and unknowable divinity 'He whose name is hidden'. Freud also saw him as the contemporary of Moses and detected influences in some of the hymns and religious inscriptions of the Amarnan period on what has come to be known as Mosaic teachings. As there is actually no historical evidence for the existence of Moses, the books which are ascribed to him having been written down nearly a thousand years after Akhenaten's lifetime, this association is, to express it mildly, tenuous. But this is not to denigrate the value of the literary works ascribed to Akhenaten, which have a pleasingly ethereal quality to them and which do genuinely seem to reflect a concern for all the complexities and infinite variety of life.[9] This concern for the natural world, though wholly Egyptian in nature, had seldom been expressed verbally, the natural form of expression of the Egyptian psyche having always seemed to be in the plastic arts: Akhenaten or his publicists achieved a felicity of expression which is still greatly appealing.

For reasons which must have been locked deep in Akhenaten's own psyche he chose frequently to have himself portrayed in the most grotesque manner. He is shown with a gross, distended stomach and improbably wide hips, a long thin neck and facial features of a subject in the advanced stages of a wasting disease. Sometimes, however, the skill of the sculptor gives him an expression of radiant beauty. Akhenaten was, and remains, an enigma.

It is not usual in respectable academic contexts to mention the name of Immanuel Velikovsky, the author of a number of sensational revisions of the chronology of the second and first millennia and a forceful advocate of the theory of catastrophism, other than to mock or to dismiss his speculations peremptorily. However, there is one case in which, in this writer's view at least, Velikovsky proposes a most convincing theory: this is his identification between the royal families of the two Thebes, the Egyptian Thebes and the other in Sparta, of which Oedipus was king.[10] Velikovsky manages, with considerable skill and with less than usual resort to the special pleading of which he was not infrequently guilty, to identify all the players in Oedipus' tragic destiny with those who ruled Egypt, five hundred years before the time when Oedipus limped into *his* Thebes.

Akhenaten disappeared after the seventeenth year of his reign. Nothing is known of his passing. It is probable that he was succeeded for a short time by a young prince, Smenkhkara (c.1338–1336 BC), who may have been his son, or, more likely, his nephew or cousin. Little is known of him either, other than from a few portraits of a rather epicene youth. He, too, disappeared, to be succeeded in turn by one who was amongst the least but at the same time the most famous of all Egypt's kings.

CHAPTER XI

TUTANKHAMUN AND THE
REAFFIRMATION OF AMUN

——— ·◆· ———

Apart from two world wars, the slaughter of millions by totalitarian regimes and, though less certainly, the extension of *Homo sapiens'* dominion to the moon, no single event in the twentieth century had so profound an impact, nor set up so many resonances, as the discovery of the tomb of Nebkheperu-Ra Tutankhamun (c.1333–1323 BC) in the Valley of the Kings in 1922. The story has been told countless times:[1] how Howard Carter and his employer, the Earl of Carnarvon, after years of largely fruitless excavation in Egypt, in virtually the last days of their concession to dig in the Valley came upon the burial place of the least of the monarchs of the New Kingdom and found it a treasure trove the like of which the modern world had never seen. At once all the stories which had entranced generations since storytelling began, of the finding, in a remote and secret place, of treasures beyond computation, were given the force of truth.

The effect of the discovery was extraordinary. In the immediate aftermath of a particularly dreadful conflict which had caused the deaths of millions, which had destroyed a world which had endured, largely unchanging, for centuries, and which was the prelude to world-wide repression, depression and deprivation, the discovery of this golden boy and his incalculable riches was bound to be an event of great power. It was the more so since, for the first time, the distant past could be brought to life by the application of all the techniques of modern publicity and media exploitation. This last consequence of the discovery has continued without abatement ever since.

The contents of Tutankhamun's small, hidden tomb, with its six little rooms – the very modesty of their scale made it easy for a wide public to identify with them, if not so readily with what they contained – were, in Carter's word, 'wonderful'. The abundance of gold and gilding alone would ensure that a world increasingly bereft of splendour would respond with wonder and delight at their revelation. Whilst honesty compels the observer to acknowledge that some of the objects with which the king was buried were, when judged by the highest standards of Egyptian art, of dubious taste, some are superlative: most are of outstanding craftsmanship, even when the design is not of the happiest.[2]

Tutankhamun's tomb reveals the heights which Egyptian technique, especially in wood-carving, gilding and the making of fine jewels, had achieved in the New Kingdom. Workers in precious metals and in a thousand specialisations were recruited, organised and set to work on the king's treasury for the afterlife, all to be completed in the seventy days from death to the final interment in his House of Millions of Years. His tomb was entered by robbers, probably not long after his burial. For whatever reason they left hurriedly, and did not return. The tomb was then entirely forgotten until the twentieth century.

Tutankhamun's paternity is still doubtful, though it is likely that he was a son of Akhenaten, by one of his lesser wives, not by Nefertiti. He was a child when he succeeded: a charming object from the tomb, the golden haft from a walking stick,[3] shows him as a chubby little boy, wearing the warrior's blue crown and holding himself very upright with his stomach drawn tightly in, as no doubt his tutors had instructed him. Little is known of his reign, though it is clear that the priests of Amun who had been dispossessed by Akhenaten reasserted their authority, moved the capital back to Thebes, renamed the king, hitherto Tutankhaten, and execrated 'the Heretic of Amarna', cutting away his name wherever it was to be found in inscriptions. But, though his life was obscure and his reign relatively unimportant, the excavation of Tutankhamun's tomb gave the world some idea of what it was to be a king of Egypt.

Part of the significance of the recovery of Tutankhamun, for his body was preserved as well as his regalia and possessions,[4] was accounted for by the fact that he was so small a king, amongst the least of the great monarchs who had enjoyed the Dual Kingship, whose very existence had been questioned only a short time before Carter found him in the Valley. If the discovery had been of one of the great Thutmosids or Amenhoteps, for example, paradoxically the impact might not have been as great as the finding of this boy, the formulation of whose given name was unique in all the annals of Egypt before or after his brief lifetime; he died when he was probably about 19 years old.

Thus this most obscure of the kings of Egypt became the most familiar of all, his name applied to countless objects, designs, films and books. It was as if the world had been waiting for his return; the myth of the Returning King is an enduring one and in Tutankhamun's case it had become reality. He was the archetype of the Young Prince, the Beautiful Boy, the *Puer Aeturnus*, who awaits rebirth constantly in a variety of forms, some benign, some deeply menacing.

But Tutankhamun was all light. The scenes which showed him, with his young wife, hunting in the marshes on his skiff and in the myriad of *ushabti* figures, some of the finest carvings in the tomb, portray a young prince, carefree and by no means especially god-like.

The portraits of Tutankhamun in his tomb show a remarkable consistency which suggests that they are close to actual likeness. He is represented as quite exceptionally beautiful, an essential quality of the archetype; following the reign of Akhenaten, when there was some attempt to represent the royal family naturistically, a practice which continued in Tutankhamun's lifetime, it can, with reasonable assurance, be assumed that the portraits show the king much as he was. In later years, had he lived, he would no doubt have grown as portly as his likely grandfather, Amenhotep III, whom he somewhat resembles. But Tutankhamun was never to be old.

The circumstances of his burial were remarkable enough. His mummified body, badly affected by the action of the resins in the process which was supposed to preserve it, was contained in a series of magnificent gold coffins, each one with a representation of the king, each subtly different as though the craftsmen were representing the king in different moods, or, simply, as he was seen to each. One of the coffins, the second, was probably intended originally for Smenkhkara and hence is not a portrait of Tutankhamun at all.[5] The coffins, one inside the other, are hugely bulky; in turn they are contained inside a series of three wooden shrines, which carry on them a version of the Book of the Dead, the spells and prayers designed to carry the King safely to the afterlife, which descend ultimately from the ancient Pyramid Texts, through the Coffin Texts of the Middle Kingdom. The shrines are built on the scale of rooms; the outer shrine is notable for the four exquisite figures of goddesses who stand by them, their wings and arms outstretched protectively around the king's mummy. Even so small a king as Tutankhamun could expect to have gods and goddesses at his service.

But the noblest of all the representations of Tutankhamun, which emphasises his divinity and the majesty of his office, is the immense gold mask which was placed over the head of his mummy, in the innermost of the coffins; after the Pyramids it is perhaps the most universally reproduced of all Egyptian artifacts. This is not the portrait of a slender boy but of a god-king, living for ever and ever. Few photographs do the mask justice: gold is a difficult material to photograph without it assuming the consistency of brass. The most successful is perhaps the first to be taken, by Harry Burton,[6] the American photographer who was present in the tomb from the time of its opening.

In Burton's photograph the mask appears still wreathed with the garlands which were laid around it more than three thousand years before. The presence of the flowers and the little smudges of dust which Burton and Carter did not remove, to avoid destroying the garlands, give the mask an extraordinary living presence.

When cleaned and cleared of the scattering of flowers the mask is magnificent, a triumph, if not of high art, then certainly of the highest craftsmanship. But it is clearly an artifact whereas, in Burton's photograph, the king lives.

The impact of the discovery of Tutankhamun can perhaps best be appreciated by comparing the finding of his tomb with the near-contemporary excavation of the Royal Tombs at the Sumerian city of Ur by Sir Leonard

Figure 17 The gold mask which covered the head of King Tutankhamun is one of the most familiar of Egyptian icons. The most moving reproduction of the mask is this photograph, less familiar than those which show it after it was cleaned. This was the first record of the mask, taken when it was uncovered by Howard Carter in the king's tomb in the Valley of the Kings. The dust and the remains of the garlands which were placed in the king's coffin give this image a living, deeply moving quality.

Woolley. For barbaric splendour combined with *grand guignol*, the great death pits at Ur should totally have eclipsed Tutankhamun, yet they did not do so.

Woolley found a number of burials, sunk deep in what was evidently a royal or sacred burial site, on the outskirts of Ur, one of the most important of Sumer's city-states. The burials were much earlier than Tutankhamun's, c.2600 BC, and thus earlier even than the Giza Pyramids. Altogether Woolley found sixteen burials which he believed were of royal personages. In the stone-lined vaults, deep in the earth, were found the remains of high-status burials, attended by the most elaborate panoply of death. The principal occupants of the tomb were attended by ranks of courtiers, musicians, soldiers, wagoners (with their wagons and the oxen which drew them) all neatly laid out, for a carefully organised ceremony of death.

The artifacts which were buried with them were of the most superb craftsmanship, elegant, austere but at the same time extremely rich in material and adornment. They are, it must be said, very un-Sumerian in design and craftsmanship.

Unlike the excavation of Tutankhamun's tomb, which has never been professionally published, Woolley unleashed a stream of sumptuous and detailed reports on his excavations, supported by many popular publications.[7] Yet for every thousand people who know the name Tutankhamun there may be one who recognises Ur and its royal burials, even when it carries its biblical ascription 'of the Chaldees' with its putative connection with Abraham, the Friend of God.

The reason for the lesser impact of the Royal Tombs of Ur is that they were not redolent of the archetypes in the way in which the tomb of Tutankhamun was so liberally provided. Sumer, despite the fact that it is probably the culture in which writing evolved into something more than a simple device for the convenience of accountants, has never caught the world's imagination in the way in which Egypt has done. Waiting in his tomb for three thousand two hundred years, Tutankhamun was the heir to all the immense accumulation of wonder and respect which Egypt had engendered and, in his own person, was to be identified as an archetypal figure such as only Egypt could apparently produce.

Tutankhamun was the last lineal descendant of Ahmose, who had founded the Eighteenth Dynasty more than two hundred years earlier. What has been interpreted as the marks of a blow behind his ear and a displaced piece of bone, possibly dislodged from the interior of his skull, have prompted suggestions that he was murdered. He left no heir though two female foetuses were found in his tomb, perhaps his children who had been born prematurely. He had married a daughter of Akhenaten, Ankhesena'amun, whose name had been changed from Ankhesenpa'aten. She brings her own small element of tragedy to the decline of the Thutmosid house. Evidently bereft at the death of Tutankhamun, for they are often depicted, like two flower children, charmingly engaged in simple pleasures (and she it was who scattered flowers in his tomb), she appealed to the great King of the Hittites, Suppululiumas, to send her one of his sons, that he might become King of Egypt. That such a message was sent at all is a measure both of the desperation of Ankhesena'amun and those around her and of the state of Egypt. Suppululiumas agreed and despatched his son Zennanza with a suitable escort south to Egypt. He never reached Ankhesena'amun for he was murdered on the way. Of Ankhesena'amun, nothing more is ever heard.

She may have had one more duty laid upon her however. As the daughter of Akhenaten she bore the right to the throne within her, hence her invitation to Suppululiumas. Now there appears a figure from the relatively distant past, Ay, a son of Yuya and Tuya, who had given their daughter Tiy to Amenhotep III and who had exercised such great influence on his reign and that of Akhenaten. Her brother had shared in the fortune which her elevation had brought to the family of Yuya. He held offices of power and influence under both Amenhotep and Akhenaten.

He now suddenly appears as King of Egypt (c.1323–1319 BC) conducting the funeral ceremonies for Tutankhamun as if he were the latter's son, despite the great difference in their ages.[8] Ay was old; he reigned for only four years and it is likely that he only secured the throne by taking the heiress in marriage.

During his reign he continued the execration of Akhenaten which the angry priests of Amun of Thebes had so vigorously initiated. He attributed all Egypt's ills to the follies and neglect of Akhenaten's reign. Like all political survivors he did not feel it necessary to explain or apologise for his part in them.

The death of Ay left another problem for the succession because he, too, was childless. By some process which is unknown a successor was found who had no familial connection with the Dynasty, though he is always counted as one of its kings. Presumably he emerged as the choice of the great magnates – and, no doubt, of the priests – who were concerned to secure the stability of the Kingdoms. Their choice, however it was made, was fortunate.

The chosen successor was one Horemhab, a senior army officer who had distinguished himself not only in campaigns but as an administrator. He seems to have been intelligent, clear-sighted and honourable; he was to make an admirable king (c.1319–1307 or 1291 BC). He had served Tutankhamun as a commanding general and had accompanied the young king on campaigns into Syria, where no doubt he provided the military experience needed. Later he seems to have had charge of Egypt's foreign relations.

After the vagaries of Akhenaten's reign and the lack of any firm direction during Tutankhamun's, and with the continued growth of the priestly bureaucracy, Egypt needed a firm hand. This precisely was what Horemhab was equipped to provide.

He seems to have had three main priorities. First, he sought to stabilize the frontiers and, so far as it was possible, to restore confidence in Egyptian rule amongst the client kings of the Empire as much as to face down the dissident princes who had seen the opportunity to assert their own authority. In this he was to be largely successful, doubtless because he was on ground which he understood, given his experience in diplomacy.

Then he set about reordering the internal administration. With the years of Akhenaten's self-imposed exile in Akhetaten followed by the weak reigns of Smenkhkara and Tutankhamun, the internal structure of the country was undermined. The old nomarchical families had long been dispossessed of their power but there were plenty of others who would not ignore an opportunity to carve out a place for themselves if they could. In this Horemhab achieved a result which was to stand his eventual successors in excellent stead.

Finally he saw himself as taking up the historic responsibility of a king of Egypt in restoring the country's great monuments and building new ones to the glory of the gods and of himself. In this, too, he was almost entirely successful.

Despite its vicissitudes Egypt was still an immensely rich land. The huge extent of what today might be called its reserves, built up in the reigns of Amenhotep III and his immediate predecessors, were still abundant and Horemhab was able both to harvest and to augment them.

The buildings which survive from his time have a particular delicacy and grace about them, a whit surprising perhaps in the inspiration of a retired general: the reliefs and portrait sculpture of Horemhab's period are as fine as any produced at any time since the end of the Old Kingdom. But Horemhab was a man of parts. He was obviously able to make use of the artists and craftsmen who had begun to change the style of Egyptian art in Amenhotep III's time and to permit the freedom which those changes occasioned to flourish, without having to overlay them with the doctrinaire Aten-dominated propaganda promoted by Akhenaten. The result is almost uniformly happy.[9]

Horemhab reigned peacefully and well, probably for twenty-eight years. When he died he was buried in a grand new tomb befitting his dignity as king, not the more modest but very pleasingly designed one that originally he had planned at Memphis, when he was still a serving soldier. It had been built before fortune and the gods of Egypt had called him to a higher, unforeseen destiny.

CHAPTER XII

THE RAMESSIDES AND THE DECLINE OF EGYPT

—— •◆• ——

Horemhab left no heir other than, it might be said, the soldiery. Before his death he prudently arranged for the crown to pass to another general of the army, whose throne name was Ramesses. This procedure was remarkable: there was at least always the pretence of continuity maintained in the succession by the choice for the Kingship marrying one of the royal women. Presumably the line of Ahmose had become totally extinct, an outcome by no means improbable when the rather effete and epicene character of the last males of the line is recalled. Not only was Ramesses merely nominated by his predecessor, he was a Northerner, the first, so far as we know, ever to hold the undisputed Kingship of all Egypt.

Ramesses was the product of a family from the eastern Delta who had a long military tradition.[1] He had served under Horemhab as vizier, thus repeating Horemhab's own career pathway. He reigned for only two years (c.1307–1306 BC); however, the succession was now secure for his son, who had been associated with him in his administration, succeeded him. He too was a senior officer and, like Horemhab, had charge of foreign affairs which, significantly, had come to be regarded as a military responsibility in Egypt.

He reigned as Seti I (c.1206–1290 BC) and consolidated the grasp of his family on the Kingship. He was remembered as a just and most honourably motivated king; he had built for himself one of the finest surviving temples in Egypt, his mortuary temple at Abydos. It contains some of the most resplendent painted reliefs, all of the very highest quality, from any period of Egyptian art. Seti's mortuary temple is also a superb architectural creation. It is clear that Seti was one of the most enlightened patrons of the arts to sit on the thrones of Egypt.[2]

He commissioned the splendid King-list at Abydos which shows himself and his young son, Ramesses, who would succeed him in the Kingship, worshipping those who had gone before them, from the time of Menes onwards. This was a skilful stroke of royal propaganda for it firmly established the new dynasty as the natural successors of the mighty line of kings which had preceded them. The quality of the art associated with Seti's reign is uniformly fine. The great relief which shows him and his young son lassoing a sacred bull is a masterpiece of formal yet finely observed art.

Seti attached much importance to the region from which his family came. It is not unlikely that one of the reasons which prompted the choice of Seti's father for the Kingship in the first place was the family's knowledge of and status in an area which had long been one of the most vulnerable of Egypt's frontiers. Nonetheless, the choice of a king from the North was to change the balance of the Two Lands and even contributed eventually to Egypt's decline, though in Seti's lifetime this must have seemed remote. He was a vigorous campaigner and his experience in foreign policy returned high dividends to Egypt. He extended and consolidated Horemhab's conquests in the Levant and he soon re-established Egyptian hegemony over an extensive area of the eastern Mediterranean coast and its hinterland. Towards the end of his reign he encountered one of the great powers of the ancient Near East, the Hittites from eastern Anatolia. Their encounter was indecisive, but in the reign of his son the confrontation was to become historic.

Seti's choice of name was interesting.[3] His family always demonstrated a reverence for the very ancient god Set (his grandfather was also Seti), but this is a little surprising since Set was associated, from very early times, with Upper Egypt, of which he probably was the tutelary divinity. Set was identified, in the period following the introduction of Osiris into the pantheon, as the murderer of his brother and, eventually, in late times, as the personification of evil. In Egyptian mythology he is the perpetual opponent, the very opposite of Horus, until the two are reconciled.

As northeners the family of the first Ramesses would not seem to have any natural affiliation with Set. It may be that he was identified with a northern, Syro-Palestinian deity like Baal or Teshub, with both of whom in Hyksos times he had been assimilated. It may equally be that the family felt the need to associate themselves with the south and courageously chose the maligned Set for their patron. Evidently they believed, as did all the greatest Egyptian kings, in conciliation. The royal name which dominates the early years of the Nineteenth Dynasty and was universally adopted by its successors in the Twentieth, Ramesses, contained the name of the sun-god of the Old Kingdom, who now made something of a comeback, after his at least partial eclipse by Osiris.

Seti I does not seem to have been any great age when he died. His son was in his early twenties and was destined to become one of the longest-reigning and most widely publicised (largely by himself) of all the kings of Egypt.

Ramesses II (c.1290–1224 BC) was obviously an intensely charismatic man, quite apart from the aura which his office gave to him.[4] He was handsome (even his mummy, as a very old man, reveals this) and powerful. He was also totally convinced of the authority of the Kingship which had come to him; he even revived the custom of referring to the king as 'the Great God'. He was a man of consuming energy, with an astonishing catalogue of great buildings and monuments raised in his reign and mostly dedicated to himself. He was a tireless campaigner; he was also a publicist of genius.

No king of any ancient land has left so many self-portraits in stone, many of them gigantic in scale, as Ramesses II. His obsession with monuments designed on such a scale has made it inevitable that he is accused of bombastic public building seldom even approached by the most self-directed totalitarian ruler of the present century. Though it is impossible not to admire Ramesses, it is difficult to love him. It is tempting to suggest that Ramesses was suffering from some degree of insecurity which made him insist with such preposterous overemphasis on his divinity, his courage, his beauty and his prowess in war. It is perhaps more to his credit that his remarkable personality contributed something to the composite figure of the archetypal King of Egypt known to the Greeks as Sesostris: Ramesses in this case is joined with Senwosret I and Senwosret III, who were also supremely charismatic kings.

Apart from his buildings Ramesses is best remembered for the effectiveness of his excursions, military and matrimonial, into Asia. Continuing the policies of his father, he ensured that Egypt once again was the greatest power in the Near East. Much of Egypt's restored position in the world was a direct result of Ramesses' enthusiasm for matrimony. He married frequently; unlike many of his predecessors he seems to have been less concerned to conciliate his own nobles by linking them to his house (the power of the old noble families in any case had been broken after the end of the Middle Kingdom) but rather to achieve diplomatic coups by marrying the daughters of powerful kings whose alliance might be beneficial to Egypt. A train of foreign princesses flowed into Egypt, as important and as influential in the changes which they wrought as the flow of treasure from conquest and tribute.

The return of Egypt to supreme authority in the ancient world was bought at a price, however: the increasing dilution of the historic Egyptian personality. But this did not perturb Ramesses as he covered the land of Egypt with a series of immense monuments which took the often carefully balanced scale attempted by the architects and artists of the early Eighteenth Dynasty, and inflated it to the proportions of gigantism. Once again, Egypt and the King were wholly identified and Ramesses was tireless in the presentation of his side of every dispute, of every battle in which he was engaged.

His architects did produce some fine works, nonetheless. The remarkable technique required to set the innermost recesses of the Osirid temple at Abu Simbel so precisely that the heads of the four divinities, deep in the

---

Figure 18 The interior of the great temple at Abu Simbel, prior to its transfer to its present site (*see opposite*). The temple was built by King Ramesses II to his glory and that of his companion gods, Amun, Ptah and Ra-Harakhty. The temple was built with great skill and precision of alignment, to permit the sun's rays at dawn on the spring and autumn equinoxes to illuminate the faces of the four gods, deep in the living rock into which the temple is cut. The temple is surmounted by a frieze of sacred baboons seemingly greeting the sun as its rays strike the temple's facade.

rock in the remotest part of the temple (including, of course Ramesses himself), were lit by the rising sun on the morning of the spring equinox, is one example of what they were capable.[5] This was the sort of engineering skill which allowed the Egyptians to alter the orientation of a temple when the star on whose position it had originally been set moved its position as a consequence of the Precession, something which seems to have happened several times during the New Kingdom.[6]

Ramesses lived to a great age. Having come to the throne in his early twenties, he reigned for sixty-seven years. That he was very old at his death is eloquently confirmed by his mummy, for not all the skills of the funerary priests could conceal the ruin which time had wrought on one of the most splendid and assertive of Egyptian kings.

Ramesses lived so long that many of his sons, including several who were nominated as Crown Prince, died before him. Amongst them was Prince Khaemweset, who is both a somewhat mysterious and an attractive figure. He enjoyed a considerable reputation as a magician. He was also a keen antiquarian and archaeologist, excavating and restoring the tombs and monuments of the earlier kings. He was evidently a cultivated and agreeable personality and, hence, it must be suspected not entirely like his father.

The thirteenth of his sons, Merneptah, eventually succeeded Ramesses. He was already a middle-aged man when he did so. He reigned well but only for nine years (c.1224–1214 BC).

He is principally remembered for an event which it is hard to believe ever happened. Merneptah is often described as 'the Pharaoh of the Exodus', though there is, as we have observed, no actual archaeological or historical evidence for the captivity of the Jews in Egypt, nor, for that matter, for the captivity of any other linguistic or confessional group.[7] The first mention of Israel as a political entity occurs in Merneptah's reign, where it is listed amongst a group of minor dissident countries beyond Egypt's borders.

The reign of Merneptah was complicated, to be sure, by troubles on his Asiatic frontier, a situation which had preoccupied his father throughout much of his reign. He continued the excellent relations established by his father with the Hittite Empire, whose border with Egypt was probably somewhere in the region of Damascus. Merneptah had also to cope with trouble in the south, where the Nubians revolted, and to the west, where the Libyans and the 'Sea Peoples', a congeries of Indo-European-speaking peoples who came in all probability from Anatolia and the Mediterranean islands, began to be troublesome. They were to become particularly threatening in years to come.

Merneptah's reign was followed by a period of disorder, when the succession was disputed. Again, a formidable woman emerged, the last of the type which had so greatly influenced the fortunes of Egypt during the New Kingdom. This was Twosret, who left behind her a distinctly ambiguous reputation; she was associated with the chancellor Bay, a particularly sinister Syrian. She survived for two years (*c.*1198–1196 BC). It was entirely in character with Egypt's often remarkable historical symmetry that the powerful queens of the beginning of the New Kingdom should be balanced in its decline by a queen, even one whose reputation was almost entirely deplored.

After the immensely long reign of Ramesses II, the large number of sons whom he left behind him, despite the premature deaths of many, meant that there was no shortage of contenders for the crown. A new dynasty emerged, the Twentieth (1196–1070 BC), founded by one Sethnakht, about whose origins virtually nothing is known. The succession devolved upon the last great Egyptian king, who took the name Ramesses III (*c.*1194–1163 BC). He and his successors over the next 120 years deliberately looked back to the reign of the second Ramesses, whose brilliant career they sought, wholly inadequately most of them, to emulate. In the case of most of them, their reigns were brief; Ramesses III was an exception, keeping the throne for nearly thirty years. He was a warrior and did much, in the short term, to hold back the pressures which, once again, were building up on the frontiers.

His greatest triumph was against the Sea Peoples, who had first emerged in the reign of Merneptah as a menace to Egypt's security. Then they were driven off but in Ramesses III's reign they returned, considerably strengthened. The Egyptians defeated them in a series of battles which Ramesses commemorated on the walls of his mortuary temple at Medinet Habu.

His Kingship was not without its domestic crises. A harem conspiracy was hatched, to kill the king and to substitute one of his younger sons, by a minor wife, who evidently led the treachery. It was discovered and, after a formal trial, the ringleaders were executed or commanded to commit suicide. There has been speculation that the king died as a result of the assassination attempt, but this is not certain. It is apparent that he died before the trial of his assailants and the other plotters was completed.[8]

Ramesses III's successors, all called Ramesses and numbered to the eleventh of the name, were most of them of brief duration in the Kingship. One of the recurring problems of the Egyptian succession plagued the house of Ramesses. Like Ramesses I, the third Ramesses in the course of his comparatively long reign produced many sons. His immediate successors were ageing men when they came to the throne. The throne in consequence was not able properly to consolidate the succession as happened, for example, in the early Twelfth or Eighteenth Dynasties, when the incumbent was able to plan his succession and, usually, to secure it for the prince of his choice.

The Twentieth Dynasty, that of the successors of Ramesses II, ended with Egypt once more falling into confusion, with warring factions each seeking the other's destruction and the elevation of their own interest, with no thought for the general good of Egypt or its people. Security collapsed with gangs of robbers, often with powerful priestly or political backing, ravaging the tombs of long dead kings and their families. The most ominous of all the factions to emerge at this time, and immeasurably the most powerful, was to be the agent of the destruction of historic Egypt whose Kingship had, by this time, descended over some two thousand years. The power that wrought the downfall of this most majestic of all human societies was that of the priests, the servants of the gods amongst whom, notionally at least, the king was numbered.

The end of the Twentieth Dynasty represented the end of the New Kingdom. It is a convenient point at which to view the course of Egyptian history, both in retrospect and on into the much less assured future. After the end of the Twentieth Dynasty Egypt was rarely ruled by a native-born Egyptian until modern times. The long centuries of Egypt's paramountcy were times of relative security, when the autochthonous culture of the Nile Valley was largely resistant to exterior forces and could always absorb such influences that impinged on it, Egyptianising them in the process. As the rest of the Near East began to develop other complex societies, Egypt, ageing and with its vital creative spark diminished, could no longer resist foreign influences and the changes which they wrought. The most corrosive of these influences were, as the Egyptians themselves always feared, to come from the desert: ultimately it was Set who defeated Horus.

For the remaining thousand years of Egypt's history, down to the time of the Greeks' transformation of its ancient mysteries into part of the intellectual heritage of the Western world, the Egyptians were still to achieve much. Some of the products of the craftsmen of the Twenty-Sixth Dynasty, for example, though obviously derivative, could still bear comparison with the original works, in this case of the Old Kingdom, from which they drew their inspiration. But it was a conscious archaicising, an admission that the past had more to give than did the present.

Nonetheless Egypt was long to exercise its immemorial fascination for the world outside the Valley, particularly that part which derived its culture from around the Mediterranean. Its political and military power may in large part have evaporated, but the mystery remained and, indeed, grew abundantly.

CHAPTER XIII

THE FINAL PHASE

—— ·•· ——

After the end of the Twentieth Dynasty the cancer which had been gnawing at the body of Egypt at least since the beginning of the Eighteenth Dynasty finally triumphed. The power which destroyed Egypt was, ironically, what might be termed 'organised religion', represented by the temple bureaucracies which had been accumulating power and wealth until they rivalled, if they did not exceed, the wealth and power of the Kingship. The irony lies in the belief that Egypt was the land which, more than any other, had given life to the worship of the gods as a state function, having even been ruled by an immanent divinity.

In the early part of the Eighteenth Dynasty something of the conflict which was to bedevil Europe in the Middle Ages, the dialogue, often most venomous, between Pope and Emperor, beset Egypt. Earlier, following the shift to Thebes in the time of the Middle Kingdom and that city's role in nurturing the line of princes who reinstated the Kingship after the Hyksos period, the power of Amun, the Theban divinity *par excellence*, had risen dramatically becoming by the early New Kingdom effectively the national divinity of all Egypt, when conflated with the sun-god Ra. With the rise of Amun came, inevitably, the rise of his priests.

The brief period of the 'Amarnan Heresy' must have been a traumatic time for the followers of Amun. Of all Egypt's kings Akhenaten seems to have detested Amun most strongly, recognising presumably that it was from the already deeply entrenched interests of the great priests of his cult that he could expect the most overt and dangerous opposition to his new – or relatively new – ideas of a universal beneficent divinity, symbolised by the sun's disk. He was right and his mysterious disappearance and eventual death may very well be set to their account.

After the restoration of the Amun cult and the re-establishment of Thebes as the capital of Egypt the priests were determined to protect and augment their power and, by doing so, to eliminate the risk of another persecution by a heretic or uncompliant king. In the reigns of Seti I and his son the centre of the country shifted northwards to the Delta. When the dynasty fell away the Ramesside kings who needed to consolidate their rule did so by associating themselves with the only other powerful constituency in the Two Kingdoms, the religious establishment and, in particular, with the temples of Amun centred, as always, on Thebes.

The power of the Kingship had, as we have seen, become greatly diminished by the end of Ramesses XI's reign. In his later years a powerful rival to the royal power emerged in the person of Herihor, the High Priest of Amun in Thebes. Gradually he began to assume many of the accoutrements and titles of royalty. He controlled much of Upper Egypt and most of the Kingdom's resources (c.1080–1072 BC). After Ramesses XI's death another powerful man, Smendes, took power in the north of the country, ruling from Tanis in the Delta where he established an independent dynasty, the Twenty-First (c.1070–945 BC). Like Herihor he was probably a Libyan, the first example of the rise to power of a people which was to play a significant part in the later stages of Egyptian history. The threat which the Egyptians had always feared from the west, as great a threat to them as that from the north, was realised, though the transition from the last of the Ramessides to the new line seems to have been effected peacefully.

Egypt was now dismembered, its two constituent parts, which the kings had sought so long and persistently to hold together, sundered. Smendes may have married a daughter of Ramesses XI, in which case, having married the heiress, he was a legitimate King of Egypt; he proclaimed himself 'Powerful Bull beloved by Ra'. Meanwhile the high priests in Thebes, who seem to have maintained relations with the Tanite kings and even sometimes acknowledged their sovereignty, continued to farm the south. But, despite the relatively tranquil beginning to the Twenty-First Dynasty, the next three hundred years were amongst the most bizarre and disturbed in Egypt's rich history.[1]

This, the Third Intermediate period, was longer in duration than either of its predecessors but it did not leave anything of the same traumata in the Egyptian collective psyche as the First and Second periods of uncertainty and invasion undoubtedly did. The first came to represent the horrors which awaited Egypt when the royal authority collapsed, the second the shameful fact of invasion by a despised opponent; the third passed with little lasting impact, for by this time Egypt was effectively defunct. Only the form remained, the creative substance was spent. That it did not create the distress amongst the people that its predecessors had done is probably because already the nature of Egypt was seen to have changed by the Egyptians themselves.

Not that the world at large realised that Egypt's decline had almost reached its terminus. Egypt was still the land which had dominated so much of the politics of the Near East for as long as there had been records kept and even before that time, Egypt was known to have been a great and powerful state, before, indeed, any of the other states which now both emulated and menaced it even existed. This reputation sustained the *image* of Egypt, even if the reality was lamentably different. Herihor was succeeded by Piankhi. Pinudjem I, Piankhi's son, took the name 'Powerful Bull crowned in Thebes' and ruled in the south (1070–1032 BC). On Smendes' death he was succeeded by two heirs, Nefekare Amenennisu and Psussenes I. The latter was a successful ruler; he reigned for nearly fifty years and developed his city of Tanis extensively (c.1040–992 BC). A succession of less accomplished rulers followed him, with the high priests in Thebes maintaining their own state though, as in previous generations, the two seem to have had quite cordial relations. Psussenes is notable for being the only king of Egypt whose burial has been found intact: it was, however, not remotely so lavish as Tutankhamun's, demonstrating how, in the intervening three centuries, the wealth of Egypt's kings had diminished.

Under the last king of the Tanite Dynasty, Psussenes II (959–945 BC), Egypt felt strong enough once again to involve itself in the larger concerns of the Near East. Of this time – and rather unreliably, in historiographical terms – the Old Testament books record the interaction between Egypt and the Kingdom of Jerusalem. The biblical reports of the contacts of David and Solomon with Egypt are not altogether to be taken seriously, however, since there is no archaeological evidence, or documentary evidence outside the biblical stories, for the existence of either David or Solomon or for the kingdom which they are supposed to have ruled.[2]

The Libyans took advantage of Egypt's poverty at the death of the last of the Tanite kings and the 'Great Chiefs of the Meshwesh', as the leaders of the Libyan tribal groups were called, now took power. At first they exercised it over a very small part of the Delta. However, during this Libyan dynasty, the Twenty-Second (945–712 BC) there is evidence of the appearance of Syro-Palestinian leaders, representing the 'new' kingdoms of Judah and Israel, on the Near Eastern scene. The importance which has been attributed to these contacts and the appearance of the names of Egyptian kings in the biblical reports of this period (evidently more reliable than their predecessors) have given a special significance to them.

The new dynasty was centred on Bubastis, also in the Delta. Initially the kings enjoyed some success, giving Egypt a recollection of what its power had once been. But now a new power was rising, ominously, in the east: Assyria, under the bloodthirsty Assurnasirpal (883–859 BC). For a time Egypt was able to hold off the Assyrians from its Palestinian clients, but eventually the king of Israel was obliged to pay tribute to Assyria.

Despite the pressures, political, economic and military, which the Bubastite dynasty undoubtedly experienced, it survived for over two hundred years. Its kings conducted themselves in the manner of those whom they claimed as their ancestors. Thus Sheshonq I (c.945–924 BC) built extensively in his thirty-year reign, including work at Karnak, in the temple of Amun.

Several of the Bubastite kings enjoyed long and relatively prosperous reigns, one of them, Sheshonq III, reigning for more than half a century (c.835–783 BC). From time to time Egypt engaged in military expeditions in Syria and Palestine, usually combining with other states to try to contain the rising power of Assyria.

After the death of the last Bubastite king, Osorkon IV, in 715 BC, a family of princes from Tanis, though perhaps connected with the dynasty

Figure 19 King Osorkon II of the Twenty-Second Dynasty is attended and protected by two goddesses. This exquisite jewel shows that even in a period of Egypt's decline from the heights of the Old and Middle Kindoms, Egyptian art could still achieve an unrivalled quality.

from Bubastis, proclaimed themselves kings, reigning for a century. This was a time of deepening confusion and the records of these reigns are very obscure. The Twenty-Fourth Dynasty (742–712 BC) consisted only of one acknowledged king, from Sardis in the Delta. The Libyans were still in the ascendancy but their power can have brought them little satisfaction since the Twenty-Second Dynasty overlapped with both the Twenty-Third and Twenty-Fourth Dynasties in its later years.

After the final eclipse of the various contenders for rule over smaller and smaller stretches of territory in the Delta, Egypt entered what was to be its final phase as a regional power. The period was troubled, though some of the kings enjoyed reasonably long and secure reigns. There were times when, once more, Egypt fell under foreign domination; not all of these, however, were resented and the last of them enabled Egypt's legend, the myth which had so powerfully built up around it in the long continuum of the centuries, to be released into the modern world.

This last phase began, remarkably enough, with the rise to power of a family from the region of Kush, which included Upper or southern Nubia and Sudan.[3] It is likely that kings with a substantial Nubian component in their ancestry had sat on the thrones of Egypt long before this time, in the Middle Kingdom and in the Eighteenth Dynasty if not earlier in the Old Kingdom, but now an acknowledged Nubian dynasty assumed the royal power, proclaiming its leaders the kings of all Egypt. The line of kings which now came to power, with a sense of great religious purpose, was from Napata, very far to the south in deepest Nubia.

These African kings saw it as their destiny to restore the gods and glory of Egypt as they had once been. They reigned in Egypt itself for something over a hundred years, and they continued to rule in their homeland for centuries more. The first to rule Egypt was Piankhy (747–716 BC), son of Kashta, evidently a great chief, who had penetrated above the First Cataract in the last years of the preceding dynasty. Piankhy ruled the south for the last thirty years of the Twenty-Fourth Dynasty and claimed that kings of all the Tanite and Bubastite dynasties paid homage to him. Finally he captured Memphis itself and in effect ruled all of historic Egypt. Piankhy was hailed as 'Bull of the Two Lands', indicating that the ancient identification of the king with the divine bull was as powerful a part of the titulary of the African kings as it had always been for their Egyptian models. When Piankhy died he was buried with his favourite horses at Napata; he was a great lover of horses and many were the stories which told of his devotion to them.

The dynasty, the Twenty-Fifth (770–657 BC), however, still had to contend with the insurrections of the Delta kings. Shabaka (712–698 BC), one of the greatest of the dynasty who succeeded Piankhy, drove out any opponents remaining in the marshes of the Delta (he is said to have burned alive one of the claimants, Buchoris of the Twenty-Fourth Dynasty) and established himself as undisputed ruler.

Shabaka was succeeded by Shabataka (the Kushite dynasty tended to have, by Egyptian standards, rather barbarous names), who adopted an aggressive policy towards the increasing threat from the Assyrians. He fought campaigns in Syria-Palestine, in which he was joined by his favourite nephew, Taharqa, who was eventually to succeed him as King of Egypt.

Taharqa was crowned king in Memphis in 690 BC. He was a powerful ruler and, having succeeded to the throne as a young man, he continued his uncle's policy of determined opposition towards the Assyrians. He was, however, eventually defeated by them when the Assyrians drove the Egyptian forces out of both Memphis and Thebes.

Despite the evident power of the Assyrians, a peculiarly ruthless and cruel people, the Egyptian–Nubian forces were still not entirely beaten. Taharqa died in 664 BC and was succeeded by Tanutamun (664–657 BC). He seems, briefly at least, to have been acknowledged as king of Upper and Lower Egypt but eventually he was driven further and further to the south by the relentless Assyrians, eventually to be buried near the Nubian dynasty's stronghold at Napata. During his reign the unthinkable occurred: Thebes was sacked, her temples destroyed and her treasure wrenched from the most powerful stronghold of the gods.

A brief interregnum intervened, at the end of the Twenty-Fifth Dynasty. The Assyrians were still largely in control, but their power was weakened by mounting political pressures in their homeland. A Delta ruler, Necho I, the first king of the Twenty-Sixth Dynasty (664–525 BC), had been killed by Tanutamun but his son, Psamtik I (Psametichus) first allied himself with the Assyrians and then, choosing his opportunity skilfully, disengaged himself from them. He was to reign for more than fifty years (664–610 BC) and he brought about the reunification of Egypt. He was, perhaps, the last great Egyptian king.

Like so many others in recent centuries Psamtik's family came from the Delta, from Sais. It was to become a handsome city, with many fine public buildings, according to Herodotus, who visited it in the fifth century.

Psamtik's reign, as its length indicates, was a time of relative tranquillity in an Egypt which had its fill of disturbance and unrest. It was certainly a time of prosperity for the country as a whole. Egypt was increasingly opened up to foreign traders and the Greeks, in particular, began to arrive in Egypt in considerable numbers. A scaraboid seal, bearing the king's name, was found as far away as the island of Bahrain in the Arabian Gulf. The process of increasing foreign contact seems to have been encouraged by the kings and, by the time of the establishment of the Greeks as the rulers of Egypt under the Ptolemies, there were extensive and influential Greek settlements in Egypt, especially in the north.

The Saite Dynasty was notable for its evidently quite conscious attempts to halt the decline of Egypt and to recall its ancient spirit by creating works of art and architecture which deliberately harked back to the past.[4] The evidence of the past lay all around in Egypt and the action of the Saites suggests that some at least of its people recognised the powerful forces to which the artists, of the Old Kingdom in particular, had access. The royal authority now encouraged the making of works of art which deliberately recalled the styles of the Old Kingdom. The results are often very fine, particularly in portraiture. The old Egyptian delight in the handling of fine, intractable or difficult stones seems once again to have seized Egyptian artists. The products of the Saite period, though they emulate the finest works of the Old Kingdom, cannot really be mistaken for them; they have their own individuality and their own distinctive aura. They represent what was perhaps the last flaring of the flame which had illuminated the Egyptian creative spirit in its finest manifestations for so very long.

As was appropriate for a conscientious antiquarian, Psamtik I paid especial honour to the gods. He greatly enlarged the Serapeum at Saqqara, where the Apis bulls, the manifestation of the god Ptah, were buried in immense granite sarcophagi, many of them weighing more than 60 tons.

Even the cult of Apis, revived so effectively at this time, was a deliberate recollection of the bull-cults of the Archaic period and earlier.

Nostalgia is a curious emotion, one which frequently is to be found in societies which are long past their prime – in individuals too – and which seek to reclaim some elements of past grandeur by simulating the outward forms of an admired antiquity. It is a rather touching emotion, even if, sometimes, it is a little absurd. In the case of the art of the Saite period the Egyptian ability to synthesise the unconscious promptings of the group came once more into play, to produce a society which, in its public and material manifestations, looked back two thousand years. No other society of the day would have had either the opportunity to do this on the scale undertaken by the Saites, or the inclination. The Greeks were much impressed by what they saw in seventh-century Egypt and later; this transmitted itself both in terms of the Egyptian influences on Greek art which can be traced to this time, such as even so very Greek a product as the naked, gently smiling *kouros*, and of the deep sense of awe which Egypt made on impressionable, and frequently rather naïve, Greek visitors. This period contributed considerably to the refinement and promotion of Egypt as the source of the archetypes of forms and social structures which the Greeks were to do so much to transmit to the world.

Psamtik seems not to have disassociated himself entirely from an alliance with the Assyrians, a policy which his son and successor Necho II also followed (610–595 BC). He was to be celebrated for his encouragement of seamanship and navigation. He was a great shipbuilder, an occupation unusual for an Egyptian king, for the Egyptians generally were distrustful of the sea. One of Necho's expeditions sailed from the Red Sea round Africa to the Pillars of Hercules, a remarkable achievement for the seventh century BC.

Necho was involved in various campaigns in Palestine and at one point defeated and killed the king of Judah. He was also a believer in opening up Egypt to external influences and in his reign the Greek presence in the country increased considerably.

Two kings dominate the latter years of the dynasty, Apries and Amasis. The former came against Nebuchadnezzar II and was defeated by him; he was overthrown by Amasis, an uncouth, drunken and boorish soldier but a man of considerable ability. He reigned long and ably (570–526 BC); he maintained an extensive diplomatic network, all round the eastern Mediterranean. His advice to Polycrates, the luxurious tyrant of Samos, not to tempt the gods by the too obvious display of his good fortune was nullified by the malice of the gods themselves. Mockingly, they returned Polycrates' sacrifice, a much treasured ring which he had cast into the sea, and so presaged his eventual downfall and horrific end.

The Assyrian threat in the Near East was now replaced by that of the Persians. Cyrus and later Cambyses II (525–522 BC) saw Egypt as the ultimate prize and, having broken a coalition of Egypt and Babylonia, conquered the Valley. Now the Persians ruled Egypt as part of their immense Empire.

The Persians seem generally to have respected Egypt and its institutions despite the story of Cambyses' blasphemy against the gods and his ensuing madness, after his alleged killing of the incumbent Apis bull.[5] Darius I, Cambyses' successor (521–486 BC), did much to restore Egyptian institutions; he even attempted to codify Egyptian laws. He restored many of the traditional prerogatives and benefices of the temples, which had become seriously depleted.

The shifting patterns of power in the Near East now brought about the rise of the Greeks. The defeat of the Persians at Marathon announced the arrival of a new player in the game of nations. Darius' successors were more concerned with the maintenance of order in the heartland of the Empire than to worry unduly about a province like Egypt; the country was largely allowed to follow its own way. More and more Greeks, traders and mercenaries, came into Egypt, as did the Jews, a community well favoured by the Persians.

In 404 BC a revolt in Egypt against the weakened Empire introduced a short period of Egyptian independence. Once again the initiative came from the Delta, from Sais, which seems to have inherited the role of Thebes as the focus for Egyptian nationalism. Only one king is recorded as representing the Twenty-Eighth Dynasty, Amyrtaios. It was he who expelled the Persians, though he reigned only for six years (404–399 BC).

The last years of Egypt's history, before the conquests of Alexander the Great changed the political map of the ancient world irrevocably, were marked by a succession of short-lived, sometimes competing and generally unremarkable kings. The Twenty-Ninth Dynasty, centred on Mendes, another Delta city, lasted less than twenty years (399–380 BC). The Thirtieth (380–343 BC) was dominated by two kings called Nectanebo, who both reigned for eighteen years. The first Nectanebo enjoyed a relatively quiet reign (380–362 BC) and so was able to follow the customary practice of Egyptian kings and restore the monuments. His grandson, Nectanebo II (360–342·BC), was less fortunate for in his reign the Persians once again became a force in the region. Nectanebo was a brave commander and an experienced ruler; he hoped to stand against the Persians but they had learned the lessons of their previous excursions against Egypt and infiltrated the cities of Egypt which, one by one, capitulated to them. Their generals were skilled and they were aided by Greek mercenaries who, by this time, had become the most formidable war bands in the world. Nectanebo II realised that resistance was impossible. He withdrew into the far south, taking with him to Ethiopia, according to Diodorus, the greater part of his possessions.

He was heard of no more, though there was a legend, quite unsubstantiated, that he was the true father of Alexander and that he visited the

Macedonian queen, Olympias, secretly, in fulfilment of a prophecy. It is an agreeable story, no more. But Alexander, whether his father was Philip II of Macedon, Amun of Thebes (as he himself was inclined to believe), Nectanebo, or a divine snake (as Olympias insisted) was to save Egypt from the Persians, draw the ancient land wholly into the culture of the Mediterranean and, ultimately, open the way to the modern world.

CHAPTER XIV

THE GREEKS IN EGYPT

—— •◆• ——

It is often considered both convenient and apt to end a survey of the ancient world with the record of the death, in Babylon in July 323 BC, of Alexander, son of Philip King of Macedon, commonly called 'the Great'. After his brief, extraordinary lifetime, the axis of world politics shifted westwards, away from the Near East. At this point a new epoch approaches which will be very different in its *mores*, philosophy and attitudes to the world in the coming centuries. The modern world, unmistakably, is in the offing.

This generalisation is not, however, wholly true of Egypt which, despite all appearances, had not yet exhausted all its benefactions to the world around it and which lay in the centuries which were to come. That this was the case is the consequence of the almost accidental decision of Alexander to absorb Egypt into his empire.

Throughout Alexander's career there are intimations of Egypt around him. There was the myth, cultivated by his dreadful mother Olympias, that she had conceived of a god in the form of a snake and that the god concerned was Amun.

Alexander was deeply sensitive to the presence and influence of the gods. He was diligent in their service and in the promotion of the proper honours which each required. Like most Greeks he was a syncretist in matters of religion, believing that the same gods were present in all lands under different guises and bearing different names. As the years of his life unfurled, few though they were, he became increasingly convinced that he was to be numbered among them, a view from which his mother did nothing to dissuade him.

The great conflict of Alexander's life was with the Persian Empire. His pursuit of Darius III assumed a curious, almost dreamlike quality; though the battles were real enough, his determination to possess the Great King took on something of a very Greek quest, of the pursuit by the lover of the beloved. Alexander's adoption of Darius' family and the honour which he paid to them is some evidence of this strange affection, as it is also of Alexander's not infrequent magnanimity.

His defeat of Darius at Issus in 333 opened the way to Egypt. Before this event there is no evidence that Alexander actually nursed any ambitions towards the control of the Nile Valley. But after Issus he dropped down from Giza and as soon as he set foot on Egyptian territory Mazaces, the Persian satrap who ruled it in Darius' name, surrendered without resistance.

Alexander was crowned in Memphis as a true King of Egypt, a choice confirmed by the oracle of Amun at Siwa. This was not one of the great religious centres of Egypt but it was identified particularly with Amun; by the act of his coronation Alexander was the Divine King and the earlier identification of Amun as his putative father may have determined his decision to make for Siwa, heading westwards across the desert, at considerable discomfort and in some danger.

At one point the king and his escort were seemingly lost in the waterless desert; then, by the intervention of one of the wonderful events which always illuminated the life and the legend of Alexander, a snake appeared on the sands, and led the party to safety. Alexander's mother, naturally enough, hinted that it was the same Amun who had visited her in the form of a snake when her son was conceived. Once in Siwa Alexander was hailed by the priests as King of Egypt and, alone, was taken into the god's shrine to receive the oracle. Whatever Alexander heard or saw made a profound impression on him, though he apparently never revealed what had occurred, even to his most intimate companions.

Alexander spent around six months in Egypt. Everywhere he was greeted rapturously, hailed as the redeemer who had driven the hated and despised Persians out of Egypt. He reorganised the administration, appointing Egyptians to many of the principal positions of authority in the state, though Greeks also were given positions of power; eventually Greeks were to replace the native Egyptians in the government of the country. Alexander never returned to Egypt as a living king.

His most enduring act in Egypt was the foundation of the city of Alexandria, one of the many cities which he scattered across his domains which bore his name. The Egyptian Alexandria was sited on the Mediterranean coast near Canopus and Lake Mareotis. The story of the choice of the site is another of the marvellous tales which attached themselves to him. He put his cloak on the ground and instructed his architect, Deinocrates, to lay the city out in the cloak's shape. The outline of the cloak was marked with grain. At once birds came down and ate the grain, as birds are wont to do. Alexander's attendants were dismayed, believing that the birds' actions presaged the destruction of the city. The King at once said it was not so, for now Alexandria had been taken up into the sky and so would endure for ever. Thus far, the prophecy has held.

Alexander did eventually return to Alexandria, his mummified corpse borne on an immense catafalque. Ptolemy, one of his most trusted commanders, who was perhaps the son of Philip II, Alexander's father, and hence the conqueror's half-brother, probably always intended to seize Egypt and to establish his own kingdom there in the confused aftermath of Alexander's death. He captured the funeral procession on its way from Babylon and diverted it to Memphis. In the reign of his son, Ptolemy II (285–247 BC), the mummified corpse of Alexander was brought to Alexandria. There, amid great pomp, Alexander was laid in his mausoleum, according to the stories in a crystal coffin, his mummy, a golden circlet round its head, seated on a throne. The mausoleum apparently survived until the Moslem conquests in the seventh century AD. Its location has now been lost but the possibility that Alexander is still in his city has continued to intrigue more romantic spirits.

Ptolemy I (323–282 BC) was a resourceful and determined commander. He was also a brilliant politician, who changed the character of Egypt profoundly and established what was to be one of its longest-lasting ruling families (323–30 BC), though it was always entirely Greek in manner, language and in most of its customs.

The Ptolemies adopted the useful convention of the divinity of the king and, sometimes that of his sister-consort. They adopted the practice of brother–sister marriage early on, though such incest was wholly unacceptable in Greek lands. The Ptolemies happily discovered that they were descended both from Herakales and from Dionysos, the one a hero, the other a god, each with a tendency towards the ecstatic and the unbridled.

The new dynasty soon imposed a pervasive, military-based authority over all parts of the population. Egypt was, in the convention of Macedonian tradition, 'spear-won' and hence was ruled as the property of the king. The country was, early on, ruled as a conquered territory, but generally speaking the native Egyptian population seems to have accepted the foreign nature of the ruling power and the presence, at all levels, of a large Greek, and Greek-speaking, population. Perhaps, knowing that the ancient dignity of Egypt was consumed, they did not much concern themselves with such matters, though the ancient practices and the worship of the gods in the old ways still continued.

The existing Greek populations, which had been established for centuries in the trading centres, were considerably enlarged and Greek immigration was vigorously encouraged. The transfer of a Greek population to the Nile Valley, where entire cities were founded and older ones assumed Greek names, must be seen against the remarkable overseas expansion which the Greeks undertook in late antiquity.

The Greeks had long made use of a very sensible procedure whereby, when a *polis* reached a certain level of population or whenever signs of tension and stress, the consequences of over-population, became apparent the parent city would bud off a daughter settlement, often far away from the parent. Thus Greek communities were established as early as the seventh century BC in the western Mediterranean, in Spain, in the islands, notably in Sicily and in southern Italy. Similarly Greek influences spread eastwards, into Anatolia and beyond, in Syria, the Levant and even Mesopotamia, to the borders of Persia. Alexander himself encouraged the practice and provided incentives for his time-expired soldiery to establish Greek enclaves in the most distant of his conquests.

These settlements established by the Greeks served to establish and consolidate immense trading networks. These reached, most improbably, deep into the Arabian desert where, at sites like Qariyat al-Faw, some 400 miles into the deep desert south of the modern capital, Riyadh, a flourishing caravanserai was established and continued to serve the eastwards incense and spice trade for several hundred years.[1] All the way across the south-eastern desert regions, by the lakes of Laila for example, small towns, quite unmistakably Greek, served the travellers who carried their merchandise to and from the Gulf, in this case, incense for trans-shipment northwards to Mesopotamia. In the Bahrain islands there was a substantial Greek colony in the last centuries BC, when the principal island was known by a Greek name, Tylos.[2] At the same period, a Greek community lived on the island of Failaka in the Bay of Kuwait, intriguingly named Ikaros apparently by Alexander himself, where a pretty little Greek temple, a gymnasium and a shrine with an international reputation, dedicated to Artemis the Slayer of Bulls, served the community and, no doubt, the many traders who must have sailed up and down the Gulf then as they had done for at least two thousand years earlier.[3] Further down the Gulf, in what is today the United Arab Emirates, similar colonies were established.[4]

In the Nile Valley itself the Greeks reached down into Nubia; Alexander himself had sailed as far as the First Cataract, at the southern frontier of Egypt, during his Egyptian visit. It was familiar territory for Greeks; from an earlier period, a long inscription in Greek, carved by (or on behalf of) two Greek soldiers is still to be seen on the legs of one of the great seated statues on the facade of the temple at Abu Simbel.

All of this gave the Ptolemies a sound base on which to found their peculiar and distinctive Egyptanised Hellenic culture, known to history as the Hellenistic.[5] It cannot be doubted that there was a deliberate attempt to achieve a synthesis of two such disparate cultures, though Alexander had himself foreseen something of the sort when he attempted to unite east and west, symbolically and physically, by the marriage of 10,000 of his Greeks to an equal number of Persian women at Susa.

The integration of two such powerful and distinctive cultures as Egypt and Greece was bound to produce a remarkable progeny. For a while Egypt must have seemed almost as ideal a land as it had been at the height of its greatness in much earlier times, except that now it was wholly liberated, open to every sort of influence. Every conceivable idea, experiment, innovation and speculation flowed in and out, in particular, of Alexandria, which within decades of its foundation became the intellectual centre of the world which Alexander had left behind him. It was also notorious for its luxury and all manner of sophisticated wantonness. Alexandria became the byword for intellectual adventure and for cultivated and imaginative licentiousness.

The mixture of Greek and Egyptian did, however, evidently produce some curious anomalies. Thus the lamentable Greek custom of exposing unwanted offspring was adopted in Egypt, where the generous land had always been able to provide for all its children. The problem was solved by all such unfortunate babies being collected, declared the property of the king and sold into slavery.

The Greeks brought to the embellishment of Alexandria – 'the city' as it was always called, as if no other could pretend to the same status – their sense of proportion and elegance in the design of the buildings, which, though perhaps they did not know it, echoed forms first developed long ago in Egypt itself. The city was a new phenomenon for Egypt for it was built beside the sea, rather than the river which had always rated higher in the Egyptians' consciousness than any other natural feature of their country. The sea provided new perspectives and new uses of light, which the architects of Alexandria fully exploited. In a short time immense structures, gleaming white and splashed with vivid colour, rose on the Mediterranean shore. These included the Palace of the king (as Ptolemy I proclaimed himself in 305 BC) and the Museum, in which learned men, relieved from the concerns of everyday living, worked at intellectual, academic and scientific projects to which they were set by the king himself. Alexandria's greatest glory was its immense library which, by the first century BC, probably contained at least three-quarters of a million texts. The city was an appropriate setting for its ruling dynasty, which in a few generations became the richest and most brilliant in the known world.

The library at Alexandria was not unique to Egypt. State libraries were founded in Antioch, Pergamum, Rhodes and Smyrna. But it was the library in Alexandria, at the Bucheion, founded largely by the first two Ptolemies, which was of universal importance. It was one of the main factors in ensuring the continuation of Alexandria's status as the known world's principal centre of scientific enquiry and encouraging the creation of works of literature, which drew scholars, irresistibly, from all parts of the world. This process was not to be repeated on such a scale until the foundation of some of the great modern centres of learning a thousand years and more later.

Julius Caesar has been accused of burning the library of Alexandria but an accident during his entry into the city in fact resulted only in the burning of a quantity of largely discarded papyri. The great library itself was broken up and destroyed in AD 272 by the Emperor Aurelian.

The work of Alexandrian savants spread not only the fruits of Hellenistic science and literature across the known world (the extent of which was quadrupled by Alexander's conquests) but also ensured that the reputation and mystery of Egypt grew. The great wall enclosing the city, which was said to be 10 miles in length, contained a rich miscellany of talents, more, perhaps, than has been found in any city till modern times. Writers like Menander, Callimachus of Cyrene, who celebrated his friend Heraclitus so memorably, Meleager, Philodemus, Theocritus and Apollonius called the

Rhodian, were writers who flourished in Alexandria, and who gave the tradition of letters to the later world of Western Europe.

One of the most enduring works from Alexandrian times, which was to provide an incalculably rich resource for the study of the history of Egypt, was a product of the Ptolemies' rule, though not directly of Alexandria. This was the history, the *Egyptiaka*, written by Manetho, a Hellenised Egyptian, the High Priest, no less, of Heliopolis in the reign of Ptolemy I, who was himself a historian.

There have been few more convincing evidences of the extraordinary change which the coming of the Greeks brought to the ancient world than Manetho's work. The spirit of enquiry which so absorbed their intellectual energies is well demonstrated by his attempt to produce a coherent and reasonably objective summary of the sequence of the kings, not in a formal, hierarchic context inscribed in monumental hieroglyphs on a temple wall, but as a piece of considered research, treating the succession of the kings, really for the first time, as history.

The cosmopolitan, liberal and enterprising society which evolved in Ptolemaic Egypt appealed greatly to the numerous, increasingly prosperous and assertive Jewish communities of the eastern Mediterranean. The Ptolemies encouraged the Jews to settle in Egypt and a special quarter of Alexandria became associated with them, though they probably never ranked as citizens; the Greeks tended always to be niggardly with the awarding of the rights of citizenship to strangers. Ptolemy IV (222–205 BC) seems to have had the rather curious idea that the god of the Jews was identical with, of all equivocal divinities, Dionysos. Since he was descended from Dionysos Ptolemy thought that he could promote himself as the incarnate god of Jews, Egyptians and Greeks alike. He found little support for the idea. His successor, Ptolemy V, appears to have been the first of the line (other, of course, than Alexander himself) to have had himself crowned according to the immemorial Egyptian rituals.

The Jews made an important contribution to the intellectual and artistic life of Hellenistic Egypt. Their own culture changed significantly meanwhile: Aramaic, the vernacular of the Jewish people in post-Exilic times, went the same way as the spoken Hebrew which it had replaced. Both were subsumed by Greek, which became the language of Jewish scholarship and, as such, exercised a considerable influence on the intellectual development and literary expression of early Christianity.

There were, from time to time, outbursts of anti-Jewish feeling in the Greek cities but generally the communities lived together peaceably enough. Only the dreadful excesses of the Hasmoneans, the family of bloodthirsty despots who ruled in Palestine for a time in the second and first centuries BC, represented a threat to the hegemony of the Ptolemies, though a temporary one, as much as it was a threat to all those who lived in second-century Palestine.

The attraction which the city exercised on the minds of the most adventurous spirits of the day was of profound importance in laying down the foundations of the early modern world, and in establishing the myth of Egypt in the consciousness of succeeding generations. Throughout much of its early history, before the impact first of Christianity and then of Islam, Alexandria seems to have been something of a genuinely open society in which the ideas of the day could be explored, debated and pursued to their logical ends. At this time the Near East was changing profoundly; the outpouring of new, or at least markedly different ideas of philosophy and religion, from both east and west, acted on the dying embers of the ancient societies which lay around the Mediterranean in various stages of either exhaustion or the promise of a new age. The antics of the Olympians had finally become too much for them to be taken seriously. Even with a family ruling in Egypt who seemed to mimic them in many of their more deplorable ways, the time had clearly come for their eclipse.

The intellectual and philosophical currents which were running in the eastern Mediterranean were complex; frequently they flowed closely together. Greece provided a substantial input of empirical, observation-based scientific theory and practice which the extensive network of Greek communities ensured was distributed internationally and enhanced by the experience and ideas of scholars and practical men alike drawing on many different disciplines, backgrounds and intellectual environments. From the east there poured in an extraordinary mélange of speculations about the nature of man and the gods, and about their interaction. The predisposition of Semitic-speaking peoples to this type of speculation and their ready response to faiths with a substantial component of mysticism and miracle-working meant that a myriad of wonder-workers, prophets and holy men converged on the eastern Mediterranean, their speculations striking a ready response from a world which was grown weary of the proliferation of divinities and conflicting sects which all clamoured for attention, status and support.

This is, of course, a gross over-simplification of a subtle and complex process which extended over several centuries. But the mixture of Greek analytical procedures with the rich heritage of cosmological myth from eastern lands, all of which seemed to converge in Alexandria, did produce, for a brief two or three hundred years, at either side of the turn of the epochs, an exciting and intensely creative atmosphere and the circumstances in which the Hellenistic genius becomes apparent. In the plastic arts, in painting, sculpture, jewellery and architecture, the Hellenistic style, its intellectual dynamic so largely established in Alexandria, changed the appearance and the life-styles of the entire population of the region and far beyond it. In literature, too, a new freedom and delight in the exercise of literary composition becomes apparent, in effect for the first time, though with the great originals of the past, even, in Egypt itself, of the distant past, still in mind.

For the Greeks Egypt was a land of wonders where the gods, even in the days of its decline, were still very close. Much of the most intense speculation and debate amongst the Alexandrians was about the nature of the gods and their relationship with the visible world. The Ptolemies, following Alexander's own clearly expressed ideals of the synthesis of peoples and faiths, promoted a composite divinity, who became especially identified with the city. This was Serapis, a patriarchal god who was the conflation of Osiris, the god of regeneration and Apis, the sacred bull, with whom, from the very earliest times, the creator god Ptah had been identified. Serapis' cults spread over much of the ancient world, extending, under Roman influence, into Europe. Similarly the cult of Mithras, though it originated in Persia, made great inroads in the last centuries of the ancient world and in the first centuries of the Christian era.[6]

The two most powerful divinities to become associated with this last, dying phase of Egypt's history were Dionysos, an Asiatic god adopted by the Greeks, and Isis, the compassionate mother goddess. She was especially identified in Egyptian mythology with the life and death of Osiris and the upbringing of his heir, Horus.

Alexandria, and the influence of Hellenism generally, brought into sharp relief the idea of the individual. The emergence of individual awareness had been the product of the process which resulted first in the recognition of the identity of Egypt and of its people, over many hundreds of years. In late antiquity recognition of the individual accelerated and became one of the dominant themes in the philosophy of the period, as expressed most notably by scholars such as Epicurus and Zeno. Closely associated with this was the concept of individual salvation, which had been implicit in Egyptian beliefs from the earliest days, eventually to become the attainable goal of all people.

Many of the cults of late antiquity encouraged the aspirations of the individual to seek and attain salvation. Osiris, like his composite successor Serapis, was one of the most fully realised of saviour gods; so too was Dionysos, who was really the patron divinity of Alexandria in the centuries of Ptolemaic rule. Orpheus appeared again, the epitome of the arts of which Alexandria was so richly observant. Mithras, too, was a saviour god and his cult had great appeal especially to the Roman legions who succeeded the Greeks in the rule of Egypt.

With the spread of religions which preached individual salvation there also flowed a mass of magical and occult faiths, logical enough if the idea of the individual's ability to influence his own salvation is admitted.[7] Astrology became a practice peculiarly associated with Alexandria and the Levant and by its arts the individual could predict and hence – presumably – influence his destiny and ultimately his prospects of salvation.[8]

Around the turn of the epochs, in the first century BC, these beliefs spread over a substantial part of the ancient world and then north and westwards into Europe. The Roman legions, especially after the conquest of Egypt, bore the message of Mithras and of Serapis to the most barbarous outlands, even Scotland. But the most powerful of all the images of divinity which at this time flowed out of Egypt was of the Mother holding her child on her lap. This ancient symbol of the transmission of the divine Kingship from the heiress to the Horus was transmuted into the image of Mary and her child, the Queen of Heaven and the son of man who is also the Son of God, a divine king whose divinity is mediated through his mother's impregnation by a patriarchal divinity.

The extent of Isis' cult was immense. Like that of Serapis it reached deep into Western Europe, into Gaul and the basin of the Danube. Isis was undoubtedly one of the reasons for the ready acceptance of the reverence – some would say worship – of the Mother of God when Christianity became established as the successor to all the ancient cults. These declined but they did not disappear. The image of the compassionate, caring mother, nursing her child, was the last great archetype which Egypt released to the world.

The heady mixture of divinity, the transience of mortal life, magic, great luxury and the ebb and flow of nations lends the Hellenistic period a particular but appealing intensity. Given the indebtedness of the world of medieval Europe and, especially, of the Renaissance, to Hellenism, this may account for the penetration of the idea of ancient Egypt, however bizarre and outlandish its interpretation might sometimes be, which went so deep into the European consciousness.

The crucial archetypal figure of this period is Alexander himself. It was he who, in a quite uncanny fashion, seems to have anticipated the sort of world which was waiting to be born. The idea of a universal empire, of what might, with proper qualifications and the acknowledgment of his own supreme position, high above the ordinary run of humanity, be called the brotherhood of men, existed in his complex mind at least to the extent that he saw all men as potential subjects of his *imperium*. He stands as the end of the ancient world and as the beginning of the new age, the omega and the alpha. He is the greatest of all historical enigmas, for if he had lived and turned to extend his empire to the west, whilst consolidating his Mediterranean possessions, the world would clearly have been a very different place and, perhaps, a more compassionate and liberated one.

If Alexander represents the archetype of the last great period of Egyptian history, the ultimate Great Individual, there is another, shadowy and rather sorrowful figure who may be taken as the exemplar of its end. He, too, is enigmatic, almost wholly obscure, confined to the footnotes of history. Yet his ancestry was august and in his blood may have run two most powerful inheritances.

This was Caesarion, the son of Cleopatra VII and Julius Caesar, the product of the months which Caesar spent in Egypt in 47 BC. By his descent

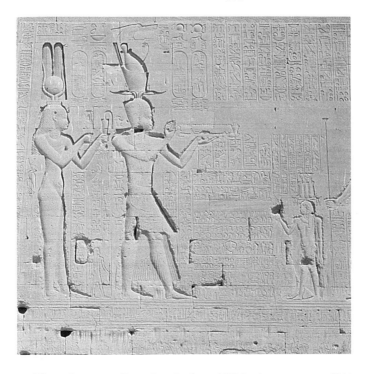

Figure 20 The unfortunate Caesarion, Ptolemy XV, in the company of his mother, Cleopatra VII, worshipping divinities. Caesarion was murdered on the orders of Augustus Caesar, after the suicide of his mother and her lover, Mark Antony, in 30 BC.

from the Ptolemies Caesarion possibly shared in the same genes as Alexander, if the parentage of Ptolemy I, from Philip II of Macedon, is to be believed. Caesar needed no justification as a parent, for he would have been the most exalted of ancestors, apart from his own acknowledged descent from the goddess Venus.

Caesar had no surviving sons by anyone other than Cleopatra. Caesarion was thus heir both to the might of Rome and to the legend of Alexander. The party of Caesar in Rome could not have resisted a living heir of his body, despite his slightly dubious Greek connections. In Egypt he reigned briefly as Ptolemy XV Caesarion (36–30 BC); he could fairly have bid to be King of the World. It is little wonder that, after the death of Cleopatra and of Caesar's successor in her affections, Mark Antony, Octavius, Caesar's nephew and heir apparent, had Caesarion put to death.

CHAPTER XV

THE MYTH OF EGYPT

—— .◆. ——

Egypt in antiquity existed not only in actuality, in the north-eastern quadrant of Africa at the point where the forces which were to mould civilisation meet and intersect, but also in the borderlands between myth and reality. The collective unconscious of the population of the Valley in the seventh and sixth millennia, when it was first permanently settled, was in a state of readiness to make a quantum leap in social and intellectual development which, in a very short space of time, would lead to the creation of one of the first and most diverse of complex societies.

When such concepts developed further, in the particular circumstances of the Nile Valley in the late fourth millennium BC, they became set in entirely Egyptian forms. Though their practical expression, their translation into forms which would survive exposure to reality, must have been problematical, survive they did, as peculiarly Egyptian institutions; thus they became forever fixed. It is in this sense that Egypt may be said to be the pristine society, its people living under a system wholly different (though not entirely out of touch with) the neolithic community and its more distant predecessors.

It is this outward flow of archetypal, primordial forms in early Egypt which gives it so particular and enduring a power to move and to fill those who contemplate even its ruins, and the destruction of its grandeur, with wonder. Because its forms are archetypal Egypt is instantly recognisable and familiar: because its institutions give rise to instant recognition, they may in turn be recognised as archetypal.

There is no agency at work in the creation of Egyptian civilisation other than the receptive responses of the minds of men. As men can conceive of gods, and give them form and substance as exemplified by Egyptian scribes and craftsmen, so gods, or demi-gods, or creatures with more than human capabilities and perceptions, become the symbols which men erect to explain what they do not understand. But all of ancient Egypt, in all its splendour, with all its marvels of creation and invention and with all the power of its intellectual processes, lay within the minds of men (and of women) living in the Valley of the Nile at this point in human history.

So far as we are able to judge, the Egyptians did not greatly concern themselves with the invention of stories to explain the inexplicable. There are Egyptian myths, of course, but they are nothing like as many or as rich as, say, the myths of the Mesopotamians or of the Semitic-speaking peoples of the Near East (who were unquenchably given to the production of myth) or of the Greeks, who really did sustain a degree of childlike wonder at the world which myth helped to express. Egyptian myths are rather matter-of-fact and, in any case, are probably rather late in their invention; many of the finest stories from Egypt in their recorded form date from the Middle Kingdom and later.

The Egyptians, certainly in the time of the Old Kingdom, did not need the support of myth for they had the archetypes to sustain them, in an immediate, physical and institutional form around them, everywhere they looked. It was only when the pressures of the combination of political circumstances and unforeseen environmental factors became intolerable that the pristine Egyptian society began to disintegrate, though, so powerful was its essential structure that its form survived for another two thousand years, for half of that period as a dominant force in the world of its time. For most of its history Egypt existed on the borderline of the mythic and the real. Its achievements were real enough, none, perhaps, more so, but the myth which it released into the world was even more enduring.

The Egyptians in the early periods of their history, down to the end of the Middle Kingdom, radiate a sort of sublime assurance, a sense that, truly for those living in the Nile Valley, all was for the best in the best of all possible worlds. The stories which they told were concerned more with the relationships of men in society, their connections with authority or their response to misfortune or injustice. But in the beginning, in the time when the expression of the archetypes was new and Egyptian society was unfolding like the lotus flower under the rays of the sun (one of the potent symbols beloved by the people) only the Kingship needed definition, tracking the course by which Egypt, and hence the known world, was to be ruled in truth. First the gods had themselves governed Egypt (and thus the world), then the demi-gods, the Followers of Horus. Finally the Kingship was transmuted into a human institution but with the qualification that its holder, rising from the seat of his coronation, was god.

The king embraced in his superhuman person all the archetypes which flowed into the Valley just as he towered above all mortals who attended him. There is no moral teaching, no promptings of right over wrong, no concern with the revelation of a divine will. If the king lives for ever, then Egypt lives for ever and men, 'the cattle of god', take their place before him, so that he may drive them forward.

The gods of Egypt are not really to be compared with the other colleges of divinities who generally plagued the lives of ancient Near Eastern societies, just as, it might be said, their successors have continued to do today. In their early form they are abstractions, though aspects of their often elusive natures will provide the key to their later appearances. Horus is the youthful god soaring into the sky, to become the ever reborn son, who occupies the throne of Egypt; eventually Osiris will be named his father.

Ma'at is truth, in whose name the king must rule, Ptah is the sublime creator.

The world of appearances was not of the first importance to the Egyptians, when contemplating the management of the Universe or the prospects of the survival of life after death. As highly intelligent men who created the most august of all human societies, they did not need to be told that life ended at death but they believed that it was possible to arrest the process or rather to transform it into another state, not necessarily for all eternity, but certainly for 'millions of years'.

Much of the world which surrounded the Egyptians was expressed in symbols; indeed, they rarely expressed a concept directly, in absolute terms. It was part of the Egyptians' psychological equipment that this should be so. As Jung wrote: 'The symbol mediates the passage of psychic energy from the unconscious in order that it may be applied consciously and turned to practical account.'[1]

All meanings are shaded; even the hieroglyphs convey meanings at one level which may be confirmed or revoked at another level of appearance or comprehension. Patterns and colours shift; just as is often the case in the white light of an Egyptian midday, things are not always as they seem.

Later, when Egypt was already in decline, this tendency towards the veiled meaning, the equivocal appearance, became a sort of game which Egypt played with the world outside its frontiers when foreigners came into the Valley to gaze with awe at a civilisation whose antiquity and splendour they could barely comprehend. Then, no doubt, the priests provided wonderful shows to impress or terrify the simple. Thus the legend of Egypt grew as, with the immense advantage of two millennia and more of high culture behind them, the reputation for magic and the presence of the gods gained currency. Though such demonstrations of Egypt's wonders were merely plays, they contained, even at the end of Egyptian history, a nub of ancient truth. All of those who have come in contact with the truth of Egypt will recognise this reality and the ancient archetypal power which it radiates.

The antiquity of Egypt focused the archetypal promptings of men living in societies around the Mediterranean and, ultimately, far beyond it. Over the centuries following the end of Egypt's dominance its myth grew, to become an essential part of the intellectual stock of the Western world.

The myth of Egypt was released into the modern world largely as a consequence of the invasion of Egypt undertaken by the young Napoleon Bonaparte in 1798.[2] Not a man much given to exaggeration or bombast, for indeed he had little need for either, Napoleon described Egypt as 'the most important country in the world'. Yet to speak thus of a country whose habitable land surface is approximately equal to that of Belgium may, at first sight, seem something of an overstatement.

After all, even in Napoleon's day, Egypt was not only a relatively small country, it was hopelessly backward, a disregarded province of the Ottoman

Empire which, though its rule was a good deal more creditable than is usually admitted, particularly by the successors of those states which eventually dismembered it, was not notable for concerning itself greatly with the advancement or aspirations of its diverse subject peoples. The Turkish élite lived in conditions of agreeable and indulgent degeneracy, indulging in every vice at whim, often with an ingenuity which would have impressed Tiberius. The Mamluks, that very strange self-perpetuating body of noble slave warriors whose addiction to homosexuality was apparently one of the criteria for advancement in their order, were still at large in the land, ruling it with caprice and, sometimes, with extraordinary elegance. Life for the native Egyptians, if not intolerable, was not greatly to be envied, subject to the depredations of the tax-gatherers and the threat of the bastinado or worse.

But one knows what Napoleon means. Even in his day the writings of the ancients, especially the Greek and Roman historians and geographers, had given a sense of Egypt's occult, seemingly impenetrable mystery. The Greeks wrote of Egypt with wonder; the Romans pillaged it and in doing so first introduced its great treasury of sculpture to Europe.

Two of the most influential writers on matters Egyptian in late antiquity were Diodorus and Plutarch. The former, writing in the lifetime of Julius Caesar, described Egypt at length in *Biblioteca Historica*. He was an enthusiast for the god Osiris who, leading his army east and west, brought civilisation to all peoples that he encountered, an amalgam, as it were, of the legendary Senwosret and the benign god Dionysos. Much of what he wrote is accurate reporting; he saw and described the monuments and he tried to understand something of the nature of the Egyptian world. He was of great influence in transmitting the image of Egypt as a land of marvels to Europe.

Somewhat earlier Plutarch, a priest of Delphi in the second century BC, provided much of the learned information on which the mystical image of Egypt was based. In particular he was responsible for the transmission of the myths of Isis and Osiris into the European consciousness. The importance of the Isis archetype, in particular, to the acceptance of Christian imagery in Europe can hardly be exaggerated.

In late medieval times both these authors, and other writers like Strabo and Pliny who approached Egypt from more specialised interests, were translated and keenly studied. Other texts, of more doubtful provenance like the supposed writings of Hermes Trismegistus, who was believed to be a contemporary of Moses, added considerably to the myth of Egypt if they did not add materially to the store of factual knowledge about the Nile civilisation.[3]

From time to time adventurous travellers entered Egypt and returned to Europe, full of marvellous tales. The primacy of Egypt, though still veiled, could yet be discerned among the nations, however dimly. The Crusaders had done something to accustom Europe to the fact of Egypt. The king of France had contrived to have himself captured on Egyptian territory; earlier, to the fury of the Church, the Hohenstauffen Emperor Frederick II had negotiated a treaty with the Shia Caliph in Cairo and, in the process, recovered Jerusalem, an outcome which all the armies of the West, the ecclesiastics and everyone else had absolutely failed to do.[4] Frederick, in consequence, was never forgiven, especially not by the Papacy which, incidentally, had appropriated some of the trappings of kings of Egypt – the portable throne, the ostrich feather fans, the seven-stepped platform on which the throne itself stood – to supplement their own state.

Napoleon knew that Egypt lay at a point which, judged from the Eurocentric view of the world which had prevailed for long before and was to prevail for long after his time, seemed plumb centre between the eastern and western hemispheres, and between north and south. To the Arabs, Cairo was the 'Mother of the World', but Cairo was a city-come-lately, a mere eight hundred years old in Napoleon's time. Egypt, very definitely, could be seen as the world's mother, and Napoleon, though speaking undoubtedly of the country's strategic importance, seems to have apprehended this admittedly rather mystical point.

Napoleon invaded Egypt principally with the objective of containing the imperial pretensions of England, which he rightly saw as the enemy of French expansionism in Europe and beyond. Where Napoleon's conduct was so remarkable was that in his preparations for the capture of Egypt he included the recruitment of a band of France's most distinguished scholars, scientists, writers and artists of the day, to accompany the Army which he had assembled. Their brief was to study and record the antiquities of Egypt and to publish their findings to the world.

Napoleon lost Egypt but the world gained an immeasurable treasure. The immediate result of the work of the savants whom he carried with him was the massive and majestic *Description de l'Egypte* published in fifteen elephant volumes between 1809 and 1829.

The *Description* had a profound effect on scholarly awareness of the riches which Egypt held. It was not of course the first such survey – one thinks of Norden, of the *Antiquities, Natural History, Ruins and other Curiosities of Egypt, Nubia and Thebes*, first published in 1755, of Montfaucon's massive *Antiquité expliquée et representée en figures* (1719–1724), and many, many more – but the *Description* was incomparably the most comprehensive, replete with wonderful drawings of the Egyptian countryside, monuments, people, costume, architecture, wildlife, plants and flowers. It was followed, throughout the nineteenth century, by a river of publications on all aspects of life in the Nile Valley which, if they did not match the splendour of the *Description* added substantially to the fields of knowledge which it had first defined. Not the least of these, published also in France, was the work of Baron Denon, who had accompanied

Napoleon. *Voyages en Haute et Basse Egypte* contains some of the finest drawings of sites in Egypt before the depredations either of the archaeologists or the modern world had harmed them.[5]

The genie which Napoleon released rapidly became a shape of tremendous and triumphant power. Egypt began more and more to feature in the creative work of European artists and writers.[6] But to speak, as some will do, of the 'rediscovery' of Egypt at this time is to misunderstand the processes at work. Egypt had never been lost to the consciousness of the lands around the Mediterranean nor of that part of the world which draws its intellectual, religious and social inspiration from them. At first consciously, as in the case of Greece or, earlier still, of some of the Levantine lands, Egypt was the model which indicated 'the way that things were done'. Later, as time went by and as societies expanded and became more sophisticated themselves, the influences began to operate at a less conscious level, though they were always likely to erupt into visibility. In Roman times, with some mediation from Greece, public buildings, the soaring columns, statuary and the exiled Egyptian obelisks themselves gave an Egyptian stamp to the Imperial city. In the Middle Ages the stories in the Christian Bible kept Egypt's name alive with the figure of 'Pharaoh' looming formidably over the fortunes of the Christians' notional confessional ancestors, the Jews and their supposed 'captivity'. Without an awareness of Egyptian architecture and many of its decorative elements, the Renaissance is hardly thinkable; the decipherment of hieroglyphs became something of a passion amongst scholars who believed that all manner of mysteries and wisdom were contained in their beautiful and innocent shapes. The practice of alchemy flourished during this time similarly, keeping alive a connection which ran back to Hellenistic Egypt and one of its more exotic products, gnosticism.

The gods of Egypt never died. Even after the demise of Egypt as an independent, self-governing nation, the gods continued to exercise their sway over the minds of men. Cults of Isis and Osiris, of the composite Serapis, of Horus, Anubis and Ptah, spread to lands of which the Egyptians themselves probably had no knowledge. These divinities contributed much to the formulation of the Christian archetypes: the bearded all-powerful father (present of course as Zeus, another appearance of the silver-backed male raised to the level of the godhead) the compassionate mother, holding the child who is to rule on her maternal lap which is also a throne, Horus himself who is the youthful warrior, who reappears as the sainted dragon-slayer, even perhaps as Siegfried in his original Burgundian character, before he was entirely subsumed into another set of myths.

The single most important element which alerted the imaginations of artists and philosophers in Renaissance and later Europe was the system of writing which had evolved in the Valley in the latter centuries of the fourth and the early centuries of the third millennia. Egyptian hieroglyphs were quite other than any form of epigraphy known to the world of late antiquity; the heirs of that world, the intellectuals who came towards the light in the more generous times which followed the end of the Middle Ages, responded to their mystery with delight and the excitement of being on the verge of an entirely new dimension of human experience. It was the Egyptian hieroglyphs, even more than the obelisks standing rather forlornly in a Roman square or the statue of a king adorning a Papal villa which, quite properly, were seen to contain the mystery of Egypt.

Post-medieval Europe was right to recognise that nowhere is the quality of the Egyptian experience, its originality and the intensely symbolic nature of its culture more vividly and directly manifested than in the system which the Egyptians evolved for recording, first the names of the kings and the principal events associated with their reigns, then the names and worship of the gods, and, eventually, the records of the daily lives, aspirations and apprehensions of the people, great and small. With a nice perception of what is right, the Greeks called Egyptian writing 'sacred signs', so wonderful did they seem to them.

As with so much associated with the ancient Egyptians, their writing appears at first sight at once familiar and deeply obscure. The form of Egyptian orthography is rooted in the capacity for observation and the love of natural forms enmeshed with a preoccupation with symbolic expression. This had the effect of concealing the deeper reality under a familiar form which would protect that reality from a too-ready or unprepared elucidation. As in all societies of a deeply conservative nature determined by hieratic principles, Egyptian forms rarely reveal their true meaning at first glance: they are therefore, to this extent, essentially symbolic and, in a literal sense, occult.

There are altogether some six hundred characters in the Egyptian signary which were in general use. The majority of these are instantly recognisable as literal representations of familiar objects: animals, objects of household or agricultural use, human figures and parts of the body, plants and the like. There are very few abstract signs and some which seem to have no parallel in the world of actuality.

One of the distinctive marks of Egyptian high culture is that it rarely chooses the easy option in any of its manifestations. All Egyptian forms, whether of architecture, in ritual practices or in political organisation, seem to be designed to survive over many centuries. The same consideration applies to Egyptian inscriptions. Egyptian hieroglyphs are unquestionably beautiful, but they are very complex. In a monumental inscription or on a vividly illustrated papyrus their creation would have represented a considerable outlay of effort and the most refined skill. In later times two forms of cursive writing were invented; *hieratic* used in formal contexts and, much later still, *demotic*, which became the vehicle of ordinary correspondence and literature. But the glory of hieroglyphs is in the form which evolved during the Old Kingdom and achieved its highest level of development in the Middle Kingdom, the classical period of much Egyptian creativity.

Hieroglyphic writing is already well established early in the First Dynasty; it is used to record the names of the earliest kings, in the *serekh* which proclaimed their 'Horus' names. The pictographic origin of hiero-glyphic writing is clear; in many of the small ivory 'labels' which record important events in the early reigns, the signs are used to show objects or events quite realistically. Swiftly, however, the technique develops until, by the latter part of the First Dynasty, complex messages can be conveyed.[7]

To compare the Egyptian system of writing with that created by the Sumerians in southern Iraq, who are usually credited with the actual inven-tion of writing, reveals both the similarities and the differences between the two systems. The earliest examples of Sumerian epigraphy appear in the latter part of the fourth millennium, some decades before any recog-nisable inscriptions appear in Egypt. The Sumerians began with a picto-graphic script, though a much simpler one than the Egyptians produced. However, they quite early discarded pictographs, which they found cumbersome, and gradually evolved cuneiform, the script which, in its final evolution having gone through some six phases, lasted into the first millen-nium BC.[8] In Egypt, once they were established during the early dynasties the hieroglyphs continued unchanged, except in small details, and with the occasional deletion or addition of a particular character, until the dissolution of all vestiges of Egyptian culture, in the fourth century AD.

Because hieroglyphs could express the most abstruse ideas, as witness the Pyramid Texts, and were employed for every conceivable use, from the royal and liturgical inscriptions, through law, commerce, storytelling, scientific observation, medical practice, surveying or mathematics, they contributed as much to the development of the historic Egyptian person-ality as they were an expression of it. As they represented known and familiar objects and creatures, they reinforced the essentially pragmatic character of the Egyptians as much as their majestic forms enhanced the already exalted idea which the Egyptians held of their place in the world.

The Egyptian language itself changed over the centuries, to an extent greater than the changes which the hieroglyphs themselves underwent. The high point of literary Egyptian is generally reckoned to be the Middle Kingdom period. Before that the written language of the Old Kingdom is relatively sparse and obscure though its literary products, particularly the Pyramid Texts, are amongst the most important expressions of the Egyptians' thought and rituals. In the New Kingdom the language became somewhat more baroque, perhaps to permit a more extravagant quality of statement to which some of the Kings and their adherents were given.

Egyptian contains traces of an Hamitic, African strain and rather more Semitic borrowings.[9] There are also, intriguingly, words, particularly those which have an agricultural connotation, which seem to be Sumerian in origin.[10] Egyptian hieroglyphs contained the rudiments of an alphabet. Some of the signs represented a single consonant; there are no vowels in Egyptian. The same sign could be employed in different contexts, conveying different meanings; in consequence, it was customary to add, at the end of the word, a determinative which indicated the group's meaning. In this practice too Egyptian and Sumerian share a similar, though not identical, technique for Sumerian determinatives precede rather than follow the word which they qualify.

Hieroglyphs tended to be reserved principally for the most monumental and formal purposes; their most frequently used medium was the inscription in stone and the finest examples are of an extraordinary beauty and power. Sometimes wood was used though inevitably fewer examples than those of stone inscriptions have survived. However, one set of inscriptions carved in wood is amongst the oldest: from the mastaba tomb of Hesy-ra, a Third Dynasty noble who was one of the chief ministers of King Djoser Netjerykhet. The hieroglyphic texts which are carved on acacia-wood panels setting out his titles and offices (amongst other attainments he was a dentist) are amongst the most elegant of all to survive from so early a time.[11]

Papyrus was widely used to carry Egyptian texts, a forerunner of paper. The papyrus sheets, formed from pounded papyrus pith, cut into lengths laid side by side with a second layer laid above the first at right angles, and then polished with a stone, were ideal materials on which to write formal inscriptions, invocations, royal decrees or to paint the marvellous scenes which were used in Middle Kingdom and New Kingdom times to guide the dead on their journeys to the afterlife.

A mastery of the hieroglyphs was the proudest achievement of an educated Egyptian. The profession of scribe was one of great prestige and the ability to write opened the way to the highest reaches of the administration, even to a man of relatively modest origins. The scribe in consequence was convinced of his own ineffable superiority, which he was not above vaunting over his less advantaged contemporaries.

It is a matter of some dispute how much 'scientific' knowledge (to use a word which would have been meaningless to all Egyptians) was contained in Egyptian writings. There are texts which deal with mathematical problems, but these seem to be little more than exercises for the education of budding scribes. There are extensive texts which are concerned with medical practice, both clinical and surgical, some alleged to be from very early times indeed. They are of a disconcerting amalgam of quite sophisticated knowledge and what a modern reader might regard as simple superstition. There is very little in the surviving texts which displays the profound knowledge and control of technique which must have supported the construction of the great monuments or the subtle observation of the stars.

Egyptian hieroglyphs are, like all the other products of the Egyptian psyche, complex and often distinctly, even wilfully obscure. Sometimes they seem designed to conceal as much as they reveal: sometimes their usage is remote from the understanding of modern minds. The Egyptians loved games with words; hieroglyphs depend for their understanding not only on their meaning, but also on their sound, for a sign may have a different sound in different contexts, and on their visual effect. No more elegant, nor more carefully veiled system of communication has yet been devised by any historic society.

It is surprising that no Egyptian-Greek inscription had been found before the Rosetta Stone, whose decipherment (a story so often told) by Champollion finally led to the uncovering of Egypt's literary heritage, opening it to Europe and the world. Many of the Greek world's most adventurous intellects were said to have studied in Egypt and to have gained wisdom from the priests: Solon, Pythagoras and Plato all claimed Egypt as the location of their higher education; but of these only Pythagoras seems to have studied the Egyptian language. None of the others apparently did so nor sought to read the inscriptions which they saw all around them. In common with other Greek travellers, including Herodotus, who went to Egypt specifically in search of information, they relied upon the often inaccurate and sometimes deliberately misleading, interpretations which were given to them.

The Romans were much less impressed by things Egyptian. This did not prevent them from exporting many Egyptian antiquities to Rome during imperial times, including the twelve obelisks which grace the eternal city's squares to this day. The emperors were all proclaimed Egyptian kings though few ever bothered to visit their Egyptian province; a notable exception was Hadrian, whose journey to the Nile in 130 AD culminated in the mysterious death of his young lover, Antinuous, subsequently deified.

The inscriptions did not, apparently, excite much interest at the time that they were taken to Rome and there are no reports of any attempt to translate them though, of course, there would still have been many Egyptians who could have done so. Though the hieroglyphs remained silent during the time of Rome's greatness, it was the inscriptions on the looted statuary which eventually were to stimulate so much scholarly interest in the centuries to come, especially during the Renaissance.

Ancient Egyptian was transmuted into Coptic and became the language of Christianity in Egypt, heavily Graecised. The language of the kings, which had evolved over the preceding five millennia at least, was lost. The overlaying of Arabic in language and culture in the seventh century of the present era contributed further to its disappearance.

The hieroglyphs really returned to the consciousness of Europe during the period which followed the Crusades, which, however uneasily, had opened up the Moslem world including Egypt, which was largely Islamised in the seventh century, to contact with Europe. There were occasional reports from European travellers who visited Egypt of the wonders which the Valley still revealed so prodigally; many of these visitors were monks who tended to be more concerned about the threat which Islam was thought to represent to Christendom.

The antiquities of Egypt were noted, but did not attract the wonder that they once had done in the days of the Greek travellers. The Pyramids were Judaised by Christian travellers, to make them acceptable to minds nurtured on the Old Testament. In this transformation they became the granaries in which Joseph stored grain in the lean years.

Even before the Reformation there were scholars who caught echoes of the classical tradition that the hieroglyphs contained the occult wisdom of the Egyptians. Some scholars, standing on the threshold of comparative linguistic studies, sought the secret of the signs and attempted to break open the secrets which it was believed they concealed.

What typified most of the early attempts to decipher the hieroglyphs was the belief that the signs were symbolic, their meaning concealed beneath the appearance of the signs themselves. This is an idea which has not been entirely discarded today. It was believed that the signs grouped together spelled out a message which could only be fully apprehended by inspiration, rather than by analysis. Attempts to provide a 'translation' became more and more remote, even bizarre. The Egyptian syllabary was complex but relatively direct; its admirers in Europe in the period from the late Middle Ages to the early nineteenth century laid obfuscation upon ignorance and in the process produced interpretations of the Egyptian mystery, like those which ultimately led to *Die Zauberflöte* in Schikaneder's wonderful if overwrought libretto.

A text, possibly originating in the fourth century AD, its authorship ascribed to one Horapollo, began to gain considerable currency amongst the cultivated, humanistic intellectual élite which was appearing in European centres of learning from the fifteenth century following its publication by Christoforo Buondelmonti, who found it on the island of Andros. Nothing is known of this Horapollo, who does not seem to have been any of the living Egyptians who bore that name. His treatise purported to reveal the meaning of the hieroglyphs and gained rapid fame in intellectual circles. It exercised a considerable influence in late medieval times and is still current in magical and occult circles.[12]

One of the first scholars to take a more or less objective view of the issue, to the extent that he sought to treat the hieroglyphs principally as a form of writing and not merely as the vehicle for the transmission of occult teachings, was Pierno, who translated a series of Hermetic treatises, works of late antiquity preserved in Greek. They were seized on by scholars of the day with enthusiasm for they appeared to open a new door to the literature of the past which hitherto had been closed to them.

This movement inevitably attracted more dubious adherents, of whom Nonnius was probably the most influential. He produced a series of fairly ridiculous forgeries of monuments bearing entirely invented hieroglyphs which nonetheless were accepted by many and served further to perplex those scholars who earnestly sought to penetrate their meaning.

Looking with twentieth-century eyes at the products of men like Nonnius it is difficult to see how anyone, with the evidence of the inscriptions on the obelisks in Rome, for example, before them, could even have thought them to have been original products of Egyptian hands. This is one of the mysteries, even of early Egyptology, for the renderings of the monuments, as much of the inscriptions, of early professional Egyptologists working in the early part of the nineteenth century, are frequently as inept. It is as though the hieroglyphs were determined to keep their secrets for as long as possible.

The early sixteenth century was characterised by a more liberal acceptance of the pagan world combined with potent manifestations of Papal supremicism. In Rome that remarkable pontiff Alexander VI Borgia was greatly intrigued by Egypt's past and, with a distinctly casual attitude to the precepts of the religion of which he was the Shepherd, sought to trace the descent of his own family from the union of Isis and Osiris. Pinturicchio painted a series of murals for the private apartments in the Vatican which celebrate the Pope's ancestry. The two gods stand together, attended by an Apis bull who, observing the Pontiff's supposed ancestors with a profoundly sceptical expression, clearly believes not a word of it.

As the intellectual climate in Europe began to change, with the dawn of the sixteenth century and later the clash of opposing ideologies dramatised brutally in the Thirty Years War, the Reformation introduced a more sceptical attitude, one much less inclined to accept wonders at their face value or as they were represented, but rather to question them. The hieroglyphs now moved increasingly into the realm of science, away from that of religious or philosophical speculation.

Paradoxically, a prime mover in this process was the Jesuit scholar Athanasius Kircher.[13] Becoming fascinated by the hieroglyphs at an early age, he set out to break their code; the paradox in his endeavours derives from his preconception that the signs were symbolic and much of his work was directed towards proving this belief. He published extensively and enjoyed the patronage of several antiquarian-minded popes. He did much to focus scholarly attention on the hieroglyphs and his work, though misguided, gave impetus to later attempts to translate them. He was constantly on the lookout for new texts and inscriptions and was tireless in promoting awareness of them.

The seventeenth century saw the foundation of some of the great European collections, first as accumulations of 'curiosities', later as more sophisticated assemblages of the art and material heritage of the ancient world. Oxford University had one of the earliest collections of Egyptian material; it was notable for the fact that, even at this early date, Egyptian antiquities were being counterfeited, for an ushabti, presented to the Bodeian Library in 1635 by Archbishop Laud, was a fake.[14]

During the eighteenth century a more penetrating view of the hieroglyphs and of the monuments of Egypt began to prevail. Savants such as Sicard,[15] though the original of his work was lost, reported accurately on the sites which he visited. Another, Benoît de Maillet, was amongst the first observers to note that, in addition to the formal hieroglyphs familiar from inscriptions, the Egyptians also had a cursive script, the recognition of which began to divest the hieroglyphs of some of their symbolic, mystical import.[16]

An English traveller, Richard Pococke, visited Egypt in 1770 and reached the source of the Blue Nile; he recorded inscriptions in the tomb of Ramesses III.[17] But of course the breakthrough in the decipherment of hieroglyphs came about, not as the result of an English traveller penetrating their secrets but by the insistence of the British authorities that a trilingual inscription, found by French soldiers at Rosetta, should be declared spoils of war. Champollion obtained a copy of the inscription, in hieroglyphs, cursive script and Greek, and was the first successfully to translate a substantial Egyptian text.[18]

At last the ancient Egyptians were able to speak. Over the next two centuries, to the present day, countless texts, preserved by the climate of Egypt and the durability of stone and papyrus, have been translated. There are still some mysteries, some words which so far defy translation and the elusive, often elliptical methods of Egyptian thought and expression have frequently conspired to render the meaning of some inscriptions, like the Pyramid Texts, virtually impenetrable. The wells of recollection of Europe's Egyptian past were opened by Napoleon's savants and those who followed them; since that time they have never ceased flowing.

※　　※　　※　　※

The past two centuries of the study of the civilisation of ancient Egypt have given access, on a scale greater perhaps than for any other ancient society, to the minds of the people who lived in the Valley over the three thousand years of Egypt's history. The textual inheritance, like the material heritage of Egyptian civilisation, is a treasury of incalculable value. If the basic contention of this book is tenable, that in Egypt men living in a complex society which was the first to become a nation-state were similarly the first to recognise and to name the archetypes which flowed out of the collective unconscious, then it may with justice be said, as Napoleon so intuitively understood, that Egypt is still the most important country in the world, the matrix in which all subsequent achievements were contained.

Further, it may be said that those who, however vicariously, have an engagement with ancient Egypt, who respect its quality and who approach the study of its contribution to the world with proper deference, have access to a treasure as wonderful as Tutankhamun's and an enduring privilege. Because of its archetypal qualities Egypt is the most humane of ancient societies, its humanity of profound and continuing value to the world of today. The observation may invite mockery but access to the mystery of Egypt puts those who enjoy that access into a hierarchic structure which reaches back over fifty centuries and more. There is no consecration required or necessary for this particular hierarchy, other than a recognition of the unique quality of the inheritance which much of the world still draws from Egypt.

The insecurities which life in mass have induced in the collective psyche of contemporary man are too evident to require description. Since the Renaissance at least, and particularly over the past century, the relics of Egyptian civilisation have been the happy hunting ground of those who seek for human destiny in the stars or who hope for a solution to the dilemma of human existence by the intervention, in the past or to come, of beings from distant space or a kindly, patriarchal divinity.

It may be recalled that Jung examined one aspect of the psychological confusions of modern man when he ascribed the appearance of Flying Saucers, of wonderful objects seen in the sky, to times of uncertainty and as the products of the psychic projections of those who observed them.[19] The 'existence' of Flying Saucers implies the existence of some other intelligence which has a concern, for good or evil, for mankind. So it is with those who believe that the builders of the Pyramids left encoded messages for the enlightenment of future generations.

For those who think in such terms it is difficult to accept that the splendours of ancient Egypt and its achievements are the products of humankind, represented by the psychic upsurge which the releasing of the archetypes, locked in the collective unconscious, made possible. That the intervention of mysterious forces, extraterrestrials or the inhabitants of other dimensions is thus sought for confirms, if confirmation were required, the generally modest view which humans tend to take of themselves and of their place in the order of things.

The Egyptians, in the finest centuries of their existence, did not suffer from such insecurities. This indeed is part of the reason for the enduring mystery of Egypt. It is also the product of the projections which the many generations of those from outside the Valley have placed on Egypt. Egypt therefore, in addition to its own undoubted quality, has borne the burden of others' apprehensions and wish fulfilment. Not even the Greatest of Seers could have foreseen so remarkable a destiny.

The mystery of Egypt is very great. It is so because it is the most creative and enduring expression of the greatest mystery of all, human consciousness. By defining the archetypes, by giving them form and so bringing a new set of concepts into the world, Egypt expanded immeasurably the boundaries of human awareness and, in consequence, of human creativity. Egypt did not invent consciousness but the psychic processes which were at work in the late predynastic period onwards gave rise to the expansion of consciousness and of what it could achieve, on a scale never before apprehended by men. The result was the creation of the entire majestic edifice which was the ancient Egyptian state.

Although the mythic quality which ancient Egypt conveys is very powerful, despite its plethora of gods, goddesses, kings, queens and assorted 'Great Ones', it is an entirely human construct, to be viewed in a human dimension. Because the development of ancient Egyptian society so precisely – and so uncannily – replicates the process whereby the individual achieves maturity, it has been possible for the individual, in all ages, to recognise the nature of the experience involved and to associate himself with it. That Egypt was a community rather than an individual does not invalidate that experience or make it less relevant: rather the opposite, for if nothing else it suggests what achievements could be realised by the individual who is aware of the process at work. The process which leads to the individuation of the Egyptian state precisely mirrors the experience of the individual moving towards the understanding of his own individual nature and existence. This emphasises that the Egyptian state, even in its richest and most complex form, was essentially a human institution. Ultimately, the King of Egypt, like all dominant figures of gods and men, fades into the awesome figure of the dominant alpha male, the old silver back, Jung's 'big ape', the ultimate ancestor of all authority and, in all his primate splendour, the fount of our humanity.

In him, amongst his closest companions the other alpha males, can be seen that most remarkable of all the incarnations of the Egyptian creative imagination, the cynocephalus Thoth, god of wisdom and of learning. His presence in the company of gods is an extraordinary witness of the Egyptians' genius at anticipating actuality and of giving form to ideas which only in our time have become understood. Thoth may stand as the embodiment of Egyptian wisdom, not occult or arcane but splendidly and assuredly primatial.

The underlying argument of this book turns back upon itself. Egypt represents what, sadly, has proved to be a unique experiment: the creation of a human society which is truly complex and not simple but which maintains a secure balance with the natural terrestrial world and with the stars and planets. It acknowledges and communicates with the psychic forces contained within the human unconscious whose power it liberates in the form of the archetypes. For almost two thousand years it kept all these forces in balance, to the immeasurable benefit of the small company of privileged humans who were fortunate enough to live in the Valley during the third and much of the second millennium BC but ultimately, for all mankind. Egypt was the land in which modern humans, after the long process of evolution from ape to king, discovered the way of living together and with nature. This was the time when man, not alone in Egypt, given the means of expression in writing and in art, first began to realise the truth about himself. As man proliferated the pristine glory of Egypt was bound to fade, though it lasted over a period which represents three-fifths of recorded history, ultimately to be replaced by other, more brutal systems of belief and government. But the experiment *had* been made and, thus far at least, its experience has not been forgotten.

NOTES

—— •◆• ——

PREFACE

1 Rice, 1990.

CHRONOLOGY

1 Manetho, trans. Waddell, 1940. Also quoted in Emery 1961.
2 P. F. O'Mara, 1979, *The Palermo Stone and the Archaic Kings of Egypt*, La Canada, Calif.
3 A. Gardiner, 1959, *The Royal Canon of Turin*, Oxford; Edwards 1971: 1–3, and *passim*.
4 One of the King Lists, originally in the Hall of Ancestors at Karnak, is now in the Louvre; the Seti list is *in situ*, at Abdyos.
5 Baines and Málek 1980.

CHAPTER I

1 Frankfort 1948a. Though it was published half a century ago, *Kingship and the Gods* remains the most authoritative study of ancient Near Eastern administrations which were based on the principle of Kingship. It demonstrates the many characteristics in common and the many differences between the Egyptian and the Mesopotamian systems.
2 Herodotus, Book II: 35.
3 O. Neugerbauer, 1957, *The Exact Sciences in Antiquity*, New York. Ch. 4 considers Egyptian mathematics largely as empirical and solution-orientated.
4 Thus G. J. Toomer in J. R. Harris (ed.), 1971, *The Legacy of Egypt*, Oxford, 45: 'The truth is that Egyptian mathematics remained at much too low a level to be able to contribute anything of value ... its interest for us lies in its primitive character.'
5 The several recensions of the Pyramid Texts are frequently referred to here; references will be found in Faulkner 1969, where the Texts are considered in their historical contexts.
6 Edwards 1947: 300–2, 304.
7 Bauval and Gilbert 1994, *passim*. The realisation that the layout of the Giza Plateau and of the other pyramid fields nearby may mimic the relative positions of the stars in Orion's belt, whilst perspicacious, should not really provoke unbridled surprise. That the Egyptians were consummate observers of the skies is an opinion constantly reiterated here; they identified the terrestrial Nile with the heavenly Nile, the Milky Way, which flowed across the brilliantly clear

night sky, which was so magical a sight before the onset of the ambient light of universal urban development. Given the equation of Osiris with Orion, which seems to have been made almost as soon as Osiris joined the pantheon, it is not surprising that they should have attempted to adapt the distribution of the principal stars in the constellation when planning the great monuments of the Pyramid Age. That they did so is yet another, if particularly remarkable, example of the ancient Egyptian ability to synthesise the practical and the mystical, by building the greatest structures the world had ever seen to replicate distant points of light in the sky.

As Orion was considered to be the location for the soul of Osiris, the Egyptian genius for synthesis might well have conceived of even so bold a plan as to bring down the stars which were to be his eternal home. It was, after all, no more daring a concept than building a stairway for him to ascend to the heavens which so evidently – as we shall see – was the intention of the architects of the stepped pyramids of an earlier generation.

8 This is an issue of some complexity and considerable dispute. The phenomenon exists: the question is whether the ancients knew that it did. The most perceptive recent study of the matter is undoubtedly de Santillana and von Dechend 1969/70. Krupp 1979 and Cornell 1981 also provide excellent commentaries on it. More recently still a remarkable work, Sellers 1992, has set the fact of the Precession firmly into an Egyptian context, to my eyes at least most convincingly.

The definition of the Precession seems to tax most writers who would comment on it, producing explanations of varying opacity and diversity. One of the more elegant, it seems to me, is that supplied by the Revd. J. Griffith, 1928, in *The Life and Work of Sir Norman Lockyer*, T. and M. Lockyer, London: 'Owing to a gradual change in the direction of the Earth's axis the north celestial pole gradually changes its position in the sky and the point of intersection of the horizon with the diurnal path of the heavenly bodies consequently changes its position also.

'The angle of the plane of the sun's apparent revolution around the Earth (the Ecliptic) and the plane of the Earth's equator undergo an alteration, so that the point in the sky measured with respect to the horizon at which the sun is situated at a given time is very slightly different from the point at which it was situated at the corresponding time in the previous year.'

9 Mellaart 1967. Mellaart's work at Catal Huyuk represents perhaps the most important single archaeological investigation in the Near East in the second half of the twentieth century. It was, sadly, interrupted after only a few seasons by a somewhat bizarre disagreement with the Turkish authorities; work has recently recommenced on the site and it is to be hoped that it may continue.

10 H. Lhote, 1959, *The Search for the Tassili Frescoes*, London (*La Découverte des fresques de Tassili*, Paris, 1958). For a more recent view of the chronology of the Saharan rock art see A. Muzzolini, 'Dating the earliest Saharan rock art: archaeological and linguistic data', in Friedman and Adams 1992: 147–54.

11 See Ch. II n. 18 for the relevant reference.

12 McClure 1971: 21, 47.

13 J. Zarins, 1982, 'Early rock art of Saudi Arabia', *Archaeology*, Nov./Dec.; M. Khan *et al.* 1985–90, 'Rock art epigraphic Survey', *Atlal*, vols 9–13.

14 See, for example, Hoffman 1980.

15 Emery 1949–58; Kemp 1966, 1967.

16 Emery 1961, using the material of his scholarly reports cited in n. 15 above, gives a brilliant overview of the development of archaic Egyptian funerary

architecture, certainly the most impressive since Reisner's *Development of the Egyptian Tomb* of many years earlier (1936).

17 H. Crawford, 1991, *Sumer and the Sumerians*, Cambridge 57–62.
18 Emery 1949–58, 1961.
19 Edwards 1947, ch. 2. Firth, Quibell and Lauer 1935.
20 Edwards 1947: 136.
21 R. M. Schoch, 1992, 'Redating the Great Sphinx of Giza', *KMT*: 53–69.
22 S. Giedon, 1957, *The Beginnings of Architecture*, The A. W. Mellon Lectures in the Fine Arts, 457.
23 Giedon, ibid., gives a number of examples.
24 Schwaller de Lubicz' work is still deeply controversial; few of those who have concerned themselves with an examination of Ancient Egyptian architecture possess the mathematical competence, other considerations apart, to judge it accurately (*pace* Neugerbauer and Toomer quoted in nn. 3 and 4 above). He has a committed partisan in West 1993. A brief review of some of his work also appears in *The Temple of Man* (Brookline, Mass., 1977) an abridgement and translation of Schwaller de Lubicz' *Le Temple dans l'Homme* (1947).

CHAPTER II

1 Jung 1963: 90; originally published in 1961 as *Erinnerungen, Träume, Gedanken*.
2 The English edition appeared in 1963.
3 'On the frontiers of knowledge': interview with Jung and Georges Duplain, *Gazette de Lausanne*, 4–8 Sept. 1959. Cited in William McGuire and R. F. C Hill, 1978, *C. G. Jung Speaking*, London, 374.
4 Jung 1963.
5 Ibid.: 256.
6 Jung 1973: 259–61, letter to Frau Johanna Michaelis, 20 Jan. 1939.
7 Ibid.
8 Jung 1963: 251, 256.
9 Jung 1973: 260, letter to Frau Johanna Michaelis, 20 Jan. 1939.
10 Most notably by de Santillana and von Dechend.
11 Jung 1973: 138, letter to B. Baur, 29 Jan. 1934; Jung 1967b: 136, 148, 150.
12 Jung 1976: 225–6, letter to Pater Lucas Menz, OSB, 22 Feb. 1955.
13 Edwards 1947: 262–5.
14 This term is explained below, see n. 20.
15 Jung 1967a: 75.
16 Jung 1968a: 1–4.
17 Ibid.: 5.
18 Ibid.: 6.
19 Ibid.: 489–90.
20 This concept owes much to the work of Lewis-Williams and his colleagues at Witwatersrand University, in their study of the !Kung San people of southern Africa. Some of the works which seem to me to bear most directly on the Egyptian experience (though they are not presented as such) are listed in the bibliography.
21 Jung 1969 [1958]: 180.
22 Jung 1968a: 117.
23 Jung 1973: 260, letter to Frau Johanna Michaelis, 29 Jan. 1939.
24 Jung 1968a: 106.
25 In particular Frankfort 1948a: 162–3, 167–8, 171–3, ch. 14 n. 69.

26 For a consideration of this term see E. Neumann, 1954, *The Origins and History of Consciousness*, Princeton, esp. 421–35.

27 Jung 1967b: 309–10.

28 Jung 1968a: 179.

29 From a seminar by Jung, quoted by James Hillman, 1989, 'Senex and Puer', in *Puer Papers*, Dallas, 44.

30 J. D. Lewis-Williams, 1983, *The Rock Art of Southern Africa*, Cambridge; id., 1986, *Reality and Non-reality in San Rock Art*, Twenty-fifth Raymond Dart Lecture, Johannesburg.

31 J. A. West (1993) has an interesting discussion of this point, relating to the work of Schwaller de Lubicz, though most Egyptologists would probably be shy of following him in it.

32 J. D. Lewis-Williams, and T. A. Dowson, 1988, 'The signs of all times: entoptic phenomena in Upper Palaeolithic Art', *Current Anthropology* 24: 201–45; eid., 1989, *Images of Power: Understanding Bushman Rock Art*, Johannesburg.

33 Wendorf 1968: 1: 954.

34 Hoffman 1982: 38–50, 54, 56.

35 Kemp 1973: 36–43; C. Aldred, 1963 *Egypt to the End of the Old Kingdom*, London, 33, ill. 21.

36 Kemp 1966, 1967.

37 Emery 1949–58, 1961, though his belief that the Saqqara tombs were the burials of kings of the First Dynasty is not now generally accepted.

38 Ibid.: Pls. 22, 24, 32A, 34, 35, and the sketch plan of 'the tomb of Enezib', showing an internal stepped structure; id., 1961: 82–4, fig. 85.

39 The evidence is summarised in S. Lloyd and H. W. Muller, *Ancient Architecture* Milan and London, 75–78.

40 Jung 1968b: 241.

41 Thomas Mann, 1936, 'Freud and the Future', in *Life and Letters*, vol. 15, no. 5, pp. 90–1.

42 Emery 1961 summarises the rather gruesome statistics of the burials at Saqqara and Abydos. Hoffman 1980: 272, 275–9, 261–2; 284 considers the practice in some detail.

43 Jung 1969: 790, 792, 797; 13: 68.

44 Faulkner 1968, 1969.

45 Faulkner 1968: unfortunately all the plates are in monochrome.

CHAPTER III

1 Kramer 1963: 116

2 Ibid.: 160–2.

3 Ibid.

4 J. Gwyn Griffiths, 1966, *The Origins of Osiris*, Berlin, 57–8.

CHAPTER IV

1 See ch. II n. 33 above.

2 G. Caton Thompson, and E. W. Gardner, 1934, *The Desert Fayum*, 2 vols, London.

3 H. J. B. Junker, *MDAIK* 1 (1930), 1–37; *AnzOAW* 5–13 (1930), 21–83; *MDAIK* 3 (1932), 168–9; *AnzOAW* 1–4 (1932) 36–97; *AnzOAW* 1–4 (1940) 55–6.

4 F. Debono, 1945, 'Helouan-El Omari: Fouilles du Service des Antiquités 1943–45', *Cd'E* 21: 50–4; 'La Civilisation predynastique d'El Omari (nord d'Helouan)', *BIE* 37 (1956) 329–39.

5 O. Menghin, and M. Amer, *Maadi – 1930–31*, Egy. Univ. Fac. of Arts, Publ. 19 (1932) and 20 (1936). Cairo.

6 Trigger *et al.* 1983: 23.

7 Ibid.: 25.

8 Quibell and Green 1902: 36, Pl. III, 1, 2; B. Adams, 1995, *Ancient Nekhen: Garstang in the City of Hierakonpolis*, London, 56, 86, (fig. 32), 88.

9 Trigger *et al.* 1983: 39–40.

10 Fig. 3 in *L'Egypte avant les Pyramides* 1973. Illustrated Pl. II in Rice 1990.

11 W. Kaiser, 1957, 'Zur inneren Chronologie der Nagadakultur', *Archaeologia Geographica* 6: (1957) 69–77.

12 Fairservis *et al.* 1971–2.

13 G. Dreyer, 1993 'Nachuntersuchungen im frühzeitlichen Konigsfriedhof. 5/6 Vorbericht', *MDAIK* 49: 23–62.

14 An excellent summary of the glyptic evidence for Western Asiatic influences in late predynastic Egypt is to be found in H. S. Smith 1992.

15 B. Williams 1986.

16 Dreyer. op. cit. n. 13 above.

17 W. M. F. Petrie, 1917, 'Egypt and Mesopotamia', in *Ancient Egypt*, Pt 1: 26–36; id., 'The geography of the gods', in *Ancient Egypt*, Pt. 3: 109–19; id. 1939: 77.

18 H. Frankfort, 1924, *Studies in the Pottery of the Near East*, 1. *Mesopotamia, Syria and Egypt and their Earliest Interrelations*, London.

19 Baumgartel, 1955: 48–56; id. 1960: 5, 7, 120.

20 H. Kantor, 1942, 'The early relations of Egypt with Asia', *JNES* 1: 174–213; id. 1964, 'The relative chronology of Egypt and its foreign correlations before the late Bronze Age', in R. Erich (ed.) *Relative Chronologies in Old World Archaeology*, Chicago, 1–46.

21 Edwards 1971: 38.

22 B. Adams, 1995 op. cit. n. 8 above: 60–3, 72–5, figs. 21, 26.

23 P. Delougaz, 1940, *The Temple Oval at Khafajeh*, Chicago, frontispiece.

24 Michael Rice, 1983, *The Temple Oval at Barbar, Bahrain*, Bahrain. Including plans and excavation photographs.

25 Baines and Málek 1980: 79.

26 Petrie 1939: 77.

27 K. Frifelt, 1991, 'The Island of Umm an-Nar', *Third Millennium Graves*, vol. 1, Jutland.

28 K. Frifelt, 1975, 'On the prehistoric settlement and chronology of the Oman Peninsula', *East and West* 25: 62–110.

29 G. Weisgerber, 1980 '. . . und Kupfer in Oman', *Der Anschnit* (Bochum) 32(2–3): 62–110.

30 Frifelt 1975 (n. 28 above), Pls. 20–21A, 29, 30.

31 This belief was once widely held especially after its espousal by Petrie. Emery 1961 also accepted the idea of an invasion, but it is now almost entirely discarded, at least to the extent of any sort of armed incursion having taken place.

32 H. A. Winkler, (1938) *Rock Drawings of Southern Upper Egypt*, London. See Pls. XXXIII–XLI for Winkler's comparison of late predynastic sea-craft from Egypt and Mesopotamia.

33 S. Ratnagar, 1981, *Encounters: The Westerly Trade of the Harappan Civilization*, Delhi, 166–72.

34 T. van der Way, 'Indications of architecture with niches at Buto', in Friedman and Adams 1992: 217–26.
35 S. AA. Al-Rashid n.d., *Al-Rabadah: A Portrait of an Early Islamic Civilization in Saudi Arabia*, Riyadh.
36 H. J. Nissen, 1986, 'The occurrence of Dilmun in the earliest texts of Mesopotamia', in Khalifa and Rice 1986: 335–9.
37 F. E. Zeuner, 1963, *A History of Domesticated Animals*, London, 177–9.
38 See Michael Rice in *The Power of the Bull* (forthcoming).
39 Extensively illustrated in Emery 1949–58 and 1961.
40 Amiet 1966: Pls. 29, 45.
41 See n. 13 above.
42 Emery 1949–58: his publications are notable for the elegance and precision of his archaeological drawings. The complexity and discipline of the earliest Egyptian buildings have never been more tellingly represented.
43 e.g. Amiet 1966: Pl. 42.
44 Rice 1994: 66–7; figs 3.1, 3.3.
45 J. Zarins, 1971–81, *Atlal* vols 1–5; id. 1982, 'Early rock art of Saudi Arabia', *Archaeology* Nov./Dec.
46 M. Khan, 1993, *The Origins and Evolution of Ancient Arabic Script*, Riyadh; M. Khan, *et al.* 1985–90 'Rock Art Epigraphic Survey', *Atlal* vols 9–13.
47 It is said that wild cattle could not survive for more than three days without access to water.
48 A. Anati, 1968–72, *Rock Art in Central Arabia* 3 vols, Louvain.
49 Khan 1988 *Atlal* vol. 11, Pl. 56.
50 McClure 1971.
51 Arabia is an admirable location for the study of micro-climates. A similar situation to that referred to in the text is the creation, flourishing and eventual depletion of a community recorded from much later times at the site of Murwab, in Qatar, eastern Arabia. In B. De Cardi (ed.) 1973, *Qatar Archaeological Report and Excavations*, Oxford, 185–6.
52 J. Zarins, *et al.*, 1981, 'The Second Preliminary Report on the Southwestern Province', *Atlal*, vol. 5: 35–6, Pls. 34, 35A.
53 This is demonstrated graphically in the displays in the Museum of Archaeology and Ethnography, Riyadh. The material is also illustrated in the Museum's handbook.
54 Rice 1994: fig. 9.5.
55 Ibid. fig. 8.2, centre row left.
56 Michael Rice, 1986, 'The island on the edge of the world', in Khalifa and Rice (1986), 116–24.

CHAPTER V

1 Frankfort 1948a: 32–5, 37.
2 Ibid.: 43–4.
3 Parkinson 1991: 43.
4 Frankfort 1948a: 71–3.
5 A. Piankoff, 1968, *The Pyramid of Unas*, Princeton.
6 Baines and Málek 1980: 134.
7 Ibid.
8 See Edwards (1971), 'Royalty and State'.
9 Ibid.: 32.

10 Ibid.: 33.
11 Ibid.
12 Ibid.: 34.
13 Ibid.: 35.
14 Saad 1969, 1947.
15 Emery 1949–58.
16 Ibid. vol. 2, Tomb 3035, Pls. I, VII, A and B.
17 Kemp 1966, 1967.
18 G. Dreyer, 1993, 'A hundred years at Abydos', *Egyptian Archaeology* 3: 11.
19 Emery remarks on this phenomenon (1961: 73); he evidently intended to return to the matter, describing it as 'of particular interest', but does not appear to have done so.
20 Emery 1961: 217–18 provides a compilation based on his 'Great Tombs' series (Emery 1949–58) of the styles of archaic Egyptian stone vessel manufacture, fig. 125; see also El-Khouli 1978.
21 Manetho, trans. Waddell (1940): 35. Fr. 8 (From Syncellus) according to Africanus.
22 Newberry 1922: 40–6.

CHAPTER VI

1 As, for example, the wonderful images of Djoser himself in faience tiles in the interior chambers of the Step Pyramid.
2 The two handsome volumes produced by Firth and Quibell with Lauer before the Second World War are masterpieces of Egyptological publishing (1935). Lauer lived on, to make the Step Pyramid, restored, his own monument. Lauer 1976 is a distinguished record of his lifetime's work at Saqqara.
3 Beautifully restored graphically by Lauer in the 1935 publication and now substantially restored on the site itself.
4 Firth, Quibell with Lauer, 1935, vol. 2, Pl. 73.
5 Ibid., Pl. 28 which shows Djoser still in his serdab, where he had waited for nearly five thousand years, and the subsequent plates which show the statue's extraordinary power. A more recent colour reproduction of the statue is to be found in Rice 1990, Pl. XI.
6 Edwards, 1947: 60–73.
7 Petrie 1903: Pl. XIV.
8 Edwards, 1947: 78.
9 M. Z. Nour, Z. Iskander, M. S. Osman and A.Y. Moustafa, 1960 *The Cheops Boats Pt. 1* (only part published), Cairo.
10 N. Jenkins, 1980, *The Boat beneath the Pyramid*, London; a disappointing text supported by a superb series of photographs.
11 W. S. Smith, 1946, 2nd edn, 1949, Boston: 145–8; figs. 55, 56, 57, Pl. 37.
12 Ibid.: 153–6.
13 Moussa and Altenmuller 1971.
14 Ibid.: Pl. 40A.
15 Ibid.: Pls. 22, 23, 24.
16 Parkinson 1991: 54, 'The tale of King Neferkare and General Sasenet'.

CHAPTER VII

1 Butzer 1976: 28–9.
2 W. Nutzel, 1976, 'The climatic changes of Mesopotamia and bordering areas 14000–2000 BC', *Sumer* 32: 20; H.J. Nissen, *The Early History of the Ancient Near East 9000–2000 BC*, trans. E. Lutzen with Kenneth J. Northcott, Chicago, 55–6, 59, 73.
3 Manetho (from Syncellus), according to Africanus. Another version of Syncellus' text, according to Eusebius, has the Seventh Dynasty consisting of five kings who reigned for seventy five days. At all events the point is made about the dynasty's ephemeral nature.
4 W. F. Leemans, 1950, *The Old Babylonian Merchant*, Leiden; id. 1960, *Foreign Trade in the Old Babylonian Period*, Leiden; P. L. Kohl, 1986, 'The lands of Dilmun: changing cultural and economic relations during the third and early second millennia', in Khalifa and Rice (1986), 367–75.
5 J. Vandier, 1950, 'Mo'alla. La Tombe d'Ankhtifi et la tombe de Sebekhotep', *BdE* 18.
6 M. Lichteim, 1975, *Ancient Egyptian Literature*, vol. 1. *The Old and Middle Kingdoms*, vol. 3 (1980). *The Late Period*, Berkeley, Calif; A. Erman, 1927, *The Literature of the Ancient Egyptians*, trans A. M. Blackman, London; Parkinson 1991.
7 See Lichteim above, 1975: Pt 1, section V, Old Kingdom (Didactic Literature); Pt 2 III (The Instruction Addressed to King Merikare) Pt 3 III (Middle Kingdom Didactic Literature).

CHAPTER VIII

1 Baines and Málek 1980: 14, 15.
2 Saleh 1977.
3 King Wahank Intef 'The Dog Stela' illustrated and translated in Parkinson 1991: 112–13.
4 H. E. Winlock, 1947, *The Rise and Fall of the Middle Kingdom at Thebes*, New York, 29 nn. 21 and 22.
5 For a careful and perceptive study of Middle Kingdom coffins as works of art, see E. L. B. Terrace 1968, *Egyptian Paintings of the Middle Kingdom*, London.
6 See ch. I n. 8 above.
7 Lichteim 1975: Pt III: 135 'Instructions of King Amenemhet I for his son Sesostris I'.
8 Ibid.: 139, 'The Prophecies of Neferti'.
9 Ibid.: 222, 'The Story of Sinuhe'.
10 Herodotus 2, 102; Diodorus 1; Pliny 33, 3; Strabo 16; Lucan 10, 276.
11 T. S. Eliot, 1922, *The Waste Land*: 1. 43–6.
12 William Hayes in 'The Middle Kingdom in Egypt' *Cambridge Ancient History* (3rd edn, 1970), vol. 1, pt II: 501, 508, describes the campaigns of Senwosret I and Senwosret III in Palestine and Syria, referring to the 'hill country' adjoining the Mediterranean.
13 G.A. Reisner, D. Dunham and J. M. A. Janssen, 1960, *Semna Kumma (Second Cataract Forts)*, vol. 1, Boston.
14 P. Lacau, and H. Chevrier, 1956/69, *Une Chapelle de Sesostris Ier à Karnak*, Cairo.

15 Terrace 1968 (n. 5 above); Faulkner 1969.
16 Terrace 1968, Pl. II.
17 W. A. Ward, 1977, 'Neferhotep and his friends: a glimpse of the life of ordinary men', *JEA* 63: 63–6.
18 Parkinson 1991: 114–15, 'A monument for a favourite harpist'.
19 H. E. Winlock, 1934, *The Treasure of El-Lahun*, New York.
20 J. de Morgan, 1895–1903, *Fouilles à Dahchour*, 2 vols, Vienna.
21 From Byblos, now in the Beirut Museum. See P. Montet 1928–9, *Byblos et l'Egypte: quatre campagnes de fouilles a Gebeil 1921–1924*, Paris.
22 For the presence of Egyptians in Ankara at this time see *Cambridge Ancient History* (3rd edn, 1970), vol. 1, pt II: 504.

CHAPTER IX

1 Redford, 1992, esp. chs. 5 and 14.
2 V. Hankey, 1992, 'Egypt, the Aegean and the Levant', *Egyptian Archaeology* 3: 27–30; M. Bietak, 1992, 'Minoan wall paintings unearthed at Ancient Avaris', *Egyptian Archaeology* 2: 26–8.
3 Bietak 1992: 28.
4 A. Evans, 1921–35, *The Palace of Minos at Knossos*, 4 vols, Oxford.
5 Hankey 1992 (as n. 2).

CHAPTER X

1 Trigger *et al.* 1983: 202.
2 This strange episode was brilliantly recreated by Shadi Abdulsalaam in his film *The Night of the Counting of the Years*. George B. Johnson, 1992, 'The Royal Cache: Tomb DB320 revisited', *KMT* 4(2): 52–57.
3 The exhibition 'Egypt's Dazzling Sun: Amenhotep III and his World' revealed the extraordinary opulence of Amenhotep's reign.
4 There are many studies of the life and reign of Akhenaten, most of them tending towards the over reverential. One of the best which concentrates particularly on the aesthetics and the artistic styles associated with his reign is Aldred 1968.
5 Ibid.: 233–8
6 Ahkenaten seems to have placed himself under some sort of deliberate constraint not to cross the boundaries which he had designated as the city's limits. The boundary stelae which he erected make this clear.
7 The series of events by which the Stela of Bak was lost to the British Museum and then reached its present home in Berlin is one of the more improbable, if not indeed farcical, episodes in twentieth-century Egyptology.
8 The story has not, so far as I am aware, ever been published. When the newly elected National Socialists were establishing themselves in government in Germany it was decided that the supposed influence of the British in the Moslem world was potentially inimical to Germany's interests. Egypt was recognised as the most important of the Moslem countries represented in Berlin. Overtures were initiated and German diplomats were instructed to discover what act or gesture might with advantage be directed towards Egypt to begin the process of disengaging the country from Britain's embrace. The Egyptians sensed an opportunity; they were angry at the circumstances under which they believed

Nefertiti had been taken to Germany before the First World War. A young Egyptian diplomat was given the responsibility for negotiating her repatriation; all went swimmingly until the Prime Minister of Prussia, Hermann Goering, on the point of signing the authority, enquired whether Adolf Hitler had been advised. In view of his well-known expertise in matters of art, Goering insisted that he should be told.

At this point something approaching fantasy intervened. The Nazi predilection for large events prompted the suggestion that a grand occasion should be organised for the corps diplomatique, the Party and the *haut ton* of Berlin at which Hitler should meet Nefertiti. It was to be held in the Museum; Hitler arrived, late, was swept into the presence of the Queen, gazed at her silently, turned on his heel and announced that, so perfect an example of Ayran womanhood was she that there could be no question of her ever leaving the Fatherland.

9 S. Freud, 1955, *Moses and Monotheism*, in *Standard Edition*, vol. XXIII, trans. James Strachey.

10 I. Velikovsky, 1960, *Oedipus and Akhenaton: Myth and History*, New York.

CHAPTER XI

1 Most recently by T. G. H. James, 1992, *Howard Carter: the Path to Tutankhamun*, London.

2 I. E. S. Edwards, 1977, *Tutankhamun: His Tomb and its Treasures*, Catalogue of the exhibition 'Treasures of Tutankhamun' at various locations in the United States.

3 Ibid.: 100–101.

4 But, sadly, in a deplorable state little helped by the fact that his head was detached when the mummy was removed from its coffin, despite Carter's meticulous supervision.

5 N. Reeves, 1990, *The Complete Tutankhamun: The King – The Tomb – The Royal Treasure*, London, 108–9.

6 Edwards 1977 (n. 2 above) Pl. 133.

7 C. L. Woolley, 1934, *Ur: The Royal Cemetery*, 2 vols. (text and plates), London and Philadelphia.

8 Desroches Noblecourt 1963: Pl. 147.

9 Martin 1991: 24, 25, 36, 43.

CHAPTER XII

1 Kitchen 1982.

2 W. Stevenson Smith 1958: ch. 19, provides a comprehensive commentary on early Ramesside art and architecture but is perhaps a little wanting in enthusiasm for Seti's legacy: 215–29.

3 Habachi 1974.

4 Kitchen 1982.

5 W. MacQuitty, 1965, *Abu Simbel*, London, 96–104.

6 Lockyer 1964/1884. *The Dawn of Astronomy* is a remarkable work: inspired astronomy mixed with distinctly flawed archaeology, which is an exceptional source, if handled carefully, for an understanding of the Egyptian capacity for

exploring the heavenly bodies. Lockyer examines the orientation of a number of important Egyptian temples, including Karnak and Denderah, and concludes that their orientation was changed to perpetuate the temple's lock on to a particular star to which it was aligned when it was originally constructed.

7 See Redford, 1992. Also Michael Rice, 1994, *False Inheritance: Israel in Palestine and the Search for a Solution*, London, esp. chs. 5 and 6.
8 Grimal 1992: 276.

CHAPTER XIII

1 See Kitchen 1973 for a rewarding examination of an intensely confused period.
2 See the references in Rice, *False Inheritance* (ch. XII n. 7) Redford 1992; and Thomas L. Thompson, 1993, *Early History of the Israelite People*, Leiden, who, *inter alia*, examines the historicity of David and Soloman.
3 O'Connor 1993 provides a picture of the extent of the Kushite and Nubian kingdoms, their relations with Egypt and their remarkable record of survival.
4 W. Stevenson Smith 1958: 245, 250; Kitchen 1973.
5 For a review of this curious episode see L. Depuyot, 1995, Murder in Memphis: the story of Cambyses' mortal wounding of the Apis bull (ca. 523 BC)', *JNES* 54(2): 119–26.

CHAPTER XIV

1 A.R. Al-Ansary, 1981, *Qaryat al-Fau: A Portrait of a Pre-Islamic Civilization in Saudi Arabia*, Riyadh.
2 D. T. Potts, 1990, *The Arabian Gulf in Antiquity*, vol. 2: 103–5.
3 Ibid.: 183–95; K. Jeppesen, 1989, *Ikaros, The Hellenistic Settlement. The Sacred Enclosure in the Early Hellenistic Period*, Jutland, 72–104.
4 Potts 1990 (n. 2 above), chs 5 (North-eastern Arabia) and 6 (South-eastern Arabia).
5 Tarn 1961.
6 F. Cumont, (1903; 1956, *The Mysteries of Mithra*, New York; D. Ulansey, 1989, *The Origin of the Mithraic Mysteries*, New York and Oxford. Jung was deeply interested in Mithraism and saw it as a bridge between Ancient Egypt and the alchemists of the late Middle Ages and the more scientific minds of the Renaissance.
7 A brief survey of mystery religions of late antiquity is Joscelyn Godwin (1981) *Mystery Religions in the Ancient World*, London.
8 Jung on Astrology, in McGuire and Hill, *C. G. Jung Speaking* (ch. II n. 3 above): 349, 370, 398.

CHAPTER XV

1 Jung 1967a: 344.
2 Herold, J. Christopher (1962) *Bonaparte in Egypt*, New York
3 G. Boas, 1950, *The Hieroglyphics of Horapollo*, Bollingen ser., Princeton; A. J. Cory, 1840, *The Hieroglyphics of Horapollo Nilus*, repr. London, 1987.

4 D. Abulafia, 1988, *Frederick II : A Medieval Emperor*, London, ch. 5: 164–201.

5 Baron V. Denon, 1802, *Voyages en Haute et Basse Egypte*, 2 vols.

6 National Gallery of Canada, 1994, *'Egyptomania': Egypt in Western Art 1730–1930*, Ottawa; J. S. Curl, 1994, *'Egyptomania' – The Egyptian Revival: A Recurring Theme in the History of Taste*, Manchester.

7 *Cambridge Ancient History* (3rd edn, 1970), vol. 1, pt. I: 131–3.

8 Kramer, 1963: 302–7, fig 6.

9 See n. 7 above.

10 E. S. Meltzer, 1970, 'An observation on the hieroglyph *mr*', *JEA* 56: 193–4.

11 W. Stevenson Smith 1946/1949: 139–41, 268–70, Pl. 31b, 'Hesi-Ra'.

12 Cory 1840/1987 (n. 3 above).

13 J. Godwin, 1979, *Athanasius Kircher: A Renaissance Man and the Quest for Lost Knowledge*, London.

14 P.R.S. Moorey, 1983, *Ancient Egypt*, Oxford, 3, Pl. 1 (right).

15 C. Sicard, 1845, *Description de l'Egypte*, Lyons.

16 Benoît de Maillet, 1735, *Description de l'Egypte, contenant plusieurs remarques curieuses*, Paris.

17 R. Pococke, 1743–5, *A Description of the East and Some Other Countries*, London.

18 J.-F. Champollion, 1822, *Lettre à M. Dacier*, Paris; id., 1841, *Mémoire sur les signes employées par les anciens Egyptiens*, Paris.

19 Jung 1970: 307–436, 'Flying saucers : A modern myth'.

SELECT BIBLIOGRAPHY

———— •◦• ————

There follows a list of the principal works which have been consulted or to which reference is made in the text. A more extensive list of books relating specifically to the earliest periods of Egypt's history will be found in Rice 1990.

Adams, B. (1974) *Ancient Hierakonpolis*, with supplement, Warminster.
—— (1988) *The Fort Cemetery at Hierakonpolis* (excavated by John Garstang), London.
Adams, W. Y. (1968) 'Invasion, diffusion, evolution?', *Antiquity* 42: 194–215.
—— (1970) 'A reappraisal of Nubian culture history', *Orientalia* 39: 269–77.
—— (1977) *Nubia: Corridor to Africa*, London.
Aldred, C. (1968) *Akhenaten: Pharaoh of Egypt. A New Study*, London.
Amiet, P. (1966) *Elam*, Paris.
Arkell, A. J. (1963) 'Was King Scorpion Menes?', *Antiquity* 37: 31–5.
—— (1975) 'The prehistory of the Nile Valley', in *Handbuch der Orientalistik*, Leiden, vol. 7, pt 1.2.
Arkell, A. J. and Ucko, P. J. (1965) 'Review of Predynastic development in the Nile Valley', *Current Anthropology* 6: 145–66.
Arnett, W. S. (1982) *The Predynastic Origin of Egyptian Hieroglyphs*, New York.
Baines, J. and Málek, J. (1980) *Atlas of Ancient Egypt*, London.
Baumgartel, E. J. (1955) *The Cultures of Predynastic Egypt*, 2nd edn, vol. 1, Oxford.
—— (1960) *The Cultures of Predynastic Egypt*, vol. 2, Oxford.
—— (1966) 'Scorpion and rosette and the fragment of the large Hierakonpolis mace-head', *Z. aegypt. Sprache u. Altertumskunde* 92: 9–14.
—— (1970a) 'Predynastic Egypt', in *Cambridge Ancient History*, 3rd edn, vol. 1, Cambridge.
—— (1970b) *Petrie's Naqada Excavation: A Supplement*, London.
Bauvel, R. and Gilbert, A. (1994) *The Orion Mystery: Unlocking the Secrets of the Pyramids*, London.
Bell, L. (1985) 'Luxor Temple and the cult of the royal ka', *JNES* 44: 251–94.
Bernal, M. (1991) *Black Athena: The Afro-Asiatic Roots of Classical Civilization*, vol. 2. *The Archaeological and Documentary Evidence*, London.
Boussian, J. (1981) *Pottery from the Nile Valley*, Cambridge.
Brice, W. C. (ed.) (1978) *The Environmental History of the Near and Middle East*, London and New York.
Brunton G. and Caton Thompson, G. (1928) *The Badarian Civilization*, London.
Budge, E. A. W. (1969[1904]) *The Gods of the Egyptians*, 2 vols, New York.
—— (1970[1920]) *An Egyptian Hieroglyphic Dictionary*, 2 vols, New York.
Butzer, K. W. (1971) *Environment and Archaeology: An Ecological Approach to Prehistory*, Chicago.
—— (1975) 'Patterns of environmental change in the Near East during late Pleistocene and Holocene times', in F. Wendorf and A. E. Marks (eds) *Problems in Prehistory: North Africa and the Levant*, Dallas.

—— (1976) *Early Hydraulic Civilization in Egypt: A Study in Cultural Ecology*, Chicago.

Canada, National Gallery of (1994) *Egyptomania: Egypt in Western Art* (catalogue), J. M. Humbert, M. Pantazzi, Christiane Ziegler.

Carter, H. and Mace, A.C. (1923–33) *The Tomb of Tut.ankh.amen*, 3 vols, London.

Cialowicz, K. M. (1992a) 'Problème de l'interpretation du relief Predynastique tardif. Motif du palmier et des girafes', *Zeszyty Nankowe Universytetu Jagiellonski MLXVII Prace Archaeologiczne* 53.

—— (1992b) 'La Composition des scènes avec des animaux sur les Palettes Predynastique tardives', *ZNUJ MLXXII – Prace Archaeologiczne* 54.

—— (1993) *Symbolika Przedstawien Wladey Egipskiego w Okniesie Predynastycnym* (French abstract), Krakow.

Clark, J. D. (1971) 'A re-examination of the evidence for agricultural origins in the Nile Valley', *PPS* 37: 34–9.

Clayton, P. A. (1994) *Chronicle of the Pharaohs*, London.

Crowfoot Payne, J. (1968) 'Lapis lazuli in early Egypt', *Iraq* 30(1).

Cornell, J. (1981) *The First Stargazers: An Introduction to the Origins of Astronomy*, London.

Curl, J. S. (1994) *Egyptomania. The Egyptian Revival: A Recurring Theme in the History of Taste*, Manchester.

David, A. R. (1982) *The Ancient Egyptians: Religious Beliefs and Practices*, London.

De Manuelian, P. (1994) *Living in the Past: Studies in Archaicism of the Egyptian Twenty-Sixth Dynasty*, London.

de Santillana, G. and von Dechend, H. (1969/70) *Hamlet's Mill: An Essay in Myth and the Frame of Time*, London.

Derricourt, R. M. (1971) 'Radiocarbon chronology for Egypt and North Africa', *JNES* 30: 271–92.

Derry, D. E. (1956) 'The Dynastic Race in Egypt', *JEA* 42: 80–5.

Desroches-Noblecourt, C. (1963) *Tutankhamon*, London.

Dodson, A. (1994) *The Canopic Equipment of the Kings of Egypt*, London.

Dunbar, J. H. (1941) *The Rock Pictures of Lower Nubia*, Cairo.

Dunham, D. (1978) *Zawiyet el-Aryan*, Boston.

Edwards, I. E. S. (1947; rev. 1985) *The Pyramids of Egypt*, Harmondsworth.

—— *The Pyramids of Egypt*, London.

Edwards, I. E. S., Gadd, C. J. and Hammond, N. G. L. (1971) *Cambridge Ancient History*, 3rd edn, vol. 1 pt 2. *Early History of the Middle East*, Cambridge.

L'Egypte avant les Pyramides: 4e millenaire (1973), Paris: Editions des Musées Nationaux.

Emery, W. B. (1949–58) *Great Tombs of the First Dynasty*, 3 vols, Cairo and London.

—— (1961) *Archaic Egypt*, London.

Ertman, E. E. (1972) 'The earliest known three-dimensional representation of the god Ptah', *JNES* 31: 83–6.

Fairservis, W. A., Jr, Weeks, K. and Hoffman, M. (1971–2) 'Preliminary report on the first two seasons at Hierakonpolis', *J. Am. Res. Cent. Egypt* 9: 7–68.

Fakhry, A. (1959) *The Monuments of Sneferu at Dahshur*, vol. 1. *The Bent Pyramid*, Cairo.

—— (1961) *The Monuments of Sneferu at Dahshur*, vol. 2. *The Valley Temple*, 2 parts.

Fattorovich, R. (1976) 'Trends in the study of Predynastic social structure', in D. Wildung (ed.), *First International Congress of Egyptology: Abstracts of Papers*, Munich.

Faulkner, R. O. (1968) *The Pyramid of Unas*, Bollingen ser. 5, Princeton.
—— (1969) *The Ancient Egyptian Pyramid Texts*, Oxford.
—— (1973–8) *The Egyptian Coffin Texts*, 3 vols, Warminster.
Firth, C. M., Quibell, J. E. with Lauer, J.-P. (1935) *Excavations at Saqqara: The Step Pyramid*, 2 vols, Cairo.
Fouilles de El Kab (1954) *Documents Livraison*, Brussels.
Frankfort, H. (1948a) *Kingship and the Gods*, Chicago.
—— (1948b) *Ancient Egyptian Religion*, New York.
—— (1956) *The Birth of Civilization in the Near East*, London.
Frankfort, H., Frankfort, H. A., Wilson, J. A. and Jacobsen, T. (1949) *Before Philosophy*, London.
Friedman, R. and Adams, B. (eds) (1992) *The Followers of Horus*, Oxford.
Gardiner, A. (1969) *Egyptian Grammar*, Oxford, 3rd edn.
Giedon, S. (1962) *The Eternal Present*, vol. 1. *The Beginnings of Art*, Oxford.
—— (1964) *The Eternal Present*, vol. 2. *The Beginnings of Architecture*, Oxford.
Goedicke, H. (1969–70) 'An Egyptian Claim to Asia', *JARCE* 8: 11–27.
—— (1981) 'The Chronology of the Palermo Stone and the Turin Canons', *JARCO* 4.E 18: 89–90.
Goneim, M. Z. (1956) *The Buried Pyramid*, London.
—— (1957) *Horus Sekhem Khet*, vol. 1, Cairo.
Griffiths, J. G. (1960) *The Conflict of Horus and Seth*, Liverpool.
—— (1966) 'The Origins of Osiris', *Münchner Agyptolgische Studien*, 9.
Grimal, N. (1992) *A History of Ancient Egypt*, trans. Ian Shaw, London.
Habachi, L. (1974) 'Sethos I's devotion to Seth and Avaris', *ZAS* 100: 95–102.
Hassan, F. A. (1980) 'Radiocarbon chronology of Archaic Egypt', *JNES* 39: 203–7.
Hayes, W. C. (1953) *The Sceptre of Egypt*, vol. 1. *Before 1600 BC*, Cambridge, Mass.
—— (1959) *The Sceptre of Egypt*, vol. 2. *1675–1080 BC*, Cambridge, Mass.
—— (1965) *Most Ancient Egypt*, Chicago.
—— (1970) 'Chronology I. Egypt to the end of the Twentieth Dynasty', *Cambridge Ancient History*, 3rd edn, vol. 1, pt I, Cambridge.
Hays, T. R. (1975) 'Neolithic settlement of the Sahara as it relates to the Nile Valley', in F. Wendorf and A. E. Marks (eds), *Problems in Prehistory: North Africa and the Levant*, Dallas.
Hepper, N. (1969) 'Arabian and African frankincense trees', *JEA* 55: 66–72.
Herodotus (trans. 1954) *The Histories*, trans. Aubrey de Selincourt, London.
Herrman, G. (1968) 'Lapis lazuli: the early phases of its trade', *Iraq* 30(1).
Hoffman, M.A. (1979) *Egypt before the Pharaohs: The Prehistoric Foundations of Egyptian Civilization*, New York.
—— (1980) 'A rectangular Amratian house from Hierakonpolis', *JNES* 39: 119–37.
—— (1982) *The Predynastic of Hierakonpolis: An Interim Report*. Cairo.
Hornung, E. (1971–83) *Conceptions of God in Ancient Egypt*, trans. J. Baines, London.
Iversen, E. (1961) *The Myth of Egypt and its Hieroglyphs in European Tradition*, Copenhagen.
James, T. G. H. (1984) *Pharaoh's People: Scenes from Life in Imperial Egypt*, London.
Jenkins, N. (1980) *The Boat beneath the Pyramid*, London.
Jung, C. G. (1963) *Memories, Dreams, Reflections*, recorded and edited by Aniela Jaffe, London and Glasgow.
—— (1940) *Collected Works*, vol. II. *Psychology and Religion: West and East*, 2nd edn, London.

—— *The Collected Works*, edited by Sir Herbert Read, Michael Fordham, MD, MRCP and Gerhard Adler, Ph.D. Trans. from the German by R. F. C. Hill, London:

(1967a) vol. 5. *Symbols of Transformation*, 2nd edn.

(1967b) vol. 9 Pt II. *Aion: Researches into the Phenomenonolgy of the Self*, 2nd edn.

(1968a) vol. 9 Pt I. *The Archetypes and the Collective Unconscious*, 2nd edn.

(1968b) vol. 13. *Alchemical Studies*.

(1969) vol. 8. *the Structure and Dynamics of the Psyche*, 2nd edn.

(1970) vol. 10. *Civilization in Transition*, 2nd edn.

—— *Letters*, selected and edited by Gerhard Adler in collaboration with Aniela Jaffe. Trans. from the German by R. F. C. Hill, London:

(1973) vol. 1. *1906–1950*.

(1976) vol. 2. *1951–1961*.

Kanawati, N. (1977) *The Egyptian Administration in the Old Kingdom*, Warminster.

Kees, H. (1961) *Ancient Egypt: A Cultural Topography*, ed. T. G. H. James, trans. J. F. D. Morrow, London and Chicago.

Kelly, A. L. (1974) 'The Evidence of Mesopotamian Influence in Predynastic Egypt', *Newsletter Soc. Study Egypt. Ant.*, 4: 2–22.

Kemp, B. J. (1966) 'Abydos and the Royal Tombs of the First Dynasty', *JEA* 52: 13–22.

—— (1967) 'The Egyptian First Dynasty royal cemetery', *Antiquity* 41: 22–32.

—— (1973) 'Photographs of the Decorated Tomb at Hierakonpolis', *JEA* 39: 36–43.

—— (1976) 'A review of Hellstrom's 'The Rock Drawings', *JEA* 62: 9–26.

—— (1982) 'Automatic analysis of Predynastic cemeteries: a new method for an old problem', *JEA* 68: 5–15.

—— (1989) *Ancient Egypt: Anatomy of a Civilization*, London.

Al-Khalifa, K. A. and Rice, M. (eds) (1986) *Bahrain through the Ages: The Archaeology*, London.

El Khouli, A. (1978) *Egyptian Stone Vessels*, 3 vols, Mainz am Rhein.

Kitchen, K. (1973) *The Third Intermediate Period in Egypt (1100–650 BC)*, Warminster.

—— (1982) *Pharaoh Triumphant: The Life and Times of Ramesses II, King of Egypt*, Warminster.

Kohl, P. L. (1978) 'The balance of trade in southwestern Asia in the mid-third millennium BC', *Current Anthropology*, 19(3).

Kramer, S. N. (1963) *The Sumerians*, Chicago.

Krupp, E. C. (ed.) (1979) *In Search of Ancient Astronomies*, London.

Krzyzaniak, L. (1977) *Early Farming Cultures on the Lower Nile: The Predynastic Period in Egypt*, Warsaw.

—— (1979) 'Trends in the socio-economic development of Egyptian Predynastic societies', *Acts of the First International Congress of Egyptologists*, Cairo.

Larsen, C. E. (1983a) *Life and Land Use in the Bahrain Islands. The Geoarchaeology of an Ancient Society*, Chicago.

—— (1983b) 'The early development and hydrology of ancient Bahrain', in D. T. Potts (ed.), *Dilmun*, Berliner Beiträge zum Vorderen Orient, 2, Berlin.

Lauer, J.-P. (1976) *Saqqara*, London.

Lockyer, J. N. (1964[1884]) *The Dawn of Astronomy: A Study of the Temple Worship and Mythology of the Ancient Egyptians*, with a Preface by Giorgio de Santillana, Cambridge, Mass.

Lucas, A. and Harris, J. R. (1962) *Ancient Egyptian Materials and Industries*, 4th edn, London.

Lupton, C. (1981) 'The other Egypt: in search of the lost pharaohs', *Lore*, 31(3): 2–21.

MacDonald, J. (1972) 'Egyptian interests in western Asia to the end of the Middle Kingdom: an evaluation', *Austral. J. Bibl. Archaeol.* 2: 72–98.

McClure, H. A. (1971) *The Arabian Peninsula and Prehistoric Populations*, Miami.

Manetho, trans. W. G. Waddell (1940) Loeb Classical Library, Cambridge, Mass. and London.

Martin, G. T. (1991) *The Hidden Tombs of Memphis*, London.

Mellaart, J. (1967) *Catal Huyuk: A Neolithic Town in Anatolia*, London.

Mendelssohn, K. (1974) *The Riddle of the Pyramids*, London.

Mercer, S. (1959) *Earliest Intellectual Man's Idea of the Cosmos*, London.

Michalowski, K. (1969 *The Art of Ancient Egypt*, London.

Moorey, P.R.S. (1983) 'From Gulf to Delta in the fourth millennium BCE: the Syrian connection', in *Ancient Egypt*, Oxford, 62–9.

Morenz, S. (1973) *Egyptian Religion*, trans. A. E. Keep, London.

Morgan, J. de (1925–7) *Préhistoire Orientale*, 3 vols, Paris.

Moussa, A. M. and Altenmuller, H. (1971) *The Tomb of Nefer and Ka-Hay*, Mainz am Rhein.

Muhly, J. D. (1973) *Copper and tin*, New Haven, Conn.

Newberry, P. E. (1922) 'The Set rebellion of the IInd Dynasty', *Ancient Egypt* 1922, pt 2.

Nibbi, A. (1969) *The Tyrhennians*, Oxford.

—— (1975) *The Sea People and Egypt*, Park Ridge, NJ.

—— (1981) *Ancient Egypt and some Eastern Neighbours*, Oxford.

O'Connor, D. B. (1974) 'Political systems and archaeological data in Egypt 2600–1780 BC', *World Archaeology* 6: 15–38.

—— (1993) *Ancient Nubia: Egypt's Rival in Africa*, Pennsylvania.

Parkinson, R. B. (1991) *Voices from Ancient Egypt: An Anthology of Middle Kingdom Writings*, London.

Petrie, W. M. F. (1900) *The Royal Tombs of the First Dynasty*, pt I, Egypt Exploration Fund Memoir 18, London.

—— (1901) *The Royal Tombs of the First Dynasty*, pt II, Egypt Exploration Fund Memoir 21, London.

—— (1902) *Abdyos*, pt I, Egypt Exploration Fund Memoir 22, London.

—— (1903) *Abydos*, pt II, Egypt Exploration Fund Memoir 24, London.

—— (1920) *Prehistoric Egypt*, London.

—— (1939) *The Making of Egypt*, London.

—— (1953) *Ceremonial Slate Palettes: Corpus of Predynastic Pottery*, London.

Piankoff, A. (1968) *The Pyramid of Unas*, Princeton.

Posener, G., Sauneron, S. and Yoyotte, J. (1962) *Dictionary of Egyptian Civilization*, London.

Quibell, J. E. (1900) *Hierakonpolis*, pt I, London.

—— (1907) *Excavations at Saqqara (1905–6)*, London.

Quibell, J. E. and Green, F. W. (1902) *Hierakonpolis*, pt II, London.

Raphael, M. (1974) *Prehistoric Pottery in Egypt*, Washington.

Redford, D. B. (1992) *Egypt, Canaan and Israel in Ancient Times*, Princeton.

Reisner, G.A. (1936) *The Development of the Egyptian Tomb down to the Accession of Cheops*, Cambridge, Mass.

Renfrew, C. (1972) *The Emergence of Civilization*, London.

Reymond, E. A. E. (1969) *The Mythical Origin of the Egyptian Temple*, Manchester.

Rice, Michael (1990) *Egypt's Making: The Origins of Ancient Egypt, 5000–2000 BC*, London.

—— (1994) *The Archaeology of the Arabian Gulf*, London.

Romano, J. F. and von Bothmer, D. (1979) *The Luxor Museum of Ancient Egyptian Art*, Cairo.

Rundle Clark, R. T. (1969) *Myth and Symbol in Ancient Egypt*, Manchester.

Saad, Z. Y. (1947) *Royal Excavations at Saqqara and Helwan 1941–45*, Cairo.

—— (1969) *The Excavations at Helwan: Art and Civilization in the First and Second Egyptian Dynasties*, Norman, Oklahoma.

Saleh, M. (1977) *Three Old Kingdom Tombs at Thebes*, Mainz am Rhein.

Sanlaville, P. J. (1986) 'Shoreline changes in Bahrain since the beginning of human occupation', in H.A. Khalifa and M. Rice, (eds), *Bahrain through the Ages: The Archaeology*, London.

Scamuzzi, E. (n.d.) *Egyptian Art in the Egyptian Museum of Turin*, New York.

Schaffer, H. (1974) *Principles of Egyptian Art*, Oxford.

Sellers, J. B. (1992) *The Death of Gods in Ancient Egypt*, London.

Smith, H. S. (1992) 'The making of Egypt: A review of the influence of Susa and Sumer on Upper Egypt and Lower Nubia in the fourth millennium BC', in Friedman and Adams 1992.

Smith, W. Stevenson (1949) *A History of Egyptian Sculpture and Painting in the Old Kingdom*, Boston and London; 1st edn Oxford, 1946.

—— (1958) *The Art and Architecture of Ancient Egypt*, London.

—— (1965) *Interconnections in the Ancient Near East: A Study of the Relationships between the Arts of Egypt, the Aegean and Western Asia*, New Haven and London.

Spencer, A. J. (1993) *Early Egypt: The Rise of Civilization in the Nile Valley*, London.

Strudwick, N. (1985) *The Administration of Egypt in the Old Kingdom*, London.

Tarn, W. W. (1961) *Hellenistic Civilization*, Cleveland, Ohio.

Teissier, B. (1987) 'Glyptic evidence for a connection between Iran, Syro-Palestine and Egypt in the fourth and third millennia', *Iran* 25: 27 ff.

Trigger, B. G. (1965) *History and Settlement in Lower Nubia*, New Haven.

—— (1968) *Beyond History: The Method of Prehistory*, New York.

Trigger, B. G., Kemp, B. J., O'Connor, D. and Lloyd, A. B. (1983) *Ancient Egypt: A Social History*, Cambridge.

Vandier, J. (1952) *Manuel d'archéologie égyptienne*, vol. 1, Paris.

—— (1958) *Manuel d'archéologie égyptienne*, vol. 3, *Les grandes époques, la statuaire*, Paris.

Velde, H. te (1967) *Seth, God of Confusion: A Study of his Role in Egyptian Mythology and Religion*, Leiden.

Vercoutter, J. (1992) *The Search for Ancient Egypt*, New York.

Weeks, K. (1972) 'The niched gateway at Hierkonpolis' *JARCE* 9.

—— (1979) *Egypt and the Social Sciences: Five Studies*, Cairo.

Wendorf, F. (1968) *The Prehistory of Nubia*, 2 vols, Dallas.

Wendorf, F. and Schild, R. (1970) *The Prehistory of the Eastern Sahara*, New York.

West, J.A. (1993) *Serpent in the Sky: The High Wisdom of Ancient Egypt*, Wheaton, Ill.

Wicker, F. D. P. (1990) *Egypt and the Mountains of the Moon*, London.

Wildung, D. (1964) *L'Âge d'Or de l'Egypte: Le Moyen Empire*, Paris.

Williams, B. (1980) 'The Lost Pharaohs of Nubia', *Archaeology* 33: 12–21.

—— (1986) *Excavations between Abu Simbel and the Sudan Frontier*, Chicago.

Williams, W. Y. (1985) 'Doubts about the lost Pharaohs', *JNES* 44: 185–92.

Wood, W. (1987) 'The archaic stone tombs at Helwan', *JEA* 73.

Zarins, J., Whalen, N., Ibrahim, M., Morad, A. and Khan, M. (1980) 'Preliminary Report on the Central and Southwestern Provinces Survey', *Atlal* 4: 9–36.

INDEX

———— •◆• ————

Page numbers in bold indicate illustrations and their captions